Light in the Darkness

Daily Devotions For Troubled Times

Rev. Maryesah Karelon, O.M.M.

Light in the Darkness

Daily Devotions For Troubled Times

Rev. Maryesah Karelon, O.M.M.

© Rev. Maryesah Karelon, O.M.M., 2009

Published by 1stWorld Publishing
P.O. Box 2211, Fairfield, IA 52556
tel: 641-209-5000 • fax: 866-440 5234
web: www.1stworldpublishing.com

First Edition

LCCN: 2009922805
SoftCover ISBN: 978-1-4218-9072-2
HardCover ISBN: 978-1-4218-9071-5
eBook ISBN: 978-1-4218-9073-9

All rights reserved. No part of this book may be reproduced or utilized in any form or by any means, electronic or mechanical, including photocopying or recording, or by any information storage and retrieval system, without permission in writing from the author.

This material has been written and published solely for educational purposes. The author and the publisher shall have neither liability or responsibility to any person or entity with respect to any loss, damage or injury caused or alleged to be caused directly or indirectly by the information contained in this book.

*This book is dedicated to
the many precious souls,
who walk their life path
while darkness gathers around them.
May they always know that
the God of Light and Love
is their beacon of Hope.*

*In Loving Memory of
Father G. Peter David Posthumus, O.P.,
friend and mentor,
who faced the darkness
while he walked in the Light.
Rest in peace, dear friend.*

Acknowledgements

Given that this is my first time in publication, it is quite overwhelming to look back over the years that have brought me to this moment: from the teacher in junior high who praised the writings of a shy teenager to the college professor who accused her of plagiarism because her assignment was too good to be original. But it was. So many dear souls, most of whom are now on the Other Side, have given a part of themselves to the fulfillment of this long-time dream. They know who they are and that my heart is filled with gratitude, so I will briefly name here those who have assisted in the laying of the foundation for this particular work. My deepest love and gratitude go out to:

The Most Rev. Robert Allmen, who helped give birth to the dream of the Order of St. Mary Magdalene and ordained me to the diaconate in March of 2004;

The Rev. Kathryn Que Price, my dear sister in the Light, who has walked every step of the way with me, even through the darkest hours, and who knows the sound of angels;

my dear father, E. Clair Neal, who will celebrate his 100th birthday in July of 2009, and who has spent his life exploring and questioning how faith and reason can live in harmony;

my dear friend and editor, Pamela Leach, without whose support, enthusiasm and meticulous skill this project would never have been completed;

all those at 1st World Publishing who have added their energy and expertise to making this project a reality, especially Ed Spinella;

and last, but certainly not least, the angelic hierarchy, Mary Magdalene, and her Beloved Jesus, who desired this book to become a reality, guided my every decision and whispered the prayers in my ear. To God Be the Glory. Alleluia Amen.

Rev. Maryesah Karelon, O.M.M.

Contents

Introduction 7
January............................. 11
February............................ 41
March 69
April 99
May............................... 127
June............................... 159
July 193
August............................. 223
September 253
October............................ 281
November 311
December 343

Special Days

Christian Holy Days

Ash Wednesday 378
Palm Sunday 379
Holy Thursday 380
Good Friday 381
Easter Sunday 382
Pentecost.......................... 383

First Sunday of Advent 384
Second Sunday of Advent 385
Third Sunday of Advent 386
Fourth Sunday of Advent 386
Christmas Eve 387
Christmas Day. 388

National Holidays

Mother's Day. 389
Memorial Day. 390
Father's Day. 391
Independence Day. 392
Labor Day. 393
Veteran's Day. 394
Thanksgiving Day 395

About the Author 397
Scripture Index 399
Subject Index. 405

Introduction

The material in this book began life very quietly as a private Book of Days for members of the Order of St. Mary Magdalene. The concept of a daily spiritual journal dates back to the monastic tradition in medieval times. Eventually this modern version became part of our website and available to the public at large. In the Fall of 2008, I was working on the monthly updates in the midst of the economic meltdown. I personally found reading the material comforting and uplifting and thought if these words could find their way into my heart in a time of chaos and turmoil, then perhaps they would be helpful to others. The inspiration for this book was born.

To the best of my ability, I have attempted to write and compile this material from a non-dogmatic perspective. Though I consider myself a mystical Christian, my intent is to honor all religious traditions and provide spiritual support across the tapestry of our many faiths. For instance, certainly you will find references to Jesus, but the meditations are not addressed to him specifically or in his name. This is not meant to be disrespectful in any way but inclusive.

A pyramid of three basic assumptions forms the foundation for this material. First, humanity is one family united under one Creator. Second, each human soul is precious and may freely choose to evolve to the highest level of union with the Divine, what I call "Christ Consciousness." This is our inheritance as daughters and sons of the Most High and it is our destiny. Third, thoughts are energy. Whatever we focus our attention on we create. Thus, fear creates more fear. Hope and love create more of the same. This book is designed to assist in the process of decreasing our levels of fear and anxiety as we work to manifest a world of Abundance, Peace and Joy. This may feel like fantasy now, but that feeling is simply a barometer of how much work there is to do.

For each day of the year, you will find a quotation from Scripture, a question (or questions) for deeper reflection, a pertinent quote from a well-known or not-so-well-known source, and a closing meditation. I have purposely included quotations from ancient manuscripts not found in our canonical Christian Bible because I feel these have lessons to teach us and messages for our day. At the back of the book, you will find a section of devotions for the Christian Holy Days as well as our national holidays. There are also indexes that will assist you in finding a devotion based on a specific Scriptural passage or a particular topic. To utilize this material most effectively, I recommend journaling the answers to the reflection questions during a time of quiet meditation. However, I'm well aware that many people with very active lives find it difficult, if not impossible, to find significant quiet space in their day. If this is you, then take five minutes in the morning, even if it's in the bathroom, and read through the devotion for the day. Tuck the reflection question into your mind and carry it with you as you move through your priorities. Then in the evening before bedtime return to it and see how these thoughts impacted the activities of your day. Five minutes in the morning, five minutes in the evening—your investment in a more positive, hopeful outlook on your life. It's worth it!

I am totally convinced that we are living in an absolutely critical time in human history. Each one of us has an opportunity and a responsibility to step up and make a difference in the best way we possibly can. This book is my contribution to that effort. It is my fervent hope and prayer that this material will lift your soul on angel's wings, bringing comfort and hope to your daily life. May these words provide an open door to the Spirit of Love as they become your guide to your innermost heart and soul, your own Holy Grail. Welcome to a journey of Light and Truth for all who seek the Way. May your journey be blessed.

Rev. Mother Maryesah Karelon, OMM
January 19, 2009
Kalamazoo, Michigan

January

Know that God is Love
and God is Light.
In that Light there is no darkness.
In that Love there is no fear.
Therefore, trust always in that Love
and live always in that Light,
and fear not.

Light in the Darkness

January 1

"I am about to do a new thing; now it springs forth, do you not perceive it? I will make a way in the wilderness and rivers in the desert."

Isaiah 43:19

What new changes do you choose to create in your life for the New Year?

"If we just worry about the big picture, we are powerless. So my secret is to start right away doing whatever little work I can do. I try to give joy to one person in the morning, and remove the suffering of one person in the afternoon...That is the secret. Start right now."

Sister Chan Khong

Lord of the Ages, you have told us that you are the Alpha and the Omega, the Beginning and the End. Show us how to release the past and open the door to the future. Teach us to focus on the Light ahead of us, even if it is just that one little candle. Guide our steps as we walk fearlessly into your new world, and grant to us the courage to be your voice and your hands, creating love, peace and joy as we journey onward. So it is.

January 2

"He has said, 'I will never leave you or forsake you.' So we can say with confidence, 'The Lord is my helper; I will not be afraid.'"

Hebrews 13:5-6

What does it mean to you to know that the Lord is your helper? Have you ever tried to walk your path on your own without that help? What was the result?

"Each one of you has been called. Every individual soul has work to do. None can do the work of another. Each must do his or her own work. Therefore we say accept it, my child: accept the task laid before you and pray to the Great Spirit that you may not fail."

White Eagle

Abba, you have promised never to forsake us. Forgive us when we forsake you instead. Even when we stubbornly seek our own way, you gently lead us back to the true Path with reins of Love. You give us work to do and the strength to do it. May we always remember to seek your Will for our lives and then have the courage to accept it. So it is.

January 3

"Then God said, 'Let there be light;' and there was light. And God saw that the light was good."

Genesis 1:3-4

Where do you see light in the world around you?

"And how you ask are we to walk the spiritual path? We answer: Say little; love much; give all; judge no-one; aspire to all that is pure and good—and keep on keeping on."

White Eagle from *The Quiet Mind*

Mother/Father God, you gave birth to the cosmos and all of creation, and called it good. Today we look around us and struggle to perceive that good. Yet like the sun in the midst of a storm, we know your Light is always present even in the darkest of nights. Guide our steps as we walk our destined path and gather us under your wings when darkness falls. May we sleep in safety and peace and awake to a new dawn. So it is.

January 4

"Yeshua said: I will give you that which no eye has seen, no ear has heard, no hand has touched, and no human heart has conceived."

Gospel of Thomas, Saying 17

What energies and blessings are you prepared to invite into your life?

"How many times have we called on God and then ignored the opportunities he sent? Maybe we didn't recognize them because they didn't take the form we expected. Spiritual surrender requires faith, but it also requires paying attention to opportunities and taking action. We need to look to God for guidance, to keep us on the right course, but we can't expect God to kick-start us every morning and deliver breakfast in bed."

Kathy Cordova

Holy One, you shower us with blessings far beyond our imagining, but often we feel unworthy of your gifts and overwhelmed by the responsibility. Sometimes we don't even recognize them as gifts or acknowledge you as the Source. May we always know that we are your beloved children whom you love and care for without condition. Give us the courage to say "Yes" to your many blessings so that we may truly become your Light in the world. So it is.

January 5

"Beloved, we are God's children now."

1 John 3:2

What does it mean to affirm that you are a beloved child of God? Do you believe that all people have this birthright?

Rev. Maryesah Karelon, O.M.M.

"How many times have we waited for Spirit to move for us, when in fact Spirit is patiently waiting to work with us?"

Sarah Ban Breathnach

Holy Mother/Father God, you have called us your children and so we are. We acknowledge that often we do not understand how blessed we truly are and how secure we are in your Love. Teach us to trust in that Love. Teach us to live in your Light. Teach us to be guided by your Justice and Mercy always. So it is.

January 6

"By the tender mercy of our God, the dawn from on high will break upon us, to give light to those who sit in darkness."

Luke 1:78-79

What actions can you take in your life to more fully manifest the Light?

"People are like stained-glass windows: they sparkle and shine when the sun is out, but when the darkness sets in their true beauty is revealed only if there is a light within."

Elizabeth Kubler-Ross

Sweet Spirit, you lead us out of darkness into the light of a new year and new opportunities. Help us to embrace the past and love the darkness; it serves a purpose. As we acknowledge the return of the light, open our hearts to those who still live in the darkness of poverty, despair and violence. May your Light of Peace, Love and Joy shine through us as a beacon of hope to our hurting world. So it is.

January 7

"He took a seed from the land, placed it in fertile soil; a plant by abundant waters...It sprouted and became a vine spreading out."

Ezekiel 17:5-6

As you plant new seeds in a new year, reflect on the vineyard of your life. Identify the plants that need cultivation and nurture and those that are unwelcome weeds that need to be removed so that new growth can take place.

"Life is not easy for any of us. But what of that? We must have perseverance and above all confidence in ourselves. We must believe that we are gifted for something and that this thing must be attained."

Marie Curie

Almighty God, you planted a garden in Eden and asked humankind to be your gardeners. After all these generations, we are still trying to get it right. Sometimes the rain doesn't fall; sometimes there is too much. Then the sun will burn the tender shoots or hide its warmth and the plants wither and die. Help us, Creator God, to be attentive stewards of your Creation. May our gardens bloom and our vineyards blossom abundantly. So it is.

January 8

"For the creation waits with eager longing for the revealing of the children of God."

Romans 8:19

If we truly walked in our world as children of God, how would our world be different?

"A knowledge of the path cannot be substituted for putting one foot in front of the other."

M. C. Richards

Eternal and Loving God, you show us the way and light our path. Now it is our turn to step forward in faith to do your work in the world. Give us the strength and the courage to reveal our true Selves as your daughters and sons. May your Light and your Love shine through us as we become ever closer to your Image of us. So it is.

January 9

"The Spirit of the Lord is upon me...He has sent me to proclaim release to the captives and recovery of sight to the blind, to let the oppressed go free, to proclaim the year of the Lord's favor."

Luke 4:18-19

Two thousand years ago Jesus of Nazareth stood before his home synagogue and read these powerful words from the prophet Isaiah. He is no longer physically in our world. Can we take his place? Visualize yourself proclaiming these words before a group of your family and friends. What feelings does this image evoke?

"I have walked that long road to freedom. I have tried not to falter. I have made missteps along the way. But I have discovered the secret that after climbing a great hill, one only finds that there are many more hills to climb. I have taken a moment here to rest, to steal a view of the glorious vista that surrounds me, to look back on the distance that I have come. But I can rest only for a moment, for with freedom comes responsibilities, and I dare not linger, for my long walk is not yet ended."

Nelson Mandela from <u>The Long Road to Freedom: The Autobiography of Nelson Mandela</u>

Holy God, you have gifted us with the freedom to choose and we do not always choose well. But you love us still as a loving parent loves a willful child. Guide us onto the Path of Wisdom and Light, which so often is the narrow and difficult way. May we truly proclaim your message of Freedom and healing to a hurting world. So it is.

January 10

"Heal me, O Lord, and I shall be healed; save me, and I shall be saved; for you are my praise."
Jeremiah 17:14

What issues or challenges in your life need to be healed? Are you ready for that healing to manifest?

"Two roads diverged in a wood, and I—I took the one less traveled by, and that has made all the difference."
Robert Frost from *"The Road Not Taken"*

Source of all Healing, you wrap us in your cloak of Comfort and Love. May we know the power of your Presence that may come in a whisper or a blinding flash; in a surge of energy or a quiet, gentle peace. Thank you, Mother/Father God, for uplifting us and caring for us and never abandoning us to darkness and despair. So it is.

January 11

"She said to herself, 'If I only touch his cloak, I will be made well.' Jesus turned, and seeing her he said, 'Take heart, daughter; your faith has made you well.'"
Matthew 9:21-22

What role does faith play in the process of healing?

"We can make conscious contact with God, transcend the limitations of a dichotomous world, and regain the power that is only available to us when we're connected to the Source. This is what I call getting in the gap. It's where we create, manifest, heal, live, and perform at a miraculous level. The gap is the powerful silence we can access through meditation."

Wayne W. Dyer from *Getting In the Gap*

Loving and Merciful God, we know that your intent for us is to live in joy, peace and harmony. Heal our minds and hearts of all that is less than your perfect Will for us. Where there is hatred, let us sow Love; where there is injury, Pardon; where there is doubt, Faith; where there is despair, Hope; and where there is sadness, Joy. So it is.

January 12

"Be kind to one another, tenderhearted, forgiving one another, as God in Christ has forgiven you."

Ephesians 4:32

What role has forgiveness played in your spiritual growth? Have you ever found it impossible or nearly impossible to forgive? What was the situation and how has it affected your life?

"Radical forgiveness is much more than the mere letting go of the past. It is the key to creating the life that we want, and the world that we want. It is the key to our own happiness and the key to world peace. It is no longer an option. It is our destiny."

Colin C. Tipping

Source of All Being, you shower us with your Love and Forgiveness. How can we fail to recognize your Love and Care as the model of what we are to become? Help us to forgive even when it is difficult. May our hearts expand as we release the pain and hurt of the past. May our arms embrace the world as our neighbors and may we learn truly to love our neighbors as ourselves. So it is.

January 13

"Jesus answered, 'The first [commandment] is...you shall love the Lord your God with all your heart, and with all your soul, and with all your mind, and with all your strength. The second is this: You shall love your neighbor as yourself.' There is no other commandment greater than these."

Mark 12:29-31

What does it mean to you to "Love your neighbor as yourself?" Do you truly love yourself? If you don't, what happens to this commandment?

"Do not give yourself more attention than you need, but take care of yourself and do not continually slay the God within you. Give opportunities in your daily life for the Christ within to manifest itself. This is what we mean by loving yourself, and this is what Jesus meant when he said, 'Thou shalt love thy neighbor as thyself.' Love peace of mind, love doing the right thing, love living according to divine law."

White Eagle from *The Quiet Mind*

Loving Mother/Father God, you teach us that each and every one of us is a temple of your Spirit; a holy place for the indwelling Christ. Remind us of this truth when we look into the eyes of our neighbor. Even when that neighbor is very different from us, even when we strongly disagree, they are still a dwelling place for the Christ. Teach us to behold the living Christ in everyone we meet. So it is.

January 14

"Do you not know that you are God's temple and that God's Spirit dwells in you?"

1 Corinthians 3:16

Do you treat your body as the temple of God? What changes could you make to honor the Christ within you more fully?

"There is a place in each of us that is so beautiful, angels smile in its presence. That presence is who you really are. When you can stand spiritually naked, look at yourself and like what you see, you have achieved a great feat."

Ray Rathbun from *The Way Is Within*

Holy One, you created us in your image, male and female, and called that creation very good. Forgive us when we fail to see that goodness in each other and ourselves. Teach us how to connect with the Christ within, our true Self, and allow that Self to illuminate our lives. Teach us to focus on the very best in each person we encounter and affirm that goodness even when they cannot see it. May we live as your Light in the world. So it is.

January 15

"Let your adornment be the inner self with the lasting beauty of a gentle and quiet spirit, which is very precious in God's sight."

1 Peter 3:4

What qualities do you feel are most important for a spiritually-centered life?

"You have to leave the city of your comfort and go into the wilderness of your intuition. What you'll discover will be wonderful. What you'll discover is yourself."
Alan Alda

Light of the World, you illuminate our darkest nights and bring radiance to our lonely days. Let us seek you within our own inner temple and light the lamp in the deepest recesses of our soul. Only then will we come to know you by encountering ourselves. And as we come to know ourselves, we will be drawn ever closer to you. Thank you for showing us how to be whole in holiness. So it is.

January 16

"Let the light of your face shine on us, O Lord."

Psalm 4:6

How do you recognize God's Presence in the world?

"As a single footstep will not make a path on the earth, so a single thought will not make a pathway in the mind. To make a deep physical path, we walk again and again. To make a deep mental path, we must think over and over the kind of thoughts we wish to dominate our lives."

Henry David Thoreau

O God, our Help in ages past, our Hope for years to come, our Shelter from the stormy blast and our eternal Home; you draw us forward into the future even as the darkness gathers around us. Teach us to focus on your Light before us as our guide. May we walk the path of the present in faith and trust, knowing that the past is complete and the future is yet to come. So it is.

January 17

"We look not at what can be seen but at what cannot be seen; for what can be seen is temporary, but what cannot be seen is eternal."

2 Corinthians 4:18

Do you feel that focusing on the good and positive is a way of denial or does it empower and give energy to the Light? How do we balance being "in the world but not of the world?"

"God doesn't ask that we succeed in everything, but that we are faithful. However beautiful our work may be, let us not become attached to it. Always remain prepared to give it up, without losing your peace."

Mother Teresa of Calcutta from <u>The Joy in Loving</u>

Loving Mother/Father God, you have called us out of the world, and yet we know that the world desperately needs your Light, your Love and your Peace. Teach us how to follow your Way even in the everydayness of life. Teach us the holiness of washing dishes and baking cookies; of a job well done and workdays complete; of little hands that need holding and fragile bodies that need hugging. Hold us close in the shadow of your arms for we do not always see where we are going. So it is.

January 18

"Nothing is hidden that will not be disclosed nor is anything secret that will not become known and come to light."

Luke 8:17

Reflect on the hidden secrets of your life. Would you be prepared for them to come into the light of day? What might be the results?

"What you do speaks so loud that I cannot hear what you say."

Ralph Waldo Emerson

Almighty and Everlasting God, we know that everything is known to you. There are no secrets that we can keep from the One who knows us better than we know ourselves. Teach us the transparency of truthfulness with each other, in love and gentleness. May your Light shine into the darkest recesses of our hearts and bring healing to our fear. So it is.

January 19

"Ask God, who gives to all generously...and it will be given you. But ask in faith, never doubting."

James 1:5-6

Have you ever asked God for something and not received it, at least not in the way you expected? How do you reconcile that with the promise that you may ask and you will receive?

"Mankind must evolve for all human conflict a method which rejects revenge, aggression, and retaliation. The foundation of such a method is love."

Martin Luther King, Jr.

Loving and Merciful God, you hear us when we pray, and respond in Love and Compassion to the requests of our hearts. We know that your response may not always be what we expect.

Remind us that it is always what we need most. Help us to trust in your judgment, for your vision is far better than ours. May we always steer our lives by your compass and leave the navigating in your hands. So it is.

January 20

"To set the mind on the Spirit is life and peace."

Romans 8:6

What would change in your life if you were to live your life focused on Spirit?

"The more faithfully you listen to the voice within you, the better you will hear what is sounding outside."

Dag Hammarskj

Holy God, you guide us with your Spirit and show us the way with your Light. Open our eyes and ears so that we may hear your whisperings and follow your path. Open our hearts so that we may feel your tender loving care for each and every one of your children. As we listen, as we see, as we feel, move us forward in action for Justice and Mercy in our world. So it is.

January 21

"Then Mary arose, and embraced them all, and began to speak to her brothers: 'Do not remain in sorrow and doubt, for God's grace will guide you and comfort you. Instead, let us praise God's greatness, for God has prepared us for this. God is calling upon us to become fully human.'"

Gospel of Mary Magdalene 9:12-18

What does it mean to you to "become fully human?"

"We must give up our will, give up control, and release our expectations about a specific result. This is where the going starts to get tough. We want what we want, and usually we want it yesterday. We need to open ourselves up to the possibility that we don't always know what's best for us."

Kathy Cordova

Source of All, we come to you often as we struggle with our need to be in control of our lives. And yet we know that is an illusion. Teach us that the true control is in letting go and letting you take over the pilot's seat. Help us take that deep breath of release, knowing that your Will for us is always the highest and the best. So it is.

January 22

"Look at the birds of the air; they neither sow nor reap nor gather into barns, and yet your heavenly Father feeds them. Are you not of more value than they?"
Matthew 6:26

Has there been a time of lack in your life? How did you survive it and what lessons did you learn?

"We each have the choice in any setting to step back and let go of the mind-set of scarcity. Once we let go of scarcity, we discover the surprising truth of sufficiency. By sufficiency, I don't mean a quantity of anything. Sufficiency isn't two steps up from poverty or one step short of abundance. It isn't a measure of barely enough or more than enough. Sufficiency isn't an amount at all. It is an experience, a context we generate, a declaration, a knowing that there is enough, and that we are enough."
Lynne Twist

Mother/Father God, you give so generously when we ask but often asking is the hard part. Trusting and having faith is the hard part. Letting go is the hard part. And yet we know you are always there for us, ready to give good gifts to your children. Teach us to believe in our own goodness and worthiness so we may believe in yours. So it is.

January 23

"We know that all things work together for good for those who love God, who are called according to his purpose."

Romans 8:28

Have there been some times in your life when you doubted the above statement? How did you get through that time? Do you see things differently now?

"Those who do not know how to weep with their whole heart don't know how to laugh either."

Golda Meir

God of the Morning Dawn, remind us that joy often comes sweetest after the darkest of nights. Strengthen our faith and courage when the tests descend upon us. Show us your ever-loving Presence by lifting us on the wings of eagles. We may not always be able to fly over our pain, but we always know that you will walk with us, help us stand when we fall and carry us when we can go no further. You will never forsake us and for that we give you thanks and praise. So it is.

January 24

"Surely God is my salvation; I will trust, and will not be afraid, for the Lord God is my strength and my might; he has become my salvation."

Isaiah 12:2

What does it mean for you to trust in God?

"Every time you are tempted to react in the same old way, ask if you want to be a prisoner of the past or a pioneer of the future."
Deepak Chopra

God of all the Encircling Years, we trust in you. In our loneliest hours, you are there. When our courage fails us, you are there. When the lions and alligators gather round, you are there. Thank you for showing us a way through the wilderness and new paths to freedom. May we know the celebration of a new day dawning when fear will be no more. So it is.

January 25

"The wisdom from above is first pure, then peaceable, gentle, willing to yield, full of mercy...And a harvest of righteousness is sown in peace for those who make peace."
James 3:17-18

What steps can you take to create new and positive habits in your life?

"Thoughts lead on to purposes; purposes go forth in action; actions form habits; habits decide character; and character fixes our destiny."
Tryon Edwards

Mother/Father God, you know how frightening change can be for your children. We stubbornly cling to old worn-out patterns even when we know they are harming us and blocking our growth. You have gifted us with a new year and a new beginning. With your help and guidance, we can create a new life and new opportunities beyond our wildest dreams. Inspire us to dream, dear God, and then build the foundations under our dreams. So it is.

January 26

"It shall be said, 'Build up, build up, prepare the way.'"

Isaiah 57:14

What are your dreams and goals for this year?

"The breeze at dawn has secrets to tell you; don't go back to sleep. You must ask for what you really want; don't go back to sleep. People are going back and forth across the doorsill where the two worlds touch. The door is round and open. Don't go back to sleep."

Rumi, Sufi Mystic Poet

O God, you are the master builder. Teach us to dream and to embrace the impossible, because you have the power to make the impossible happen. Teach us to ask for what we truly desire and then wait in silence for your response. Let your Divine Will be our will and may all be in Divine Order as we act to create our dreams. So it is.

January 27

"For God alone my soul waits in silence; from him comes my salvation. He alone is my rock and my salvation, my fortress; I shall never be shaken."

Psalm 62:1-2

How does silence play a role in your life?

"I mean by the word mystical; entering into conscious direct relationship with the divine. It must be conscious and it must be direct to be mystical. Mystical is not theological; it's not having a series of ideas about God, however lucid or wonderful. It's not emotional; it's not having a series of feelings, however deep and adoring about God. And it's not intellectual, in any sense, even in the most refined sense."

Andrew Harvey

Holy One, Moses encountered you in the burning bush and removed his sandals because he was standing on holy ground. May we discover that holy ground in our lives. We invite you to an intimate communion with us. Help us to make time in our hectic lives for the Source of our Being. Take us into the silence and meet us there. So it is.

January 28

"Then they were glad because they had quiet, and he brought them to their desired haven."

Psalm 107:30

What is your desired haven of rest? How do you get there? If it is only a dream, how can you begin to make it a reality?

"When the solution is simple, God is answering."

Albert Einstein

God of Simplicity and Peace, it is we your human children that make our world so complex. In you, the knots are untied, the puzzles are solved and questions receive answers, even if those answers are unexpected or difficult for us to understand. As we move into our new beginning, help us to seek your simplicity in our daily lives. Bigger is not better; faster is not greater; more technology is not necessarily the solution. Slow us down, Lord, so we may hear your quiet whisper and feel your haven within us. So it is.

January 29

"Strive first for the kingdom of God and his righteousness, and all these things will be given to you as well."

Matthew 6:33

Reflect on your priorities for the New Year. Where does God fit into your list?

"There is a law of compensation which states 'As you give, so shall you receive—and God will provide it!" Faith expands when you give. The more you give, the more faith you're going to have. You will find out that Emerson spoke true when he said, 'You can't outgive God.'"

Greg Barrette

Holy Sophia, so often we let everything in our lives come first before we stop to listen for your voice. Yet we know deep in our hearts that nothing else truly matters. You are the solution to the impossible conundrums, the days that need 30 hours, the rat race that takes us nowhere we want to go. Bring us home, dear Mother, to the hearth of our soul and quiet the many voices of resistance. Let your Peace hover over us as a dove. So it is.

January 30

"Go in peace. The mission you are on is under the eye of the Lord."

Judges 18:6

What does peace mean to you?

"Be a sweet melody in the great orchestration, instead of a discordant note. The medicine this sick world needs is love. Hatred must be replaced by love, and fear by faith that love will prevail."

Peace Pilgrim from <u>*Her Life and Work in Her Own Words*</u>

Almighty God, we look around us and we see war and violence everywhere. There is so much hatred even in your Name. Teach us how to love each other as your beloved children. You are One God, no matter what name we call you, and we are your family. We pray for peace in our time, that we may truly come to embody your compassionate Love, your Justice and your Mercy. May we be your instruments of Peace. So it is.

January 31

"It is you who light my lamp; the Lord, my God, lights up my darkness."

Psalm 81:28

How can you bring the light of peace and love into your world?

"Holding on to resentment is like taking poison and hoping the other person will die."

Carolyn Myss

"Harboring a grudge completely blocks our ability to have peace of mind. Forgiveness is not something we do for the sake of another person. Forgiveness is something we do for ourselves."

Greg Barrette

Holy Mother/Father God, you have shown us how to forgive but sometimes it is very difficult. There is so much pain in our world, so much injustice. Teach us to see with a broader vision through your eyes. Allow your Light to flood our hearts so that we may truly embrace our brothers and sisters. May we light our lamps and set them on lamp stands as a sign of hope in the darkness. So it is.

February

Walk daily in the garden of your soul and
allow the Risen Christ to meet you there,
for in him you will find the living waters
of Peace and Healing.
In all you do, let Love
be the guiding principle,
for thus you will show yourselves
to be children of the God of Love.

Light in the Darkness

February 1

"It is like a mustard seed, which, when sown upon the ground, is the smallest of all the seeds on earth; yet when it is sown it grows up and becomes the greatest of all shrubs, and puts forth large branches, so that the birds of the air can make nests in its shade."
Mark 4:31-32

How do you see transformation birthing within your own life?

"In the midst of winter, I finally learned that there was in me an invincible summer."
Albert Camus

Mighty God, you plant the seeds within us for transformation and renewal. Teach us how to nurture them so that we may grow into our true Selves. Remind us to cherish this time of incubation and turn our attention within to the quietness and silence of your Presence. May we listen with our hearts so we may sprout new shoots in the springtime. So it is.

February 2

"No one sews a piece of unshrunk cloth on an old cloak, for the patch pulls away from the cloak, and a worse tear is made. Neither is new wine put into old wineskins; otherwise, the skins burst, and the wine is spilled."
Matthew 9:16-17

Have you ever tried to "patch" something in your life when a fresh start seemed too difficult? What was the result?

"Become a student of change. It is the only thing that will remain constant."

Anthony D'Angelo

Loving Mother/Father God, you lead us into the future where you are. Reveal to us the path of Light and Love so that we may walk in your Way. Give us the courage to let go of the baggage of the past so that our focus may be on the present, which is the only thing that is real. With our eyes fixed on your Vision, with our feet firmly grounded on your precious Earth, we journey ever onward. Walk beside us and never let us walk alone. So it is.

February 3

"Where there is no vision, the people perish."

Proverbs 29:18

What role does "vision" play in your life, both in terms of vision as goals and dreams, and vision as a spiritual epiphany?

"The Vision you hold is the calling out of your inner soul, the higher self, encouraging you to pursue its fulfillment. The experience of realizing your Vision will help you grow into what you are meant to be."

Jim Lees

Holy One, so often we are blinded by your Light and distracted by the daily emergencies of our lives. Keep our eyes focused on you until your brightness becomes our home. Expand our vision of what is possible, what is real, what is Truth. Come to us and reveal your Holiness so that we may see in the mirror, ever so dimly, what we truly are meant to be. So it is.

February 4

"*Beloved, since God loved us so much, we also ought to love one another...God lives in us, and his love is perfected in us.*"

1 John 4:11-12

How do you demonstrate that God's love lives in you?

"Look at every path closely and deliberately, then ask yourself this crucial question: 'Does this path have a heart?' If it does, then the path is good. If it doesn't, then it is of no use."

Carlos Castanada

Beloved of my Heart, you shower me with Love and I am so grateful. Open the creaky doors of my heart and flood me with the healing power of your loving Presence. Show me how to reflect that Love outwards to a hurting world that desperately needs to be loved. I offer a piece of my heart to you, my God. Replace it with the sweetness of your True Love and may it reside in my heart forevermore. So it is.

February 5

"We have gifts that differ according to the grace given to us: prophecy, in proportion to faith; ministry, in ministering; the teacher, in teaching; the exhorter, in exhortation; the giver, in generosity; the leader, in diligence; the compassionate, in cheerfulness."

Romans 12:6-8

What gifts do you bring to God's table and how are they being revealed in your daily life with friends, family and co-workers?

"Everything you need you already have. You are complete right now, you are a whole, total person, not an apprentice person on the way to someplace else. Your completeness must be understood by you and experienced in your thoughts as your own personal reality."

Wayne W. Dyer

Generous and Ever-Loving Father, show us the reality of our wholeness and completeness in your Love. Bring us face-to-face with the abundance that you offer to us. May we accept your gracious invitation to sit and dine at your banquet, at a table that is overflowing with all good things beyond our imagining. Instill in our hearts the courage to accept the gifts you offer to us. May we reveal them to the world and give you the glory. So it is.

Rev. Maryesah Karelon, O.M.M.

February 6

"So I tell you, whatever you ask for in prayer, believe that you have received it, and it will be yours."

Mark 11:24

What role does prayer play in your spiritual life?

"True prayer isn't a matter of executing a script; it's an intention of the heart."

Alan Cohen

Mother of all Mercies, as a mother loves and supports her children, so you wrap us in your loving arms and gather us under your wings. Strengthen our tired hearts when the darkness gathers. Guide us with your gentle Wisdom. Lift us to our feet when we fall and inspire us to continue onward. Gift us with a clear intention of your Will for our lives and instill in us the truth that nothing is impossible within the arms of your Love. So it is.

February 7

"For mortals it is impossible, but for God all things are possible."

Matthew 19:26

What gifts have you received from God through prayer?

"Formulate and stamp indelibly on your mind a mental picture of yourself succeeding. Hold this picture tenaciously. Never permit it to fade. Your mind will seek to develop the picture."

Norman Vincent Peale

Source of All Being, you draw us to you as your beloved children. When we face obstacles we cannot surmount, when we encounter challenges we cannot solve alone, help us to remember that you are always there for us, a well of energy and inspiration that will never run dry. Remind us that life is a journey that often requires more from us than we think possible. Do the impossible through us, O God, and expand the envelope of our vision so we may reach beyond our limits to the stars. So it is.

February 8

"The Lord said to him, 'I have heard your prayer and your plea, which you made before me; I have consecrated this house that you have built, and put my name there forever; my eyes and my heart will be there for all time.'"

1 Kings 9:3

What "house" has the Lord helped you to build in your life? What building is yet to be accomplished?

"Wisdom has to do with our relationship to the whole, to the cosmos, to nature, to both the feminine and the masculine powers of nature. Wisdom is finding the balance between the head and the heart, upper chakras and lower chakras, earth and sky, masculine and feminine, joy and sorrow, yin and yang, energy and rest, human and divine, cosmos and psyche."

Matthew Fox from *Creativity*

Holy Wisdom of God, we call on your Name and ask your assistance in building a house with a firm foundation. Too often we are tempted to build in haste, on shifting sands, and then we witness the results when a storm blows into our life. Teach us the patience of "one step at a time." Teach us to put our trust in the Master Builder who knows the blueprint of the future. With your Help and Guidance, may we build strong and well. So it is.

February 9

"It is impossible for anyone to see the everlasting reality and not become like it. The Truth is not realized like truth in the world: those who see the sun do not become the sun; those who see the sky, the earth, or anything that exists, do not become what they see. But when you see something in this other space, you become it. If you know the Breath, you are the Breath. If you know the Christ, you become the Christ. If you see the Father, you are the Father."

Gospel of Philip, verse 44

How does your spirituality impact your daily life?

"If we are facing in the right direction, all we have to do is keep on walking."

Buddhist Saying

Holy Sophia, we seek your Wisdom but often only when all else fails. We call you and invite you to make your tent among us and cover us with the cloud of your glory. Holy Shekinah, you were with our Father from the beginning, his beloved partner in heaven as on earth. Gift us with the understanding of true balance, harmony and partnership in our relations with one another. Born in wholeness and Love, may we reflect that Divine Oneness in our lives and our loves. As above, so below. So it is.

February 10

"If two of you agree on earth about anything you ask, it will be done for you by my Father in heaven. For where two or three are gathered in my name, I am there among them."

Matthew 18:19-20

Have the goals for your spiritual life ever been challenged by family or friends who disagreed with your path? How did you deal with this challenge?

"It is often easier to fight for one's principles than to live up to them."

Adlai Stevenson

Almighty and Ever-Present God, it is often a fine line between taking a stand and becoming intolerant within the diverse tapestry of our world. Teach us how to find that balance point and live there even when it's uncomfortable. Teach us to stand strong for what we believe while allowing the same opportunities to our friends, our families, our neighbors, even those who appear to be our enemies. We are all your children, created in your Divine Image. May we always see that Image in our neighbor's eyes. So it is.

February 11

"The fruit of the Spirit is love, joy, peace, patience, kindness, generosity, faithfulness, gentleness, and self-control."

Galatians 5:22-23

What can you do in your life to manifest more fully these fruits of the Spirit?

"Be aware of wonder. Live a balanced life—learn some and think some and draw and paint and sing and dance and play and work every day some."

Robert Fulghum from <u>*All I Really Need To Know I Learned In Kindergarten*</u>

Wondrous God, you surround us with such incredible beauty and yet it is so easy to focus on what is ugly in our world. Expand our narrow vision and gift us with your higher perspective.

Allow us to feel the joy of an innocent child, for it is through a child's eyes that we see heaven. Slow us down, Lord, and remind us that the race is not always won by speed but often by determination and patience. So it is.

February 12

"They are like trees planted by streams of water, which yield their fruit in its season, and their leaves do not wither. In all that they do, they prosper."

Psalm 1:3

What steps can you take to be more open to God's gracious abundance and prosperity?

"Keep a grateful journal. Every night, list five things that you are grateful for. What it will begin to do is change your perspective of your day and your life."

Oprah Winfrey

Dear God, we are so thirsty for the living water of your Truth. Show us how to send our roots deep into your good Earth so our branches may reach out to embrace a troubled world. Teach us how to bear the best fruit, fruit of the Spirit, which will manifest goodness and prosperity for all. Remind us again and again that you are the source of our abundance, and we are grateful. Thank you, thank you, thank you. So it is.

February 13

"According to the grace of God given to me, like a skilled master builder I laid a foundation, and someone else is building on it."

1 Corinthians 3:10

In what ways are you laying a foundation in your life that others may build upon? How are you having a positive influence on the lives of those you interact with: family, friends, co-workers and casual encounters?

"As we express our gratitude, we must never forget that the highest appreciation is not to utter words, but to live by them."

John F. Kennedy

Abba, we acknowledge that you are truly the Master Architect of our lives. Forgive us when we insist on going it alone and building by our own design. You laid the foundation when you created us. Remind us that a strong and blessed house needs to be built on the firm, established foundation of your Love. Let us not only speak your words of Light and Truth, but live them from our hearts. Only then will we become true temples of your living Spirit. So it is.

February 14

"Love is patient; love is kind...It bears all things, believes all things, hopes all things, endures all things. Love never ends."

                         1 Corinthians 13:4, 7-8

How would you define love and how do you express it in your life?

"You don't have to go looking for love when it's where you come from."

                                     Werner Erhard

Loving Mother/Father God, we look to you for an example of what love can be. We know that you hold us always in your loving embrace. Open our hearts to the wondrous ecstatic risk of love. Show us how to love others as you love us; without conditions, without counting the cost, without expecting anything in return. Only by giving ourselves away in love can we hope to find ourselves. So it is.

February 15

"He will guide them to springs of the water of life."

                                       Revelation 7:17

In what ways can love make a difference in our world of today? What are the risks and the blessings when you live your life from a place of love?

"Divine am I inside and out, and I make holy whatever I touch or am touched from...Why should I wish to see God better than this day? I see something of God each hour of the twenty-four, and each moment then. In the faces of men and women I see God, and in my own face in the glass. I find letters from God dropped in the street, and every one is signed by God's name."

Walt Whitman

God of Mercy, you have taught us not to judge, but so often we forget. It is so easy to assume we know better than you. Cleanse our hearts of all bitterness and anger. Let your purest Love flow through us as a river flows inevitably to the ocean. In a world of violence and bloodshed, may we stand tall for your principles of Love, Mercy and Forgiveness. Inspire us to become wells of living Love and beacons of everlasting Light. So it is.

February 16

"Those who wait for the Lord shall renew their strength, they shall mount up with wings like eagles, they shall run and not be weary, they shall walk and not faint."

Isaiah 40:31

How has your relationship with God brought change into your life?

"You cannot change your destination overnight, but you can change your direction overnight."
Jim Rohn

O God of all Ages, you call us to our right and perfect path, but there are times when that path is anything but clear. We find ourselves fighting brambles and climbing over huge boulders. Sometimes we stumble and fall and search for the strength to rise again. At that moment, you are always there with us, holding us by the hand and lifting us on outstretched wings. We give you thanks, gentle God, for never letting us go. So it is.

February 17

"See, the former things have come to pass, and new things I now declare; before they spring forth, I tell you of them."
Isaiah 42:9

How can you be more open to God's messages?

"If you go to God with a thimble, you can only bring back a thimbleful."
Randolph Wilkerson

Generous and Ever-Loving One, you offer us more than we can imagine and so often we are unprepared for your gifts. Empty our hearts and minds of the trivia of everyday life so that we may make room in our hearts for you. Remind us of what is truly important and help us to order our lives according to your priorities. And always, dear God, help us to keep it simple even when our world is a very complex place. So it is.

February 18

"Let the peace of Christ rule in your hearts...And be thankful."

Colossians 3:15

Count your blessings and make a list of what you are thankful for in your life.

"Gratitude is not only the greatest of virtues, but the parent of all others."

Cicero

Holy Spirit, you come to us in the stillness and speak in gentle whispers. You come to us in grandeur and incredible beauty, and speak in the rush of rivers. You come to us in the storms of life and speak in the language of the heart when no words will do. Open us to your Presence and your messages. Allow us to experience the Peace that only you can bring. So it is.

February 19

"Not by might, not by power, but by my spirit, says the Lord of Hosts."

Zechariah 4:6

Have you ever tried to make something happen by sheer force of will? What were the results and what did you learn from the experience?

"There is a soul force in the universe, which, if we permit it, will flow through us and provide miraculous results."

Mahatma Gandhi

Almighty God, we acknowledge your greatness. All your actions show your Wisdom and Love. Teach us to wait with patience for your solutions and allow your power to work through us. Even when we feel alone, when we cannot sense your Presence, you are there waiting for us to invite you to be our answer. Remind us, dear Holy One, that might does not make right and that your Way is the Way of Love. So it is.

February 20

"Come away to a deserted place all by yourselves and rest a while."

Mark 6:31

When was the last time you spent time alone with God? Do you have a special daily meditation time? If not, is this something that could be of benefit? What would need to change for you to spend more time in communion with God?

"In the solitude of your mind are the answers to all your questions about life. You must take the time to ask and listen."

Bawa Mahaiyaddeen

Mother/Father God, sometimes we are so tired. There are so many people and responsibilities that demand our time and attention, so many "shoulds" in our lives. You call us to rest a while in the peace and safety of your Love. Teach us how to take "minute vacations." Remind us to stop to breathe in your Spirit and breathe out our frustration, our hurry, our panic of not being good enough. Now, in your Peace, is all we have and all we need. So it is.

February 21

"Surely I know the plans I have for you, says the Lord, plans for your welfare and not for harm, to give you a future with hope."

Jeremiah 29:11

Recall a time in your life when hope was nearly gone for you. What was the cause and what was the result? What did you learn from this experience and how did hope return to your life?

"When the night has been too lonely, and the road has been too long, and you think that love is only for the lucky and the strong; just remember, in the winter far beneath the bitter snow, lies the seed that with the sun's love in the spring becomes the Rose."

Bette Midler

Source of All Being, you give us Hope when our hope is all but gone. When we're at the end of our rope, you give us the strength to tie a knot and hang on. Remind us that the dormancy of winter hides great growth and wonderful potential for life. One of the most powerful forces in the universe is a little seed pushing its way up through the soil to the sun. May we be that seed, ever reaching out for the warmth of your Light and Love. So it is.

February 22

"For now we see in a mirror, dimly, but then we will see face to face. Now I know only in part; then I will know fully, even as I have been fully known."

1 Corinthians 13:12

What parts of your self do you keep hidden from others, and for what reason? Would you like to bring this part of you more into the light? How could this be accomplished?

"Do not be discouraged. Learn not to be disappointed in anything, or any person. You are disappointed because your will, your desire, has been frustrated. Learn to submit to the divine will, for God's will is all-wise. Wait, then, for God's appointments, learning to tread the path, wisely, serenely."

White Eagle from *The Quiet Mind*

Gentle and Merciful God, waiting in patience is never easy. So often we insist we know what has to be done; we strike out in anger and frustration when in reality we have only a partial vision. Teach us to fly above the chaos of life so that we may see clearly and choose wisely. Remind us to take a deep breath before we speak words of hurt and anger. Open us to your divine appointments in our lives. May we place them on our calendars as top priority. We cherish your Presence, which gifts us with Serenity, Courage, and Wisdom. So it is.

February 23

"You did not choose me but I chose you. And I appointed you to go and bear fruit, fruit that will last, so that the Father will give you whatever you ask him in my name."

John 15:16

What does it mean to be chosen by God? Can this happen to anybody or only a special few?

"If you seek to be among the chosen, choose yourself."

Solara, Visionary and Mystic

Abba, it is difficult for us to look in the mirror and see ourselves as your chosen child. It is much easier to allow your Beloved Son Jesus to carry that title alone. But something within us knows that there is more to the story. We are all chosen, in different ways, for different work, with different gifts. May we become open to the blessings and responsibilities of our being chosen by you, and never let us assume that this makes us any better or any more perfect than anyone else. We are all laborers in your vineyard. So it is.

February 24

"When I bring clouds over the earth and the bow is seen in the clouds, I will remember my covenant that is between me and you and every living creature."

Genesis 9:14-15

As God's chosen ones, what is our responsibility to the other kingdoms of the earth; plant, animal and mineral? How can we be better stewards of our earth?

"The day of my spiritual awakening was the day I saw—and knew I saw—all things in God and God in all things."

Mechtild of Magdeburg, Medieval Mystic

Creator of All, you made all things and called them good. You created humanity as caretakers for your Creation. Forgive us when we have assumed that meant taking from the store of Mother Earth's resources and never giving back. Forgive us for despoiling your beautiful garden and teach us how to be good stewards of all your Creation. So it is.

February 25

"When the Spirit of truth comes, he will guide you into all the truth; for he will not speak on his own, but will speak whatever he hears, and he will declare to you the things that are to come."

John 16:13

What is truth for you? Have you ever felt God's spirit flowing through you in prophetic utterance or vision? How did that feel?

"By the accident of fortune a man may rule the world for a time, but by virtue of love and kindness he may rule the world forever."

Lao Tsu, Chinese Philosopher, from *Tao Te Ching*

Holy One, thank you for your indwelling Spirit as guide and teacher. Reveal to us your Truth and your message that you would have us speak. May we become your mouthpieces of Peace and Justice, and may we share your words with courage and strength. We are your voice, O God, to a hurting world. When we are silent, your Light and your Love dim among us. So it is.

February 26

"I urge that supplications, prayers, intercessions, and thanksgivings be made for everyone, for kings and all who are in high positions, so that we may lead a quiet and peaceable life."

1 Timothy 2:1-2

How does the current state of world affairs impact your spiritual faith? Do you think we can make a difference by prayer and meditation?

"Within you is one of the most beautiful oases you will ever find: it is absolute love. Seek the oasis within your heart, mind, and soul. If you cannot find your oasis, you are living in a desert. Walk out of the desert, into the openness of your mind, and you will see your oasis. Start your journey by loving yourself each day. Fill your chalice with love from your oasis within so when you meet others who are thirsty on the road of life, you have something to share."

Ron Rathbun from <u>The Way Is Within</u>

Ruler of all the Earth, we come to you in despair for the world around us. Violence and bloodshed surround us. For many terror and war are ways of life, often in honor of you. We know that this is not your Will or your Way. Guide the leaders of the world and teach them the Path of Peace. Give them and us the courage to walk the narrow and difficult way of Love and Justice. Reveal to us your Truth that all humanity are brothers and sisters, one family, embraced by your Love. Stretch out our arms to embrace our neighbors wherever we find them. So it is.

Rev. Maryesah Karelon, O.M.M.

February 27

"But there is forgiveness with you, so that you may be revered. I wait for the Lord, my soul waits, and in his word I hope."

Psalm 130:4-5

Is there anything that is unforgivable?

"Heaven is where you'll be when you are okay right where you are."

Sun Ra

Loving and Forgiving Father, you gift us over and over again with the power of your Forgiveness. We know that we are works in progress. Teach us how to love and forgive ourselves for failing to be perfect. You do not ask us for perfection on this earth plane, but you do call us to be holy and holy is what we become when we become whole. Bind up our wounds and heal us with your Love and Grace. So it is.

February 28

"There is no fear in love, but perfect love casts out fear."

1 John 4:18

It has been said that the opposite of love is not hate but fear. How do you see this demonstrated in your life and how are you working to overcome fear with love?

"Come and fill my days with dreams. Empty me of all the empty things that I hold onto. Come and fill my heart with You."

> Lyrics from "Come and Fill My Heart" by Grant Cunningham and Matt Huesmann

Beloved One, when love touches our lives so often we run away in fear; fear of being hurt, being vulnerable, surrendering our freedom. Teach us how to love as you love; without conditions, without limits, without boundaries and fears. Empower us to be true reflections of your Light and Love here on earth. May we speak and feel and walk the Way of Love, with open hearts and open arms. So it is.

February 29

"Yeshua said: If they ask you from where you come, say: We were born of the Light, there where Light is born of Light. It holds true and is revealed within their image. If they ask you who you are, say: We are its children, the beloved of the Father, the Living One. If they ask you what is the sign of the Father in you, say: It is movement and repose."

> **Gospel of Thomas, Saying 50**

How would you answer those questions: Where do you come from and who are you?

"Meister Eckhart met a beautiful naked boy. He asked him where he came from. He said: 'I come from God.' Where did you leave him? 'In pure hearts.' Where are you going? 'To God.' Where do you find God? 'Where I let go of all creatures.' Who are you? 'A King.' Where is your kingdom? 'In my heart.' Be careful that no one take it from you. 'I shall.' Then he led him to his cell and said to him: 'Take whatever jacket you would like.' 'Then I would be no king!' And he disappeared. For it was God who had been amusing the divine self at Eckhart's expense."

Holy One, you come to us as a mirror reflecting the Divine Light that is within each of us. Open our eyes so that we may truly see who we are as children of Light. Guide our footsteps as we walk along the pathway of Light. May we speak your words of Light and Truth to the world from our hearts. Fill us with your Compassion for all our brothers and sisters. Beloved One, become the still point in our lives between movement and repose as we rest in your Love. So it is.

March

Find enough security within yourself
to admit your mistakes
and humbly ask for forgiveness
when you have harmed your sister or brother.
Know that our Loving and Merciful God
has already forgiven you,
for "if you, O Lord, should mark iniquities,
Lord, who could stand?
But there is forgiveness with you,
so that you may be revered." (Psalm 130:3-4)
Therefore, forgive yourself,
forgive others that hurt you,
and ask for that gift in return.
Then release the hurt, the pain,
the anger and let it go.

Light in the Darkness

March 1

"As for me, I would seek God, and to God I would commit my cause."

                                             Job 5:8

What does it mean to commit your cause to God?

"Human beings, vegetables, or cosmic dust—we all dance to a mysterious tune, intoned in the distance by an invisible piper."

                                     Albert Einstein

Holy One, when we feel lost and alone, remind us that you are always near. When we stumble and fall, lift us to our feet again and support our halting steps. When we are overwhelmed and discouraged by the challenges and darkness around us, shine your Light into our lives, that we may always follow your Path. Thank you for never abandoning us and for seeking us when we lose our way. So it is.

March 2

"When you search for me, you will find me; if you seek me with all your heart, I will let you find me."

                                  Jeremiah 29:13-14

When you look within your heart, what barriers do you find that keep God at a distance? How might these barriers be removed?

"...I am there. You cannot see Me, yet I am the light you see by. You cannot hear Me, yet I speak through your voice. You cannot feel Me, yet I am the power at work in your hands...I am your assurance. I am your peace. I am one with you. I AM. Though you fail to find Me, I do not fail you. Though your faith in Me is unsure, My faith in you never wavers, because I know you, because I love you. Beloved, I am there."

James Dillet Freeman

Mother/Father God, you love us with a Love that will never end. We are your beloved children and like children, we sometimes make mistakes, and rebel and stray from the Path of your Light and Love. Forgive us for our blindness and stubbornness. Teach us how to forgive each other and ourselves when we fail to reflect your Image that resides within us. Guide us as we journey and lead us to your garden of Peace. So it is.

March 3

"Do not judge, and you will not be judged; do not condemn, and you will not be condemned. Forgive, and you will be forgiven."

Luke 6:37

What is more difficult for you—to forgive someone who has hurt you, to receive forgiveness when you have hurt another or to forgive yourself?

"When we want to move beyond the pain, when we want to feel better, when we are ready to move beyond where we are, emotionally and spiritually, we must forgive."

Iyanla Vanzant from *The Value in the Valley*

Loving and Merciful God, you offer us forgiveness when we stumble. You pick us up when we fall. You surround us with your ever-present Love when we are in despair and desolation. Give us the inner strength and awareness to guard our thoughts and words. Teach us the power of what we say and think so that we manifest love, joy and peace in our lives and with each other. So it is.

March 4

"They will scarcely brood over the days of their lives, because God keeps them occupied with the joy of their hearts."

Ecclesiastes 5:20

Do you find yourself brooding or worrying about issues in your life? How can you focus more on the "joys of your heart" and trust in God's Divine Order?

"Your vision will become clear only when you look into your heart."

Carl Jung

God of Peace and Joy, show us the path to the garden of our heart. Meet us there in the serenity and beauty of sacred silence. Open our eyes so that we may see your Presence in the world around us. Open our ears to the soft whisper of your voice in the sighing of the wind in the trees. Open our hearts, dear God, to the rush of your Spirit of Love. Teach us to sing your song even in our darkest nights. So it is.

March 5

"Let anyone who is thirsty come to me, and let the one who believes in me drink. As the scripture has said, 'Out of the believer's heart shall flow rivers of living water.'"

John 7:37-38

If you allow the living water from your heart to flow into the world around you, what effect will it have?

"How far you go in life depends on your being tender with the young, compassionate with the aged, sympathetic with the striving and tolerant of the weak and the strong. Because someday in life you will have been all of these."

George Washington Carver

Holy Wisdom of God, you teach us that words are not enough. We must reach out to those around us in need. Teach us how to act and not just react; to bind up wounds instead of causing hurt; to be tender, gentle and loving even in the face of fierce opposition. Show us your divine patience so that we may learn to show it to other people in our lives who push our buttons. May we watch our words as carefully as our actions so that we may become your messengers of reconciliation in a divided world. So it is.

March 6

"*Clothe yourselves with the new self, created according to the likeness of God.*"

Ephesians 4:24

If you allow the living water of God to flow through you, what changes will occur in your own life—body, mind and spirit?

"When you look for the good in others you discover the best in you yourself."

Martin Walsh

Wondrous God, you make all things new and open up the vistas of a new future. Create in us a clean, pure heart so we may cease to live in the past, with our mistakes, regrets and frustrations, and instead voyage into your future that is the now of today. Keep us centered in the present so that we learn to love and be loved every day of our lives. So it is.

March 7

"I am about to create new heavens and a new earth; the former things shall not be remembered."

Isaiah 65:17

As you look around you, what are the obstacles to the fulfillment of this prophecy? How can you assist in removing these obstacles?

"Your task is not to seek for love, but merely to seek and find all the barriers within yourself that you have built against it."

Rumi, Sufi Mystic Poet

Source of All Being, you go before us to light our way. Forgive our hesitation and fear when change looms before us. We are creatures of habit. We like the security and comfort of the familiar. Inspire us with your Vision of Truth and Justice. Guide our actions with your Wisdom and Courage so that we may become agents of change for a transformed world. So it is.

March 8

"And he has inspired them to teach...He has filled them with skill to do every kind of work done by...any sort of artisan or skilled designer."

Exodus 35:34-35

What specific skills do you have that can aid in the building of a new Heaven and a new Earth? How are you using these skills now in your life?

"However many holy words you read, however many you speak, what good will they do you if you do not act upon them?"

Buddha

Almighty God, you created us in your likeness and gave us many gifts to use in your work in the world. Help us to seek your Guidance and Wisdom to bring these gifts to full bloom and use them more fully as you intended. Heal our unworthiness and our lack of self-confidence. Show us the difference between humility and lack of commitment. May we never run away from your challenges and may we always stand for your principles. So it is.

March 9

"The human mind may devise many plans, but it is the purpose of the Lord that will be established."

Proverbs 19:21

What is the difference between creating your own plans and following the purpose that God has created for your life?

"In order to hear your calling and answer it, you must generously give yourself the gift of time. It's not how fast you make your dreams come true, but how steadily you pursue it."

Sarah Ban Breathnach

Ever-Patient One, you remind us that even you did not create the universe and all its wonders in a single day. Slow us down, Lord, so that we may truly listen for your Wisdom and Guidance. We acknowledge that you have created each one of us with a unique and special purpose. Our task is to find it and embody it. As we probe more deeply into our inner selves, we will discover the treasure that you have hidden there. Keep us faithful to your teaching and never let us be parted from you. So it is.

March 10

"But truly it is the spirit in a mortal, the breath of the Almighty, that makes for understanding."

Job 32:8

What role does your breath play in your life? Have you ever meditated on your breathing, or become very aware of your breath? What insights did this bring to you?

"The breath of God is breathing me and resting in the breath of God, I know that all is well."

Rickie Byars Beckwith from her song "The Breath of God"

Come, Holy Spirit, and breathe into us and through us. Enliven us with your Presence. Quiet our hearts and minds so that we may hear your sweet voice. Flow over and around us with your protection and power. Penetrate the deepest recesses of our bones and organs with your healing. You are Life, you are Love, and you are Light. So it is.

March 11

"Let your light shine before others, so that they may see your good works and give glory to your Father in heaven."
Matthew 5:16

What are the advantages and disadvantages of "letting your light shine?" How have you met this challenge in your own life?

"When we find ourselves looking at the world and saying, 'There's nothing out there for me,' we should probably also look into our hearts and ask, 'If there's nothing out there, is there anything in here?' We need to examine our inner dialogue to discover where we might be blocking the conscious energy flow, then remove the ego, step out of the way, and let the fire of the soul shine through us."

Deepak Chopra from <u>*The Spontaneous Fulfillment of Desire*</u>

O God of Light and Love, we are reflections of you and yet sometimes that reflection grows so dim. Help us to keep the candle burning even in the darkest times. Remind us that we are not the source of the flame so that we will always turn to you for support, encouragement and the true Image of our being. May your Light continue to bring hope to those in darkness through we who see and live in that Light. So it is.

March 12

"Now hope that is seen is not hope. For who hopes for what is seen? But if we hope for what we do not see, we wait for it with patience."

Romans 8:24-25

What is the difference between wishing and hoping for some result, and knowing that it will manifest? Does God always answer on your time schedule?

"Faith is the strength by which a shattered world shall emerge into the light."

Helen Keller

Holy Shekinah, your pillar of fire turns our darkness into the brightness of day and leads us out of the wilderness, even though we have no map to guide us. May we have such trust and faith in your empowering Presence that miracles become every day occurrences. Through the fire of your Spirit within us may we discover our own power to create and manifest what we desire. Teach us to use this power wisely for the healing and transformation of our despairing world. So it is.

March 13

"By faith Abraham obeyed when he was called to set out for a place that he was to receive as an inheritance; and he set out, not knowing where he was going...For he looked forward to the city that has foundations, whose architect and builder is God."

Hebrews 11:8,10

Have you ever been in Abraham's position and made a major life decision based on faith and intuitive knowing rather than outer evidence? Recall the feelings at different stages of your journey. What was the end result?

"Put aside ambition for public recognition, and simply do what you do because it feels good inside."

Alan Cohen

Faithful God, you call us to leave our comfort zones behind and follow you into the unknown. Forgive us when we insist on a road map to the future and a guarantee of the path ahead. Give us the strength and the courage to trust in your Love and Care. Your Way may not be the easy way and it may not be the accepted way of the world. But we know it is Divine Wisdom that guides our journey and lights our path. Thank you for never leaving us and for leading us into a future beyond our imagination. So it is.

March 14

"Know that I am with you and will keep you wherever you go, and will bring you back to this land; for I will not leave you until I have done what I have promised you."

Genesis 28:15

Reflect on the promises that God has made to you and that you have made to God. What role have they played in your life?

"No one can give you wisdom. You must discover it for yourself, on the journey through life, which no one can take for you."

Sun Bear

Holy Sophia, in our foolishness and worldly folly we seek your wise counsel. We turn to you when all else fails, when our plans and schemes create chaos around us. Teach us to listen for your Voice in our lives and all our decisions so that we may truly walk in your Light. Thank you for the comforting promise of your Presence and Guidance. May we always walk on your pathway of Light. May we speak only your words of Light and Truth and seal the door where evil may dwell in our lives. So it is.

March 15

"How beautiful upon the mountains are the feet of the messenger who announces peace, who brings good news, who announces salvation, who says to Zion, 'Your God reigns.'"

Isaiah 52:7

What good news can you find to announce as a messenger of God? How and where do you see beauty in your world?

"Seeing beauty is about broadening our ability to recognize the interconnectedness of all manifestations of life and delighting in how the smells and sounds and tastes and sights that surround us conspire to draw us toward living fully."

Oriah Mountain Dreamer from *The Invitation*

O God of Shalom, we live in a world of war and violence. We desperately need the good news of your Peace. Show us how to live in peace and love with each other. Open our hearts to the needs of our neighbor and the wounds of our enemies. Allow us to look beyond our differences and see our shared humanity. May we embrace your Earth and your children as members of one family. So it is.

March 16

"Yeshua said: Recognize what is in front of you, and what is hidden from you will be revealed. There is nothing hidden that will not be revealed."

Gospel of Thomas, Saying 5

Is this promise a positive or negative for you? Are you attempting to hide something from yourself or others, or are you seeking hidden truth and knowledge?

"Many times people stay in places they don't like because they are afraid to move. Staying in the same place because of fear and apprehension is like living on a hamster wheel. Step off the hamster wheel by flowing with the changes in your life. Be it a mental or physical change, flow with it."

Ron Rathbun from *The Way Is Within: A Spiritual Journey*

Hidden and Holy One, many of us have sought you for so long that we have almost given up hope. We are so used to stumbling in the dark. Reveal your Light to us in fulfillment of your Promise. Show us how close you truly are; in every blade of grass, in every sunset and sunrise, in every cycle of our lives you are there. Open our eyes to see your Presence in our world of darkness and lead us within ourselves so that we may seek you where you find a home in our hearts. So it is.

March 17

"You have made known to me the ways of life; you will make me full of gladness with your presence."

Acts of the Apostles 2:28

Distinguish between earthly joy and celebration, and the joy that comes from the Presence of God. Do you have both in your life?

> "May the blessings of light be upon you,
> Light without and light within.
> And in all your comings and goings,

May you ever have a kindly greeting
From them you meet along the road."

Irish Blessing

God of Joy and Gladness, so often we find time to draw near to you only in the challenging and dark times of our lives. Remind us to invite you to celebrate life with us each and every day. Open our hearts to the exquisite Joy of your Presence. Flood our bodies with your Light and Life so that we dance with joy. Show us that this joy can continue throughout our days, throughout our lives, for you will never leave us and you are the inspiration for our true Joy and Gladness. So it is.

March 18

"*Whenever you stand praying, forgive, if you have anything against anyone; so that your Father in heaven may also forgive you your trespasses.*"

Mark 11:25

What is the result of holding on to a grudge?

"Not to forgive is to be imprisoned by the past, by old grievances that do not permit life to proceed with new business. Not to forgive is to yield oneself to another's control…to be locked into a sequence of act and response, of outrage and revenge, tit for tat, escalating always. The present is endlessly overwhelmed and devoured by the past. Forgiveness frees the forgiver. It extracts the forgiver from someone else's nightmare."

Lance Morrow

Loving and Merciful God, there is so much hatred and misunderstanding in our world. It feels like the greatest light does indeed attract the greatest darkness. So as we draw closer to your Light we face more obstacles, more tests, more difficult choices. Help us to respond to hatred with Love, to injury with Pardon, and to embrace doubt with Faith and sadness with Joy. Show us that it is in giving and forgiving that we receive beyond our imaginings from your boundless store of Love. So it is.

March 19

"Be strong and bold; have no fear or dread...because it is the Lord your God who goes with you; he will not fail you or forsake you."

Deuteronomy 31:6

Do you remember a time in your life when the wisdom of the world and your perception of Divine Wisdom were in conflict? What was the result?

"When we set aside time each day for deep communion with the infinite, then, as surely as day follows night, the light of inspiration will illumine our beings."

Michael Beckwith from <u>New Thought: A Practical Spirituality</u>

Loving Mother/Father God, you lead us forward even when we fear to take the next step. You protect us from all harm even when darkness gathers all around us. You shine the Light of your Truth into our hearts even when our worldly logic whispers that it is folly to listen. Thank you, dear Lord, for your never-failing Love and Care. May we truly learn to listen to your Voice and journey without fear into your future of transformation. So it is.

March 20

"The Lord will guide you continually...and you shall be like a watered garden, like a spring of water, whose waters never fail."

Isaiah 58:11

What do you thirst for in your life? What is missing and how will you plant your garden to create positive results?

"If doubt, despair, and denial threaten to dismantle your dreams today, let Love rear up in your defense."

Sarah Ban Breathnach

Fountain of all Life, we are like travelers in a desert wilderness, sore of foot and parched with thirst. Lead us inward to the fountain of your Love and Light that you planted within each of us. Remind us as we chase after fame and fortune in our material world that our thirst can be quenched only by your life-giving water. May we become bubbling springs of living water flowing out into our world, bringing hope and nurturing dreams. So it is.

March 21

"In him all things hold together."

Colossians 1:17

What happens in your life when the "center does not hold?" How do you put the pieces back together?

"We must offer ourselves to God like a clean, smooth canvas and not worry ourselves about what God may choose to paint on it, but at each moment, feel only the stroke of His brush."

Jean Pierre de Caussade from *Two Suns Rising*

Divine Potter, you molded us in your Image. You are the glue that holds our lives together. You are the artist that paints glorious colors on the canvas of our reality. Teach us how to open our hearts to your Presence so that we may become true co-creators with the genius of your Love and Light. When our center is not holding, draw us back to our true Source of center and balance in you. Remove our fears of the future even in the midst of the storm. May we go forth as your vessels of transformation and become masterpieces of Peace. So it is.

March 22

"For God alone my soul waits in silence, for my hope is from him."

Psalm 62:5

What keeps hope alive for you in the gathering darkness?

"With every ending, something new begins."
Maxine Cates

God of all Hope, in the stillness of the night you come to us. You cleanse our hearts of darkness and despair, and fill them with your Light and Truth. We give you thanks and praise for never giving up on us. Even when there is one candle shining, we know that the morning will come. Increase our faith and strengthen our courage so that in the dark times we may not lose hope but gain faith. When the road becomes too difficult to bear and the night so dark that we lose our way, remind us that you have promised to carry us forward in your loving arms. We are never alone. So it is.

March 23

"Draw near to God, and he will draw near to you."
James 4:8

Where do you see the Presence of God in your life?

"There is a force within that gives you life—seek that. In your body there lies a priceless jewel—seek that...If you are in search of the greatest treasure, don't look outside. Look within and seek That."
Rumi, Sufi Mystic Poet

Gentle and Ever-Loving God, as a wise and caring shepherd you search for us and find your lost sheep. Even when we are unaware of how far we have strayed, you never forget us. You never forsake us. Thank you, thank you, Beloved of my Heart, for showing me the way Home. Open my eyes that I may see the beauty of your Light. Open my ears that I may hear the harmony of your Love. Open my heart that I may feel and know beyond measure the power of your Presence. Open my life that I may become One with you. So it is.

March 24

"Satisfy us in the morning with your steadfast love, so that we may rejoice and be glad all our days."

Psalm 90:14

Describe how you experience God's Love. How does it bring healing, wholeness and joy to your life?

"Come now, noble souls, and take a look at the splendor you are carrying within yourselves! But if you do not let go of yourself completely, if you do not drown yourself in the bottomless sea of the Godhead, you cannot get to know this divine light."

Meister Eckhart from
<u>Two Suns Rising: A Collection of Sacred Writings</u>

Ever-Loving God, we hunger and thirst for your Love and your Presence. Fill us with your powerful Spirit. We open ourselves to be healed, transformed and made whole by the miracle of your Grace in our lives. Teach us to let go of our need to control and to empty ourselves of our ego-self, our little self, so that you may lead us to our true Self, our soul that is the divine spark of you. With joy we surrender to your Love and Care, knowing that in you is our true wholeness. So it is.

March 25

"My child, be attentive to my words; incline your ear to my sayings...For they are life to those who find them, and healing to all their flesh."

Proverbs 4:20, 22

What aspects of your life are in need of healing? How can you accomplish this?

"Our willingness to do the work to become more conscious is what paves the way for us to recognize the unmistakable touch of grace."

Cheryl Richardson from <u>The Unmistakable Touch of Grace</u>

Gracious God, you reach out and embrace us when we are lost. You touch us with your healing Grace when we are sick in soul, mind or body. Thank you for being the Great Physician. Thank you for never giving up on us. As we heal, teach us to turn to your Light. As we become more and more whole, remind us that it is your Power within us that is doing the work. It is your

Light, your Love and your Truth that show us the way to grace. May we surrender to your Loving and Divine Will to rediscover our true Selves. So it is.

March 26

"Render service with enthusiasm...knowing that whatever we do, we will receive the same again from the Lord."

Ephesians 6:7-8

What is your service for God and the world?

"Alas for those that never sing, but die with all their music in them!"

Oliver Wendell Holmes

God of Wonder, you inspire us to be more than we ever believed we could be. Open our eyes to the greatness that you have hidden within us. Give us the courage and strength to nurture your gifts so that we may manifest them in the world for the benefit of all and to your Glory. Teach us to sing the song you have given to us in harmony with our brothers and sisters. In joy and thanksgiving we praise you for your abundant and generous Compassion and Care. May we become true reflections of you in our world. So it is.

March 27

"Yeshua said: If those who guide you say: Look, the Kingdom is in the sky, then the birds are closer than you. If they say: Look, it is in the sea, then the fish already know it. The Kingdom is inside you, and it is outside you. When you know yourself, then you will be known, and you will know that you are the child of the Living Father; but if you do not know yourself, you will live in vain and you will be vanity."

Gospel of Thomas, Saying 3

Reflect on how your inner awareness of God and your attitudes of faith and trust affect what manifests in your outer life.

"I have faith in the truth, in its ability to find us…If the truth often seems elusive when we seek it directly, perhaps it is some consolation that it also relentlessly reveals itself to us in our lives, our dreams, and the stories we tell one another."

Oriah Mountain Dreamer

God of the Visible and the Invisible, you reveal yourself to us in subtle whispers as well as loud thunderclaps. Remind us that what we feel and perceive about our reality on the inside manifests in the outside. Everything is interconnected. We are all part of a wondrous and beautiful tapestry called Life. We may be individual threads but we are all one whole within the space of your Love. Show us how to weave our part of this tapestry with integrity and harmony. May we create a pattern that demonstrates our oneness with you. So it is.

March 28

"God will fully satisfy every need of yours according to his riches in glory in Christ Jesus."

Philippians 4:19

What issues of abundance are currently surfacing in your life? How does your faith assist you in solutions?

"We make a living by what we get, we make a life by what we give."

Winston Churchill

Generous and Ever-Loving One, you shower us with blessings and abundance beyond our imagining. Yet we often do not even recognize your gifts and our secure, good fortune. Teach us to trust in your Way and let go of our way. Show us the power of giving our resources and ourselves away, without fear or thought of the future. Guide us into the flow of your abundant universe, where there is no lack or need and everyone's cup is full to the brim. We offer you thanks and praise for all you give to us. May we receive with gratitude and give with generosity. So it is.

March 29

"God's love has been poured into our hearts through the Holy Spirit that has been given to us."

Romans 5:5

If you go within to the Temple of your Heart, what do you find there? Are there feelings residing in your heart that keep you from experiencing all of God's love? Are you ready to release them so there will be more room in your heart for love?

"Make peace with all your experiences, and work through those that still cause you pain."

Sonya Friedman

Loving Creative Spirit, flow through us. Heal our pain, bind up our wounds and strengthen our shaky knees. We invite your Love to make a home within our heart. Cleanse us within and without so that our temple may welcome you with joy. Allow us to experience the depth and the fullness of Divine Love. We are ready to be transformed in your Image. Then as we have received, so let us give. So it is.

March 30

"As the Father has loved me, so I have loved you; abide in my love."

John 15:9

What does it mean to abide in the love of God and of the Christ?

"Life's most persistent and urgent question is, 'What are you doing for others?'"

Martin Luther King Jr.

Beloved of my Heart, you came to us to show us how to Love. But your Love does not sit by the fireside but goes out into the streets where people are homeless and hungry. Send us out into the world with your Love as our commission. Teach us that we are all your children, sisters and brothers around the world. A child starving in Africa could be my neighbor's child across the street. The teenager forced into prostitution in India could be my daughter. The angry young man with a bomb strapped to his body could be my son. There is no separation. We are all one in your Love. If one heart breaks, then our hearts will break. So, dear One, teach us to Love. So it is.

March 31

"Again Jesus spoke to them, saying, 'I am the light of the world. Whoever follows me will never walk in darkness but will have the light of life.'"

John 8:12

How do you understand this saying in an interfaith world? What message does it have for Jews, Muslims, Hindus, and Buddhists, and all others who live a life of faith different from Christianity?

"To serve the human race in the largest and highest sense, we must bring forth into living expression the truest, the best and the greatest that we can possibly find in the depths of our own sublime being. And to this end we need all the inspiration we can receive from nature, all the love and friendship we can receive from man, and all the wisdom and power we can receive from God."

Christian D. Larson from *The Pathway Of Roses*

Light of the World, we are surrounded by darkness and fear. We claim your Truth and your Light for all your children. Show us how to become your beacons of Light and Hope here on earth. You came to show us the Way of the Lightbearer, the Way of Truth and Justice. Forgive our blindness when we mistake the messenger for the message. Teach us to expand our vision and expand our beams of Light until all our beloved Earth is surrounded and protected by your Light and Love. So it is.

April

Welcome the unexpected into your life
and bless the changes that arrive on your doorstep,
for in so doing you will open the door
to a new heaven and a new earth.
Remember that creation often comes out of chaos
and rarely is birthing complete without pain.

April 1

"I have said this to you, so that in me you may have peace. In the world you face persecution. But take courage; I have conquered the world."

John 16:33

Are you at peace with yourself?

"To find the universal elements enough; to find the air and the water exhilarating; to be refreshed by a morning walk or an evening saunter; to be thrilled by the stars at night; to be elated over a bird's nest or wildflower in spring—these are some of the rewards of the simple life."

John Burroughs

Holy God, you surround us with the beauty of your Creation. Teach us how to slow down and appreciate the glory of a sunset or sunrise, the strength of a towering oak, the freshness of a spring shower and the delicate courage of a crocus in the snow. As we become more aware of your world, dear Lord, we are drawn ever closer to you. Fill us with the gift of your Peace as we walk our chosen paths. May we embrace the ugliness of life with love and see only beauty. May we greet the toads in our lives with a kiss of peace. So it is.

April 2

"Jesus, full of the Holy Spirit, returned from the Jordan and was led by the Spirit in the wilderness."

Luke 4:1

How do you manifest a balance of external activity that embraces others and an internal quiet that embraces God? Is this balancing act a challenge at times?

"Standing in the middle of the road is very dangerous; you get knocked down by the traffic from both sides."

Margaret Thatcher

O God of Simplicity and Peace, we admit that our lives become very complex with too many priorities. Help us to simplify and find a quiet place in the midst of the chaos. As you stilled the storm, so still the many voices and the prevailing turbulence of our lives. In quietness and rest, we find our peace. We breathe deeply and allow it to flow into our innermost heart and soul. When the world is too much with us, be our touchstone to the reality of what is truly important. So it is.

April 3

"Be dressed for action and have your lamps lit; be like those who are waiting for their master to return from the wedding banquet, so that they may open the door for him as soon as he comes and knocks."

Luke 12:35-36

What part does preparation play in patient waiting?

"Intent is a seed in consciousness, or spirit. If you pay attention to it, it has within it the means for its own fulfillment. Intention's infinite organizing power orchestrates countless details simultaneously."

Deepak Chopra from *The Spontaneous Fulfillment of Desire*

O God of Expectation, we admit that often we have no patience. We desire the fulfillment of our every wish in our timeframe, not yours. Remove our impatience and lack of trust. Teach us how to focus our intent and manifest what is truly our heart's desire, knowing that you have assured us that if we ask, we will receive. May our will be your Will, according to your Divine Order. Thank you for your patience with us and for your abundant blessings. So it is.

April 4

"May he grant your heart's desire, and fulfill all your plans."

Psalm 20:4

If you knew that you could have anything your heart desired, what would it be?

"It's not yesterday's regrets, nor tomorrow's challenges that matter—only the infinite possibilities of today."

Linda Knight

Generous and Ever-Loving God, you have promised us so much beyond our wildest dreams. Broaden our vision, inspire our imagination and deepen our trust so that we may create our heart's desire here on your blessed Earth. May we become your hands and voices to touch our world with love and healing. May we experience the power of your Spirit within us as we face the challenges of life. Even in the face of human betrayal, we know that you will never desert us. So it is.

April 5

"Truly I tell you, unless you change and become like children, you will never enter the kingdom of heaven."
Matthew 18:3

What do you believe Jesus meant by asking us to become like children?

"We must be willing to get rid of the life we've planned, so as to have the life that is awaiting us…The old skin has to be shed before the new one is to come."
Joseph Campbell

Abba Father, we are your children, the fruit of your loving and abundant Creation. You lead us with reins of Love and call us to grow and transform. Teach us to trust you as a loving Parent and know that we are safe in your loving arms. Teach us to meet life with innocence and joy, welcoming change as a great adventure. May we learn to celebrate birthing, growing and transforming, just as the flowers of spring burst into bloom. So it is.

April 6

"Teach me good judgment and knowledge; for I believe in your commandments."
Psalm 119:66

How do you define the knowledge of God? What are God's commandments for our day? Have they changed since the time of Moses?

"If you don't like where you are in life, there comes a point when you must give up the part of you that's keeping you back."
Sonya Friedman

Holy God, we are reflections of your Image and you have written your covenant on our hearts. Forgive us when we blur your Divine Image within us. Reveal to us who you truly are and who we truly are in relationship to you. Teach us how to manifest your Way in the world around us. May we always walk in your Truth, your Light and your Love. So it is.

April 7

"This is my commandment, that you love one another as I have loved you."

John 15:12

How do you demonstrate this commandment in your daily life?

"Say only what you mean. Avoid using the word to speak against yourself, or to gossip about others. Use the power of your word in the direction of truth and love."

Don Miguel Ruiz from <u>The Four Agreements</u>

God of Love, you command us to live our lives in Love. Help us to guard our words and actions so that we may truly reflect your Divine Love to the world around us. Teach us to love ourselves even when we are not perfect and fail to live up to your Image within us. We know that it is difficult if not impossible to give away what we do not have, so we must learn to love and respect ourselves to love and respect others. Above all, Beloved of our Hearts, teach us how to love you. So it is.

April 8

"Set me like a seal on your heart, like a seal on your arm. For love is strong as Death, passion as relentless as Sheol. The flash of it is a flash of fire, a flame of Yahweh himself. Love no flood

can quench, no torrents drown. Were a man to offer all his family wealth to buy love, contempt is all that he would gain."

Song of Songs 8:6-7

What is the difference between human love and divine love?

"Love is a state of Being. Your love is not outside; it is deep within you. You can never lose it, and it cannot leave you. It is not dependent on some other body, some other external form."

Eckhart Tolle from *The Power Of Now*

Beloved One, you have called us your beloved children. Lead us to that bubbling spring within that waters the garden of your Love for each one of us. As we drink from that life-giving water, we discover how precious we are. As we learn to love ourselves, teach us how to love each other as you love us. Teach us the power of loving service to a hurting world. Teach us the power of prayer so that our lives may become a living prayer to you. May we truly say "Our Father and Our Mother" and know the closeness of being in your family; loved, protected and cared for—united as One across our planet. So it is.

April 9

"I have said these things to you so that my joy may be in you, and that your joy may be complete."

John 15:11

How would you define joy?

"A single sunbeam is enough to drive away many shadows."

Francis of Assisi

God of Joy and Wonder, our world is filled with so much sadness that often we lose the appreciation for the beauty, the wonder and the joy of your Creation. Teach us how to find joy in the little things of life. Renew in us the childlike wonder we once had when every day was a miracle and all things were possible. Help us to spread your Joy and Love to everyone we meet, lighting candles of Hope and Peace so that the darkness may retreat a little further with each kind word and with each touch. May we dance your dance of Joy in the morning and rest in gentle Peace at night. So it is.

April 10

"If we walk in the light as he himself is in the light, we have fellowship with one another."

1 John 1:7

What does it mean to "have fellowship with one another?" Who would you include in your circle of fellowship?

"A friend is someone who knows your song, and sings it to you when you've forgotten it yourself."

Alan Cohen

Loving and Faithful God, in your constant Care and Compassion you demonstrate to us what true friendship can be. We are so privileged to have you for a friend. Learning from you, may we shower our brothers and sisters in your world with the same loving compassion that you have for us. We are all your children, dear God. Help us to remember this when we are tempted to make distinctions and separations. Draw us together as one family under the shadow of your wings. So it is.

April 11

"What do you think? If a shepherd has a hundred sheep, and one of them has gone astray, does he not leave the ninety-nine on the mountains and go in search of the one that went astray?"

Matthew 18:12

What does it mean today to be a good shepherd in our world?

"Kindness is an inner desire that makes us want to do great things even if we do not get anything in return. It is the joy of our life to do them. When we do good things from this inner desire, there is kindness in everything we think, say, want and do."

Emmanuel Swedenborg

Gracious God, we give you thanks and praise for your never-failing Love. You go in search of us when we stray from your Way, and lead us back with gentleness and tenderness. At times our lives may feel like a wilderness and we need a shepherd to lead us along the straight paths. May we choose our shepherds wisely, listening always to your inner Voice within us. Remind us that "By their fruits ye shall know them." So it is.

April 12

"But as for me, I walk in my integrity...My foot stands on level ground; in the great congregation I will bless the Lord."

Psalm 26:11-12

How would you define integrity? Can you recall a time when your integrity was challenged? What choices did you make and how do you feel about those choices today?

"When you know who you are, when your mission is clear and you burn with the inner fire of unbreakable will; no cold can touch your heart; no deluge can dampen your purpose."

Chief Seattle

Source of All Being, you created us in your Image and know us better than we know ourselves. Show us the path of Truth and Light that we may walk on it all our days. Teach us to speak your words of Truth even when the world around us says something else. May we stand strong for your Kingdom, for your Peace, for your Justice, for your Way of Love that casts out all fear and unites all humanity as brothers and sisters. May we be one with each other as we are one with you. So it is.

April 13

"Let us then pursue what makes for peace and for mutual upbuilding."

Romans 14:19

What would peace look like in our world today?

"A loving person lives in a loving world. A hostile person lives in a hostile world. Everyone you meet is a mirror."

Ken Keyes Jr.

Loving Creative Spirit, you inspire us to live in peace and love even when we are surrounded by violence and hate. Show us a broader vision that sees our little planet from your perspective. Open our hearts to a Love that has no boundaries and counts no costs. Remove our rose-colored glasses so that we may truly see the homeless, the hungry, the sick and oppressed. May we bring healing and wholeness in your Name to a world that is separated by strife and division. May we be instruments of your Peace and creators of your Love. So it is.

April 14

"And all in the crowd were trying to touch him, for power came out from him and healed all of them."

Luke 6:19

Have you ever witnessed or experienced healing that you could not explain physically? How do you understand God's role in healing? How does the attitude of the sick person affect what happens?

"It takes a deep commitment to change and an even deeper commitment to grow."

Ralph Ellison

Holy Mother/Father God, in you resides the power for our wholeness, health and healing. We bring our doubts, our fears, our weaknesses and our pain to your temple. Many times we feel weighed down with more than we can bear. Lift us up, dear God, and set us on our feet once again. Steady our shaky knees and bring us back to center in our lives. We claim strength and perfect health of mind, spirit and body in your Name. May we grow beyond our limitations and become temples of inner light for your Holy Spirit. So it is.

April 15

"My child, do not forget my teaching, but let your heart keep my commandments; for length of days and years of life and abundant welfare they will give you."

Proverbs 3:1

In your opinion, what is God's most important teaching?

"All that is required now is that you continue to till the soil of your soul. Just as you would not neglect seeds that you planted with the hope that they will bear vegetables and fruits and flowers, so you must attend to and nourish the garden of your becoming."

Jean Houston

Sweet Spirit, you fill us with your creative Power. Let your sun shine in our hearts. Let your cleansing Love nourish us as it flows through every cell, every organ, every vein and artery of our being. Break up the clods of "dirt" that block our becoming who you meant us to be. Heal us to the depth of our souls so that we may grow and blossom and bear good fruit. We honor the seeds you have planted in us. Teach us how to be attentive gardeners of our souls and spirits. Bathe us in the Light of your sunshine. Water us with the nourishment of your Knowledge and we promise to cultivate our gardens well. So it is.

April 16

"'I will put my spirit within you, and you shall live, and I will place you on your own soil; then you shall know that I, the Lord, have spoken and will act,' says the Lord."

Ezekiel 37:14

What does it mean to have God's spirit within you? Is this a reality in your life?

"Hope enfolds its light in the heart."

Allison Reed

Holy Shekinah, you make your dwelling place with us and pitch your tent in the center of our lives. As you hover over and around us, may we invite you into the center of our being. Infuse us with the Peace and Power of your Presence. Open us to the change and transformation that comes from enshrining you in our heart of hearts. May we become true temples of your Spirit and may our lives reflect your Light that glows from within us. So it is.

April 17

"Yeshua said: Whoever searches must continue to search until they find. When they find, they will be disturbed, they will marvel and will reign over ALL."

Gospel of Thomas, Saying 2

What are you searching for?

"Each willing effort is sufficient to move the soul."

Greg Barrette

O God of the Morning Dawn, with every new day we are created anew. We thank you and praise you that we always have the opportunity to begin again after the darkness of creative chaos has lifted. Give us the courage to welcome change and transformation into our lives. Help us to release and heal the past and whatever might keep us anchored to being less than you would have us become. Remind us that the first step is always the most difficult and we never have to journey alone. We just need to keep walking. So it is.

April 18

"They shall flourish like a garden."

Hosea 14:7

How would you characterize yourself in terms of what normally is found in a garden? Are you a flower or a vegetable? What kind? What attitudes, colors or characteristics created your choice?

"Every blade of grass has its angel that bends over it and whispers, 'Grow, grow.'"

The Talmud

God of all Creation, in this beautiful season help us to pause long enough in our busy lives to appreciate the beauty of your world. We thank you for the gentle spring rains that bless the grass, the trees and all that grows in your abundant Earth. May these times of new growth also nourish and bless us as we soak in the living waters of your Love. May we allow our roots to sink deeply into your good Earth so that we may produce good fruit. Remind us that there is no power greater than that of a blade of grass pushing up through the soil. May we become that blade of grass always stretching our arms toward you. So it is.

April 19

"As for me, I shall behold your face in righteousness; when I awake I shall be satisfied, beholding your likeness."

Psalm 17:15

What is your concept of the likeness of God? How do you manifest it?

"We must accept that this creative pulse within us is God's creative pulse itself."

Joseph Chilton Pearce

Holy One, you have gifted us with so many wondrous blessings and abilities. Often we fail to understand the depth of our knowledge and the breadth of our power. Allow us to become true vessels for your creative Wisdom. May we learn to listen for your Voice of inspiration and dance with the energy of your Holy Spirit within us. Teach us to walk in your footsteps and speak your words with grace and truth, with love and joy. So it is.

April 20

"God is Spirit, and those who worship him must worship in spirit and truth."

John 4:24

How would you define true worship of God? How do you worship God in your daily life?

"I cannot teach you how to pray in words. God listens not to your words save when He Himself utters them through your lips. And I cannot teach you the prayer of the seas and the forests and the mountains. But you who are born of the mountains and the forests and the seas can find their prayer in your heart. And if you but listen in the stillness of the night you shall hear them saying in silence, 'Our God, who art our winged self, it is thy will in us that willeth. . .'"

Kahlil Gibran

God of Wisdom and Truth, too often we feel trapped in ritual and rules made by human hands. Remind us that you are not confined to a particular time or place. You will meet us wherever we are, in the little things of life. You make all of life sacred, so that our life may become a living prayer. Teach us how to pray our lives to you, to speak and walk and cry and laugh and dance and sing for you. This would be our worship, to live our lives full to the brim, moment by moment, in your Love and Peace. So it is.

April 21

"Happy are those...who get understanding...Her ways are ways of pleasantness and all her paths are peace."

Proverbs 3:13, 17

How do you understand the balance of the mind and the heart? Do you have this balance in your life?

"The very nature of the mind is such that if you leave it in its unaltered and natural state, it will find its true nature, which is bliss and clarity."

Sogyal Rinpoche from *The Tibetan Book of Living and Dying*

Holy Sophia, you are our strength and our wisdom. Teach us to listen with both our hearts and minds to your messages. Show us how to manifest your ways of Truth in our world. Inspire us to dig deeper below the surface of life. As we listen for your Voice within us and around us, we hear you in the rushing waters of a stream, in the powerful winds that bend the trees and in the gentle rain that blesses your Earth. As we grow, may we be like a strong and straight oak tree, with deep roots reaching into the soil, arms stretching toward the heavens, and a heart embracing the world. So it is.

April 22

"God is a God not of disorder but of peace."

1 Corinthians 14:33

If it is true that God is a God of peace and understanding, not of disorder and chaos, how do you explain what is happening in the world around us?

"I keep my ideals, because in spite of everything I still believe that people are really good at heart."

Anne Frank

Eternal and Loving God, there is so much that we do not, cannot, understand. So much about our world seemingly makes no sense. Lift us above our narrow vision and show us the broader vistas of peace and order that you see. Help us to believe and hold fast to the hope in our hearts even when a different and terrible reality threatens to invade. Remind us that one act of kindness, one word of peace, can create a chain reaction of love and understanding. If we feel trapped by circumstances, we are limited only by our lack of clarity and vision. You hold the key to the door, so we ask for that open door and the strength to cross the threshold into a new future. So it is.

April 23

"Peace I leave with you; my peace I give to you. I do not give to you as the world gives. Do not let your hearts be troubled, and do not let them be afraid."

John 14:27

In what concrete ways can you bring more peace into your life?

"Here is your right and perfect place. Now is God's right and perfect time. Than why doesn't it always FEEL that way? Because when you are looking with human, not divine eyes, you cannot see with the clear perspective of Divine Order. Look past the appearances of third dimensional disorder into the seamless, harmonious whole. On the fourth dimension of Christ Consciousness, all is in perfect order, because everything is HERE, NOW!"

Greg Barrette

O Source of All, you are the glue that holds our world together. You are the Peace we are seeking. You are the Truth that melts all deception and fear. Teach us how to find you when our courage fails and darkness is all around us. Show us a better way, a more excellent way, for a gentler world. In your Love, in your Light, we open our hearts, our minds and our eyes to your Peace. So it is.

April 24

"*Strive for the greater gifts. And I will show you a still more excellent way.*"

1 Corinthians 12:31

How would you define the "more excellent way?"

"You are a book of secrets waiting to be opened."

Deepak Chopra from <u>The Book of Secrets: Unlocking the Hidden Dimensions of Your Life</u>

Holy God, you have gifted us with so many wondrous blessings. Now teach us how to open the gifts that you have given to us and use them to create a more harmonious world. May we become your gift to our sisters and brothers. Where there is hatred, let us sow Love. Where there is injury, Pardon. Where there is doubt, Faith. Where there is sadness, Joy. As we become your vessels of Love, your instruments of reconciliation to a hurting world, may we find a new purpose for living and a renewed sense of thankfulness for being alive, here and now. So it is.

April 25

"Call to me and I will answer you, and I will tell you great and hidden things that you have not known."
Jeremiah 33:3

What new things have you learned recently about yourself, your God and your spirituality? How can you put this new knowledge into practice?

"Your life becomes an adventure when you embrace the newness of life."
Greg Barrette

Lord of the Dance, you spread before us a grand design for our lives. Forgive us when we see this plan as more work and boredom, and less adventure. Renew in us the innocent joy of childhood that awakened to each new day with joy and freshness. Teach us to focus on the half-full glass and all the blessings, large and small, that overflow our lives. You are the source of our abundance and generosity. May we live in the NOW and dance in the Light of your dawn with joy and love. So it is.

April 26

"The disciples of Jesus said to him: 'Teach us about the place where you dwell, for we must seek it.' He told them: 'Those who have ears, let them hear! There is light within people of light, *and they shine it upon the whole world. If they do not shine it, what darkness!'"*

Gospel of Thomas, Saying 24

How do you see the manifestation of light and darkness in yourself and others?

"...deep within each of us lie goodness unimagined, wisdom, music, talents of every variety, joy, peace, humility and love...a vast gold-mine."

Eric Butterworth

God of Light and Love, you created each one of us to be your beacons of Light in a world of darkness. But how can we be a beacon when we stumble in our own darkness? Be our Light, Beloved One, and guide us ever inward to our true Selves. As we grow ever more certain who we are, may our light shine outward into the turmoil and fear around us. In a stormy sea, may we truly become lighthouses built on the solid foundation of your Presence and your Love. So it is.

April 27

"For whoever does the will of my Father in heaven is my brother and sister and mother."

Matthew 12:50

How do your family relationships affect your faith and spirituality?

"Kindness is the light that dissolves all walls between souls, families, and nations."

Paramahansa Yogananda

O God of all Nations, you gather all peoples together as one family under the shadow of your ever-lasting Love. Only humanity makes the separations between nations, between races, between genders, between classes. Teach us that we are truly all One with you as our Divine Parent, Guide and Guardian. Even as wayward children, you still love us and wait to welcome us Home. May we realize our foolishness when we seek to judge and condemn others. Unless we see ourselves as perfect, we have no right to cast stones. Instead may we offer a kind and loving embrace to all your children, weeping with those who mourn and rejoicing with those who sing for joy. May we all be reunited as brothers and sisters in your kingdom of Love and Peace. So it is.

April 28

"This is the message we have heard from him and proclaim to you, that God is light and in him there is no darkness at all."

1 John 1:5

Are the terrorists evil or are they perhaps reflections of our own shadow selves?

"Let us be very sincere in our dealings with each other, and have the courage to accept each other as we are. Do not be surprised or become preoccupied at each other's failures—rather, see and find in each other the good, for each one of us is created in the image of God."

Mother Teresa of Calcutta

O God of Light and Darkness, it is so easy in our world to see only the dark and believe in only the night. But when we keep our gaze fixed on you, we see only Light, and it is too easy to ignore a world in need. Empower us to be like stained-glass windows with your light shining through us so that we become instruments to bring Light and Love to the world. Open our hearts to the reality of the needs of others, and teach us that we are here not for ourselves alone, but as emissaries of your Love and Compassion. So it is.

April 29

"Besides this, you know what time it is, how it is now the moment for you to wake from sleep. For salvation is nearer to us now than when we became believers; the night is far gone, the day is near."

Romans 13:11-12

What signs do you see that humanity in general is "waking up?" What changes or transformations are happening in your own life?

"Time is something you spend everyday, but it cannot be bought at any price. You spend time on everything: yourself, loved ones, family, friends. The time in your life is priceless. What determines what you spend your time on?"

                        Ron Rathbun from *The Way Is Within*

God of all Times and Places, our finite minds cannot conceive of the infinite. Eternity doesn't exist when we focus on surviving the next moment, the next hour or day or month or year. Expand our vision of time and space so that we truly may wake up to the urgent and blessed opportunities that face us in our time. Remove our fear and dread, and fill us with anticipation of your Divine Order that creates in and through us only the good. Help us to reorder our priorities so that we may more truly reflect your Care and Concern for all your family, especially those in need. So it is.

April 30

"But I am like a green olive tree in the house of God. I trust in the steadfast love of God forever and ever."

                                                    Psalm 52:8

What fruit are you producing in your life? What priorities might you alter to produce better fruit?

"Your mind is a garden, your thoughts are the seeds, the harvest can be either flowers or weeds."

                                                Author Unknown

Wondrous God, it is your Will that we bear good fruit like a fruitful olive tree. Give us the courage to reorder our lives so that our will aligns with yours. May we weed our gardens attentively and carefully so that we produce only the very best. Our world is in desperate need of the spiritual fruits of Light, Love, Peace, Joy, Abundance and Compassion. Only through us as your chosen vessels of Light can your Will be done on our earth. May we bloom well and beautifully wherever you plant us, and may we bear the very best of fruit to aid in the transformation of our Beloved Mother Earth. So it is.

May

Learn to listen with your heart,
for the heart does not lie.
In the temple of your heart resides the greatest Truth
and greatest Love that you will ever know,
for "God's love has been poured into our hearts
through the Holy Spirit that has been given to us."
(Romans 5:5)
Keep this Love and this Truth locked away
and you will never discover their power.
Share them and you will step
beyond the boundaries of human limitation.

May 1

"See if I will not open the windows of heaven for you and pour down for you an overflowing blessing."

Malachi 3:10

Are you able to see blessings in the challenges of your life? How is this ability a step to creating more blessings?

"Never let your good get in the way of your better."

Jack Boland

Generous and Ever-Present One, how can we thank you for all you give to us? Teach us to look for the good instead of judging our challenges and lessons as negative. Open our eyes and our minds so that we may clearly perceive your Abundance. By focusing on the wonder and magic of our world, we become co-creators with you of a kinder, gentler planet. With your Wisdom as our guide and your Generosity as our inheritance, we promise to open our hearts and share what you have given, in trust and in faith. Thank you, thank you, thank you, wondrous God. So it is.

May 2

"Keep your heart with all vigilance, for from it flow the springs of life."

Proverbs 4:23

Spend some time focusing on your heart. What does the energy feel like? What is flowing from your heart?

"You have it easily in your power to increase the sum total of this world's happiness now. How? By giving a few words of sincere appreciation to someone who is lonely or discouraged. Perhaps you will forget tomorrow the kind words you say today, but the recipient may cherish them over a lifetime."

Dale Carnegie

Loving Creative Spirit, you flow into us and through us. As we hurry through our lives, remind us to pause and focus on that inner temple of the heart where you meet us in stillness and calm. May we be embraced by your tender Love so that we may reach out and embrace others who so need to feel cared for and loved. Even if it is only a smile or a touch, it can mean so much. As your Love flows through us, we become your heart, your arms and your hands to hug a hurting world. So it is.

May 3

"Then I heard the voice of the Lord saying, 'Whom shall I send, and who will go for us?' And I said, 'Here am I; send me!'"

Isaiah 6:8

What has God called you to do with your life? How have you responded?

"The golden opportunity you are seeking is in yourself."

Orison Sweet Marden

Mother/Father God, you created us in your Image and placed the seed of your Divine Presence within each one of us. Help us to nurture that seed so that it may grow and flourish, and as it grows within us, may you lead us to our greater purpose and work for your Justice and Truth. There is so much that needs doing in our world and the laborers are few. Teach us to listen for the call that is ours and respond with our whole hearts, for this is why we came to earth at this time. Let us not remain in our cocoons, silent and passive. Guide us as we walk our chosen Path. So it is.

May 4

"For this I was born, and for this I came into the world, to testify to the truth."

John 18:37

Were you ever asked to take a stand for an unpopular and inconvenient truth? What was the result and how has it affected your life?

"Let the world know you as you are, not as you think you should be, because sooner or later, if you are posing, you will forget the pose, and then where are you?"

Fanny Brice

Holy Wisdom of God, you gift us with a knowledge of you. You lead us with Love and Truth to knowledge of ourselves as your beloved children. Give us the courage to follow our destiny as you lift the veils from our eyes. May we see beyond our limitations and walk where your angels guide us to tread, knowing that your Wisdom is often not the wisdom of the world and your Truth may not be the most popular and profitable cause. Teach us to trust in your Wisdom so that our lives become a witness to your Truth and Love. So it is.

May 5

"For he will command his angels concerning you to guard you in all your ways. On their hands they will bear you up, so that you will not dash your foot against a stone."
Psalm 91:11-12

Have you ever been forced to let go and let God take control of your life? Is letting go of control easy or difficult for you?

"The power of losing control is about learning how to let go of trying to control the uncontrollable outcomes and circumstances in our lives. To do anything else is a blueprint for living a life that is driven by stress, fear, and disappointment. I'm not suggesting that we shouldn't do everything we can to make our dreams and desires come true. But letting go of the illusion that we have complete control over our outcomes will free us from our fears, allow us to bring more of ourselves to the work we need to do, and enable us to find happiness and power no matter what life brings our way."

Joe Caruso from <u>*The Power Of Losing Control*</u>

Gracious God, so often we cling to the illusion that we have all the answers and can solve every challenge we encounter. Loosen our grip on the precipice of our ego. May we take a deep breath and step out into the abyss, knowing that your angels will sustain us and guide us to our safe and chosen landing. There are miracles all around us if we remain open and willing to receive. Teach us how to lose control so that we may truly experience the power of your Love and ever-embracing Mercy. May you lift us on eagle's wings to fly in Freedom and Joy. So it is.

May 6

"Yeshua saw some infants being nursed at the breast. He said to his disciples: These nursing infants are like those who enter the Kingdom. The disciples asked him: 'Then shall we become as infants to enter the Kingdom?' Yeshua answered them: When you make the two into One, when you make the inner like the outer and the high like the low; when you make male and female into a single One, so that the male is not male and the female is not female...then you will enter into the Kingdom."

Gospel of Thomas, Saying 22

What can children teach us about the nature of God and God's Kingdom?

"Collaboration and reciprocity are natural, and yet in the world we inhabit, competition and the fear of scarcity often block us from seeing these ways of being with one another.

In a you-or-me world, reciprocity and collaboration don't fit. A you-and-me world is full of collaborators, partners, sharing, and reciprocity. In that world, our resources are not only enough; they are infinite. When we bring the practice of collaboration and reciprocity into conscious view in everyday life, a kind of alchemy and prosperity await discovery all around us."

> **Lynne Twist from** <u>*The Soul of Money: Transforming Your Relationship with Money and Life*</u>

Generous and Ever-Loving God, you shower us with blessings far greater than we can imagine. So often we concentrate only on our lack, and forget the wonder of your Grace and Mercy to us. Remind us to be grateful and to say "thank you." Open our eyes and our hearts so that we may truly receive all the good things that you have in store for us. As we acknowledge you as the Source of our good, may we also acknowledge our responsibility to share our abundance with all your children. As one family, may we grow together in love and compassion for your world. So it is.

May 7

"Every generous act of giving, with every perfect gift, is from above, coming down from the Father of lights, with whom there is no variation or shadow due to change."

James 1:17

What is the greatest gift that you have given? What part did God play in this gift?

Rev. Maryesah Karelon, O.M.M.

"In God we live and move and have our being. It is God who gives life to all, who gives power and being to all that exists. But for His sustaining presence, all things would cease to be and fall back into nothingness. Consider that you are in God, surrounded and encompassed by God, swimming in God."

Mother Teresa of Calcutta from *The Joy In Living*

Source of All Being, we are reflections of your Love and your Truth, but we admit that there are times that our reflection becomes distorted or that we even ignore your Truth for us. Remind us of who we truly are. Show us the Divine Plan that you have for our lives and teach us to let it be perfected in us. You are all around us and in and through us. There is no place where you are not. We can never be alone, though we can be lonely. We will never be poor, though we may be challenged to count our blessings. We are never without love, though we may indeed search for the manifestation of love in this physical world. Broaden our vision and deepen our trust, and gift us with your many blessings. So it is.

May 8

"I pray that, according to the riches of his glory...you may be strengthened in your inner being with power through his Spirit, and that Christ may dwell in your hearts through faith, as you are being rooted and grounded in love."

Ephesians 3:16-17

What is the difference between loneliness and solitude? What has been the loneliest time of your life? How did you survive it and was God there in the darkness with you?

"Language...has created the word 'loneliness' to express the pain of being alone. And it has created the word 'solitude' to express the glory of being alone."

Paul Johannes Tillich from <u>**The Eternal Now**</u>

Loving God, in the darkness of the night we feel our aloneness and we reach out for your Presence. You are indeed Emmanuel, God-with-us, always. Teach us to endure through those desert moments, and days, and months, even years. May we cling to you even when we do not see or perceive any evidence of your Goodness and Compassion. When we are filled with doubt and despair, strengthen our faith and teach us to hope in you. Even if it is one candle in the darkness, your Light will show the Way. Guide our steps and lift us up when we stumble. Carry us when we can go no further until at last we learn to rejoice in the desert solitude, for in the stillness we truly hear your call. So it is.

May 9

"For see, winter is past, the rains are over and gone. Flowers are appearing on the earth. The season of glad songs has come, the cooing of the turtledove is heard in our land. The fig tree is forming its first figs and the blossoming vines give out their fragrance."

Song of Songs 2:11-13

What message do you read in the beauty and abundance of God's springtime?

"The map of abundance and joy has always existed. It has always been about the basics. Sometimes we just forget what the basics are."
Earnie Larsen from *Destination Joy*

Holy One, all around us we see the beauty of your Creation bursting into the full bloom of your springtime. Fill our lives with the abundant joy of new growth and renewal. May we pursue a life founded upon your basic truths that assure us of the Peace of your Presence. Teach us to seek first your kingdom so that we may see clearly and walk in the Light of Hope even when the fog of despair threatens to envelop our daily existence. We believe, dear God. Help our unbelief. So it is.

May 10

"You have been born anew, not of perishable but of imperishable seed, through the living and enduring word of God."

I Peter 1:23

How do you understand the concept of being born again?

"When the voice of knowledge becomes the voice of integrity, you return to the truth, you return to love, you return to heaven, and live in happiness again."

Don Miguel Ruiz from *The Voice of Knowledge*

O God of Wisdom and Truth, send out your Spirit to guide us, for we have lost our way in the darkness. We are tired and afraid. In our fear, we stumble and fall. But we know that you are always with us as our Light and Protection. We call on your Truth and your Light. May you find a warm home in our hearts. May we learn to listen to your whispers of Truth and be led by your Wisdom to speak that Truth in our world. So it is.

May 11

"Your word is a lamp to my feet and a light to my path."

Psalm 119:105

How do you define the "Word of God?" Is God's Word just the Holy Scriptures or are there other ways that God communicates to you?

"Words can inspire or criticize. Words help us express our feelings and explore the very depths of what we understand. Yet words are simply symbols, like signs along the roadway that point beyond themselves. More than beautiful words about love, we seek an experience of the beauty that is Love. More than words about life we seek to express the Light which is life itself. As we move beyond the surface stream of our thoughts and words, we discover that there is so much more to us than words or ideas can ever describe. We are consciousness experiencing conscious awakening."

Ric Beattie

Holy Shekinah, it is Your Presence that hovers over and around us like a cloud of glory. We quiet our busy minds and still the many voices of our world, and come into your holy temple, the temple of our heart. Here we find you waiting, ready to share yourself and your Word with us. You have so much to teach us and we are hungry for your message of Life and Love. Fill us with your Spirit so that we may know and understand, and be transformed and awakened. We have been too long asleep. It is time. Awaken us now, sweet Spirit. So it is.

May 12

"I thank my God every time I remember you, constantly praying with joy in every one of my prayers for all of you."

Philippians 1:3-4

How would you define prayer?

"The most important part of prayer is what we feel, not what we say. We spend a great deal of time telling God what we think should be done, and not enough time waiting in the stillness for God to tell us what to do."

Peace Pilgrim from *Peace Pilgrim: Her Life and Work In Her Own Words*

Loving Mother/Father God, your Son Jesus taught his disciples to pray, not in words but with their very hearts. Remind us again of the truths behind the familiar words. We praise your

Name, O God, for you alone are the Holy One. We pray for your Divine Order to come into our disordered world and transform the darkness into Light. Let us never forget that you are the Source of our abundance and that you will meet our every need with blessings overflowing. Forgive us when we fail to live up to your Divine Image within us. Give us the gentle, merciful Love to offer forgiveness to all those who hurt or injure us. Walk beside us in the noisy world and whisper your words in our ear when the addictions of modern life tempt us away from your Path. We thank you, we bless you, and we praise you now and forever. So it is.

May 13

"For thus the Lord said to me: I will quietly look from my dwelling like clear heat in sunshine, like a cloud of dew in the heat of harvest."

Isaiah 18:4

How do you experience the Divine Presence in your daily life?

"Be still. Be still. Be still. God in the midst of you is substance. God in the midst of you is love. God in the midst of you is wisdom. Let not your thoughts be given to lack, but let wisdom fill them with the substance and faith of God. Let not your heart be a center of resentment and fear and doubt. Be still and know that at this moment it is the altar of God, of love; love so sure and unfailing, love so irresistible and magnetic that it draws your supply to you from the great store-house of the universe. Trust God, use God's wisdom, prove and express God's love."

Myrtle Fillmore from *Healing Letters*

O God of the Morning Dawn, you call us into the stillness of your Presence, when the world is hushed and all is at peace. For a few precious moments we savor the sweetness of the silence and find your Voice gently calling to us. You invite us into the garden when the dew is still on the roses and remind us of what we too often forget: there is more to life than speed and noise and complexity. You meet us in quiet simplicity and calm assurance. May we allow that calmness to flow into our hearts and minds so that it stays with us through our day. Walk beside us and befriend us when our pace gets harried and our breath comes too quickly. May we hear you whisper—Be still, be still, be still and know that I AM. So it is.

May 14

"He made streams come out of the rock, and caused waters to flow down like rivers."

Psalm 78:16

Do you see a connection between our current ecological issues and the denial of the Divine Feminine? What can you do to make a difference?

"The harvest I reap is measured by the attitudes I cultivate."

Iyanla Vanzant

O God of all Creation, you meet us in the beauty of your garden and call us into union with you. You call us to honor each one of your creatures and all you have made; the rocks, the trees, the ever-flowing streams that bring forth grass and flowers. In our mad rush through life, we have forgotten how to care for each other and all other living things. We need a change of heart and we need it now. May the clear stream of your Wisdom and Love flow into us, and turn our lives to a new path for a new day. Open our arms to embrace a tree. Open our eyes to see your beauty all around us. Open our mouths that we may speak your Truth even when it is difficult. May we become part of your solution, not part of the problem. So it is.

May 15

"The one who sows sparingly will also reap sparingly, and the one who sows bountifully will also reap bountifully."

2 Corinthians 9:6

What seeds are you sowing in your life today? What harvest are you anticipating? What needs to happen to assure a bountiful harvest?

"Go confidently in the direction of your dreams! Live the life you've imagined! As you simplify your life, the laws of the universe will be simpler."

Henry David Thoreau

God of Simplicity and Peace, we seek you in the complexities of our lives, but often we are too overwhelmed to know that something is missing. Teach us what is important in your Vision for us. Show us the Wisdom of the simple. May we open our hearts to the beauty and the bounty that is all around us, planting our gardens with simple pleasures and gentle words. May we give to others from the your ever-flowing stream of Divine Love, knowing that the stream will never run dry and that we will always be fed and nourished by your bounteous Goodness. We give you thanks and praise for the abundant harvest you lay before us. May we reap in equal abundance, to your Honor and Glory. So it is.

May 16

"New wine must be put into fresh wineskins."

Luke 5:38

Are you trying to put new wine into old wineskins in your life? What is sure to happen? Where are new wineskins needed?

"When you are in a low, there is a proven method of moving your consciousness up to a new high. Spend time in the silence of your heart, and let the winds of your inner spirit lift you!"

Greg Barrette

Gracious God, you make all things new and renew us like the morning dawn. Guide us into the sacred silence of our inner temple and show us what needs to be transformed in our beings and our lives. Remove the fear and doubt that change brings, and replace it with a spirit of adventure and anticipation. Grow us so that we may become ever more like you and closer to that divine reflection that is within us. Remind us of the power of a single blade of grass pushing through the soil, seeking your Light and Love. If a tiny seed can transform into that great power, nothing is impossible for your Love. We celebrate our becoming ever new. So it is.

May 17

"We have received...the Spirit that is from God, so that we may understand the gifts bestowed on us by God."

1 Corinthians 2:12

What gifts have you been given by God and how have they manifested in your life?

"What lies behind us and what lies before us are tiny matters compared to what lies within us."

Ralph Waldo Emerson

Sweet Spirit, you come to us with whisperings of wonder to announce the good news—we are being raised up to ever higher levels of consciousness. We give you thanks for this new awareness, and for the opportunities and gifts that come with it. As the petals of our lotus blossom gently unfold in the Light of Divine Love, may we find ourselves drawn ever closer to you and to the

Divine Purpose for our lives. As we become filled with your Spirit, may we by the power of your Love share that Spirit with others so that Truth and Justice may come to Earth and Peace may reign for all God's children and all of Creation. So it is.

May 18

"Now begin the work, and the Lord be with you."

1 Chronicles 22:16

What is the most difficult part of a project for you—getting started, maintaining focus and energy during the work or actually completing the work? How do you meet this challenge?

"Only when your consciousness is totally focused on the moment you are in can you receive whatever gift, lesson, or delight that moment has to offer."

Barbara de Angelis

O God of all Ages, teach us how to live in this moment and savor what you give to us now. The past is truly finished and gone; the future is not yet here and can only be perceived through a mirror, dimly. But the Now moment is where we are, this instant, alive and full of potential. May we learn to live in the Now and treasure what we create from this precious moment in time. For in an instant it will be no more. Yet we know that time is an illusion and that this moment is actually an eternity. Let us live in the paradox of time and no time, between heaven and earth. For truly we are the link between what is and what will be. Flesh and spirit unite in us and we become One with the Divine. So it is.

May 19

"For I will restore health to you, and your wounds I will heal."

Jeremiah 30:17

What needs to be healed in your life? How can you assist in healing the wounds of our world?

"The secret of health for both mind and body is not to mourn for the past, not to worry about the future, not to anticipate troubles, but to live the present moment wisely and earnestly."

Siddhartha Gautama Buddha

O God of Mercy and Healing, you know our frailties and the weaknesses we try to hide. You know that many times the pain inside us is so great that we become physically ill and sick of heart. Great Physician, heal us in mind, body and spirit. Let your fiery Love penetrate to every cell and organ, every vein and artery. Remove from our bodies that which blocks our wholeness and our reunion with you. Cleanse us from every thoughtless word or action that hurts our sisters and brothers. Fill us with your Light so that the darkness will flee from our presence. May we become beacons of Light for our world. So it is.

May 20

"He who prepared us for this very thing is God, who has given us the Spirit as a guarantee. So we are always confident...for we walk by faith, not by sight."

2 Corinthians 5:5-7

What has recently been the greatest challenge in your spiritual life? How do you stay centered and focused in the midst of life's chaos and turmoil?

"There is a fundamental difference between feeling lonely and being alone. To be alone is literally to be all one - to experience the Oneness of all things. Lonely is an emotional state that can often be transcended by reaching beyond ourselves in loving service to others."

Ric Beattie

O God of Light and Darkness, how often we look at our world and see the glass as half-empty. We wonder if you have given up on humankind completely and left us to our own agonizing destruction. Yet we know that you will never leave us because you are in us and in our troubled world. And we are in you. Even when we forget our oneness with the All That Is and all life, you are still there, patiently waiting like a long-suffering Parent for us to return Home. As your prodigal sons and daughters, we ask for your Guidance, your Patience and your Forgiveness. Show us the way Home, for so often it feels like we are lost. May we stretch out our hands in a loving embrace for all your family as we are drawn ever closer together in your Love, your Light and your Peace. So it is.

May 21

"Everyone who believes is set free."

Acts of the Apostles 13:39

What is the difference between beliefs that free and beliefs that enslave? Does your belief system set you free?

"Our ultimate freedom is the right and power to decide how anybody or anything outside ourselves will affect us."

Stephen Covey

Almighty God, you created us in Joy and in Freedom, and your Divine Will is that we continue to live as free men and women. Forgive us when we bind ourselves with limitations and restrictions that implant seeds of death, not life, in our world. Gift us with the courage to walk our path without fear in the freedom of your Divine Guidance. We know and affirm that you are within us and that you walk beside us, but you do not control us, you do not dictate our beliefs or our lives. Your Way is the open door of Freedom, not the restricted box of limitation. Thank you, God, for entrusting us with such a wondrous gift. May we use it wisely and with discretion, and never forget the Source of our freedom. So it is.

Rev. Maryesah Karelon, O.M.M.

May 22

"What is born of the flesh is flesh, and what is born of the Spirit is spirit. Do not be astonished that I said to you, 'You must be born from above.'"

John 3:6-7

What does it mean to you to be "born of the Spirit?"

"The Scriptures tell us that 'There is a spirit in man, and the breath of the Almighty giveth him understanding.' (Job 32:8) The only way you are going to know this Spirit is to act as though you believe it is there. Talk to it. Talk to it in Truth, talk to it in Love, talk to it in Light. Once you get in the habit of talking to Spirit, you will find that not only is it a good listener but that it answers you and does indeed make you understand."

Barbara L. King from <u>Transform Your Life</u>

Loving Creative Spirit, you give birth to the potential within us to be more than we ever believed we could be. Nurture that potential and give us the insight to follow where you lead us to birth ourselves anew. Our world desperately needs the Light and Love that you shower upon us. Introduce us to our true Self so that we may share that Self with the world. Strengthen our commitment to Truth and Justice so that as we walk our chosen path, we may offer a hand to the forsaken, words of encouragement to the broken and despairing and the bread of life to the hungry. Be our conscience, dear Spirit, and never let us climb to heaven on the backs of our brothers and sisters. We are all One and only One may enter. So it is.

May 23

"Yeshua said: Often you have wanted to hear the words that I speak to you now. No one else can say them to you, and the days will come when you seek me and do not find me."

Gospel of Thomas, Saying 38

What lessons is God currently teaching you? What do you still need to learn?

"Growth begins when we start to accept our own weaknesses."

Jean Vanier

Holy Wisdom of God, we have so many questions and so few answers. Often it feels like our lives and our planet are spinning out of control. We need your Wisdom, dear God, to understand and to survive in our complex world. May we be open to your teachings even when they challenge the status quo and bring changes into our lives. May we trust in your Guidance, for the wisdom of the world is often foolishness. Draw us ever closer to you so that our souls may truly be lifted into the radiance of your Presence. Out of our weakness may we find strength, and out of our folly and despair may we find your Truth. So it is.

May 24

"From his fullness we have all received, grace upon grace."

John 1:16

How would you define grace?

"Know, O my child, that each thing in the universe is a vessel, full to the brim with wisdom and beauty. Know, my child, that each thing is a drop from the burning river of His infinite beauty."

Rumi, Sufi Mystic Poet, from <u>The Return Of the Mother</u>

Gracious God, how can we thank you for all you have given to us? So often we look around and all we see is darkness, violence and turmoil. How easy it is to forget to count our blessings. We have so much to be thankful for, from our families and loved ones to an exquisite rosebud; from the birth of a new child to a life well-lived; from bread on our tables and a roof over our heads to green grass under our feet. Teach us how to say thank you by giving gifts to others. May we be your Grace in our world, for there is truly nothing and no one that is not part of you. For the complex, beautiful web of life, we give you thanks and praise. So it is.

May 25

"May my teaching drop like the rain, my speech condense like the dew, like gentle rain on grass, like showers on new growth."

Deuteronomy 32:2

What is the most significant spiritual teaching that you have put to good use in your life? How has this teaching changed you?

"The life you know is a thin layer of events covering a deeper reality. In the deeper reality, you are part of every event that is happening now, has ever happened, or ever will happen."

Deepak Chopra from <u>*The Book of Secrets; Unlocking the Hidden Dimensions of Your Life*</u>

Great Mystery, we seek to know you and to understand your teachings, but often we end our search with only more questions. Show us how to stop our compulsive drive for the newest answer and the hottest technology. Reveal yourself to us in your beautiful Creation that surrounds us everyday. Teach us to hear your Voice in the whispers of wind and the thunder of storms. Teach us to see your Presence in the moist and fertile Earth and the delicate power of a spring blossom. In this most beautiful of seasons, may we truly celebrate your bounty and deepen our appreciation of your continued Presence in our lives and our world. Open us fully to your Great Mystery of Life and Love. So it is.

May 26

"One does not live by bread alone, but by every word that comes from the mouth of God."
Matthew 4:4

Have you ever been forced to go hungry, without shelter or the necessities of life? What did the experience teach you? Where was God for you in those difficult times?

"You'll encounter many obstacles along the road to living your dreams. Some obstacles may be real, some imagined, some may be tangible, and some may be intangible. Some of these obstacles will be created by others, and some will be self-imposed. However they manifest, you will always be given the choice as to whether you give them power."
Francine Ward from *Esteemable Acts: 10 Actions For Building Real Self Esteem*

Loving Mother/Father God, you know our needs before we even put them into words. You have promised us that we will be cared for with even deeper Love than the sparrows or the lilies of the field. Yet you have also told us to ask and perhaps that is most difficult of all. "Ask and you shall receive." "Ask, never doubting, and it shall be given to you." These are your words to us, words to live by. Help us to believe in faith and ask in trust, knowing that it is your Will to give your children good gifts and many blessings. Teach us to count our blessings and believe in the impossible, for through you all things become possible. We have only to believe and ask. So it is.

May 27

"There is one body and one Spirit, just as you were called to the one hope of your calling, one Lord, one faith, one baptism, one God and Father of all, who is above all and through all and in all."

Ephesians 4:4-6

How would you understand this passage in an interfaith context? Do other world religions have a truth and a faith as valid as that of Christianity?

"When nobody around you seems to measure up, it's time to check your yardstick."

Bill Lemley

Great Spirit, you move among and through and with us in our world. Your Power is what binds us together as one family. Forgive us when we seek division when your reality is unity within our great diversity. We know that peace can only come to our little planet when there is peace among the world's religions. Let this be our hope and prayer. May we reach out and embrace others who believe differently than we, knowing that it is to this Love and this deeper understanding that you call us. No matter your name, we are all One in you. So it is.

May 28

"But the Advocate, the Holy Spirit, whom the Father will send in my name, will teach you everything and remind you of all that I have said to you."

John 14:26

How do you see the Holy Spirit at work in your life?

"Each of us sends out positive or negative vibrations, often without being conscious that we are doing so. What if we made an effort to be consciously positive, to resonate messages of the highest good for others and ourselves? What if we made a deliberate attempt to keep our thoughts aligned with God's spiritual optimism, to refuse to be stuck in self-centered fear? Our thoughts speak louder than our words. In order to change what we create, we must change our thinking. We must mind our mind."

Albert Clayton Gaulden

Gracious Holy Spirit, you come to us as a gift of God to open us to new possibilities within. Be our Teacher as we seek your Truth and Wisdom. Be our Comforter when everything seems to go wrong. Be our reminder that we are never alone and never abandoned. To you we lift our souls in grateful acknowledgement for who we are and what we may yet become. Allow us to perceive the difference one person can make in our world. Help us to mind our words and thoughts so we create in Love and Light. Bring us into alignment with your greater Purpose for us and for our planet so that we may assist you in the Great Transformation. We are here for a purpose, Great Spirit. Show us your Way and your Wisdom. So it is.

May 29

"He reveals deep and hidden things."

Daniel 2:22

What wisdom has God revealed to you? How are you sharing this with others? What questions do you still have?

"The deeper hunger in life is a secret that is revealed only when a person is willing to unlock a hidden part of the self."

Deepak Chopra from *The Book of Secrets: Unlocking the Hidden Dimensions of Your Life*

O God of Wisdom and Power, you reveal yourself to us in the strong winds of your Spirit and the gentle whispers of sacred silence. May we be open to receive your teaching and your messages for our lives. May we follow where you lead, even into the secret places where the hidden and the sacred reside. Give us the courage to become your voices and your prophets in our world, to share what we perceive and teach what we know. The day of your revealing has come and it is not a day of fear and judgment, but a day of joy and gladness. Thank you for your Presence among us and within us. Thank you for opening to us the hidden teachings so that all may be revealed now in our day. Guide us in the use of this knowledge so that it may be shared for the good of all your children. Unite us as one family, as we are One in you. So it is.

Rev. Maryesah Karelon, O.M.M.

May 30

"God has told you what is good; and what is it that the Lord asks of you? Only to act justly; to love tenderly; to walk wisely before your God."

Micah 6:8

What specifically is God asking of you today in your life?

"Put your mind, heart, intellect and soul even to your smallest acts. This is the secret of success."

Swami Sivananda

Dear God, you have given us so much and you ask so little in return. May our lives become a song of praise to your Love and Light. May we invest even the littlest and most everyday tasks with your Spirit. May we walk our path as a prayer, mindful always of your Presence with us. May that empowering, energizing Presence flow through us as a waterfall, cleansing and strengthening us for the work you place before us. Remind us always that no matter what the appearance may be, you never give us more than we can endure. Stretch our boundaries beyond limitations, and teach us to come to you when we are overwhelmed and overburdened. We know you want what is for our highest good. We trust you to reveal that good to us and show us the Way to attain that good. So it is.

May 31

"After this I shall pour out my spirit on all humanity. Your sons and daughters shall prophesy, your old people shall dream dreams, and your young people see visions."

Joel 3:1

How would you describe the gifts about which the prophet Joel was speaking? What role do visions and prophecies play in your life? Do you see yourself as a prophet?

"Many years ago, but not so long ago, there were those who said, 'Well, you have three strikes against you: You're black, you're blind and you're poor.' But God said to me, 'I will make you rich in the spirit of inspiration, to inspire others as well as create music to encourage the world to a place of oneness and hope, and positivity.' I believed Him and not them."

Stevie Wonder

O Spirit of our Living God, we trust in you. We rejoice in your Presence and dance with delight when you inspire us to dream and step forward into the future. You have gifted us with the power to create, in joy or in sadness. We ask for your Divine Guidance and Wisdom so that our visions may take form and transform our world from darkness into Light. May we embrace the friendless, feed the hungry, loose the chains of oppression and fear and proclaim the year of our Lord's favor. May your Spirit rest upon us, dear God, and appoint us to do your work in your vineyard. So it is.

June

As your daily life becomes
more and more a living prayer, detach yourself
from the material concerns of the world.
Place your trust completely in a Loving God
who knows all your needs, and
cares for you much more
than the lilies of the field and the sparrows.
Walk as one with God, in but not of the world,
and remember that the world
desperately needs your light, so stay grounded
as you reach for the stars.

June 1

"Trust in the Lord forever, for in the Lord God you have an everlasting rock."

Isaiah 26:4

What and in whom do you put your trust?

"My part is to believe; God's part is to provide all that is needed."

Jack Boland

Faithful God, you have promised to always walk beside us and never forsake us. Teach us to trust in your promises. So often we say, "I believe. Help my unbelief!" When we have been hurt by betrayal, show us the path of forgiveness. As chaos and confusion spin around us, we breathe deeply and center ourselves in your Love. This we know will never fail. This we can believe in. This we can trust to be our foundation. Thank you, dear God, for always being there for us and for lifting us up when we fall, for indeed, in God we trust. So it is.

June 2

"How precious is your steadfast love, O God! All people may take refuge in the shadow of your wings."

Psalm 36:7

Recall a time in your life when you needed to rely on God for strength and guidance. What did you learn through this experience?

"God in the midst of us is a great steady stream of renewing and cleansing and vitalizing life, and we can have the use of this life if we will open up the channels of its flowing and ourselves draw from this source."

Myrtle Fillmore from _Healing Letters_

Loving Mother/Father God, we call you to us in your healing Power. Flow through us and within us. Cleanse and renew us. Enliven us with your Spirit and inspire us with your Love. Teach us to become true wounded healers in your Name. May we embrace our hurting world with gentleness and compassion. Unite us as one family across the boundaries of race and nation, of gender and belief, of haves and have nots. We are all your children, brothers and sisters together. May we love as you love us and may we become a refuge for the forgotten and the lost. So it is.

June 3

"No one after lighting a lamp hides it under a jar, or puts it under a bed, but puts it on a lampstand, so that those who enter may see the light."

Luke 8:16

How are you allowing your light to shine in the world? What might you do to enhance the brightness of your light?

"When I stand before God at the end of my life, I would hope that I would not have a single bit of talent left, and could say, 'I used everything you gave me.'"

Erma Bombeck

O God of Light, your blessings rain upon us like the nurturing showers of spring. You gift us with talents and opportunities beyond our imagining. Give us the courage to open the gifts you give to us. Teach us how to use them for the highest and best purpose. May we become your Light in a darkened world. Remind us that we must allow our light to shine if we are to be wayshowers for others, but always in your Name and to your Glory. As you sent your Light into the world, so now you send us. May your Light find a home in our hearts and radiate out to everyone we meet. We are your Lightbearers. O Spirit of Fire, light your flame in us. So it is.

June 4

"The good person out of the good treasure of the heart produces good…for it is out of the abundance of the heart that the mouth speaks."

Luke 6:45

Spend a few quiet moments and journey to the sacred center of your heart. What do you find there? Is there anything that needs to be healed and released?

"Come, not to study the map of spiritual terrain, but to possess it for yourself; to walk about in it without fear of going astray. Why learn the theory of Divine Grace, and what it has been doing throughout history, when you can become the very instrument of its operation?"

Jean Pierre de Caussade

Beloved of My Heart, I open the door to your Love and Grace. Even the darkest recesses of my heart that I have kept under lock and key I now throw open to your healing Power. All the little hurts, the stuck places of disappointment, the black holes of grief, the fires of anger and despair—I release them all to the cleansing, healing power that is flowing through me now. I claim your Abundance as my birthright—abundance in all things; material, spiritual, emotional and physical. With the Grace of your Abundance living within my heart, I am free to speak your Love and Truth. I am free to create in your Name and for your Purpose. I am free to celebrate Life as you would have it be for all your children. So it is.

June 5

"Blessed are the peacemakers, for they will be called children of God."

Matthew 5:9

How can you be a peacemaker in your daily life?

"The fruit of prayer is the deepening of love, deepening of faith. If we believe, we will be able to pray, and the fruit of love is service. Therefore works of love are always works of peace, and to be able to put our hearts and hands into loving service, we must know God, we must know God is love, that He loves us and that He has created us—each one of us—for greater things."

Mother Teresa of Calcutta from *The Joy Of Loving*

Source of All Being, you call us to be peacemakers in a world of violence and bloodshed. You call us to love the unlovable, to forgive the unforgivable and to bind up the hearts of the broken in spirit. We hear your call. Teach us how to walk our paths of loving service without fear and often without honor. You have many vineyards, dear God, and the workers are all too few. May we bear good fruit in your Name. We offer our hearts, our hands and our voices to your service of Peace, Love, Light and Forgiveness. Create your Peace now, in us and through us. So it is.

June 6

"You have heard of this hope before in the word of the truth, the gospel that has come to you. Just as it is bearing fruit and growing in the whole world, so it has been bearing fruit among yourselves from the day you heard it and truly comprehended the grace of God."

Colossians 1:5-6

What is the hope that is bearing fruit in your life? Are you ever close to losing hope? What returns you to faith and hope?

"In this experience we call life, we are often confronted by the unexpected—that which we wouldn't choose for ourselves. During these times, it is helpful for us to be grounded in knowing that 'with God all things are possible.' Holding to this Truth allows us not only to embrace hope, but to actually shift outcomes to that which is more favorable, more in alignment with our choices. Life is always stacked in our favor. God would have only good for us. As we make an irrevocable decision to trust God, this will become our experience."

Ron Scott

O God, you are our hope, ever-present in times of change and distress. Teach us to trust in you so that we may go forth and bear good fruit. Show us that truly all things are possible through your Power and Love. May we become co-creators with you, allowing your Spirit to empower us and align us with your Holy Will for our lives. Remind us that our thoughts and words create, so it is our responsibility to stay focused on your Truth so that we may create in Love, in Light, in Peace. Freed from believing we are victims, we commit ourselves to bearing your good fruit. As we place our trust and hope in you, we journey onward to the goals and dreams that you have waiting for us. So it is.

June 7

> "Then Job answered the Lord: 'I know that you can do all things, and that no purpose of yours can be thwarted.'"
>
> Job 42:1-2

Recall a time in your life when what you desired and what actually happened were very different. What caused your desire to be unfulfilled? How was God at work in the result?

"Imagination is the beginning of creation. You imagine what you desire, you will what you imagine and at last you create what you will."

George Bernard Shaw

Mighty God, as we place our hope and trust in you, we imagine the power of your Spirit moving through our lives. In this imagining, we become co-creators with your Divine Purpose for us. Expand our horizons and explode the boundaries that we too often use to limit what is possible. We know that with your Spirit to guide us we will become greater than we ever imagined. May we look into our innermost hearts and see your Divine Image there, waiting to be born in all its glory. Gift us with the remembering of who we truly are so that we can imagine with you the kingdom on earth as in heaven. So it is.

June 8

"Lead a life worthy of the calling to which you have been called...bearing with one another in love, making every effort to maintain the unity of the Spirit in the bond of peace."

Ephesians 4:1-3

How are you manifesting your spiritual calling in your current life?

"God does not call the qualified, God qualifies the called."

Neale Donald Walsch from *Tomorrow's God*

Gracious God, we acknowledge that you call each and every one of us to a special and Divine Purpose. Guide and direct our footsteps so that we may walk according to that calling and fulfill that Purpose. Hold a mirror before our eyes so that we may truly see our divine Self reflected in your Light and Glory. You are part of me, wondrous God, and I am part of you. You know me better than I know myself, for you were there when I was created in my mother's womb. You molded my limbs and fashioned every vein, artery and organ of my body. Then you blew the breath of life into my lungs and your Spirit has lived within me ever since. I choose to be among your chosen ones, and I know that everyone of your children can make the same choice and be called in the same way. We are all your precious chosen people, called to be your servants in the world. So it is.

June 9

"And this is my prayer, that your love may overflow more and more with knowledge and full insight to help you to determine what is best."

Philippians 1:9

How do prayer and meditation assist you in fulfilling your Divine Purpose?

"Insofar as we are able to stay attentive to the moment, we can serve the will of God. Insofar as we are able to abandon our ideas about what should happen, and what we demand to happen, and allow the situation as it is to reveal itself to us, we are amenable to discerning the will of God. 'Thy will be done' is a prayer that will force us into this present moment, if we pray it from the heart."

Regina Sara Ryan from <u>*Praying Dangerously: Igniting the Inner Life*</u>

Loving God, you speak to us in the silence and the whisper of the wind if only we have ears to hear. You speak to us in the beauty of a rainbow and the diversity of your abundant Creation if only we have eyes to see. You speak to us in the touch of a baby's hand and the velvety petals of a rose if only we have the sensation to feel. You speak to us in the sweet taste of a lover's lips and the bitter tears of loss and grief if only we have the awareness to sense your Presence. You speak to us in the wonderful freshness of a spring rain and the tantalizing smell of newly baked bread if only we take a deep breath to inhale your precious Life. And yes, you speak to us in the innermost and sacred spaces of our hearts where words are unknown and unnecessary if only we will open the door and welcome you as our honored guest. Come unto us and come into us, and teach us how to pray with the power of the heart. So it is.

June 10

"We declare to you what was from the beginning, what we have heard, what we have seen with our eyes, what we have looked at and touched with our hands, concerning the word of life."

1 John 1:1

How would you define the "word of life" for you?

"To deepen the relationship with the Beloved, follow the same principles of relationship that you pursue in the human realm. Thus you live the relationship throughout the day, bringing the same sensitivity to nuance and fine tuning that you would bring to a human love relationship."

Jean Houston from <u>The Search For the Beloved</u>

Beloved of My Heart, I invite you to enter my sacred and innermost temple. I wait with eager longing to hear your Voice and feel your touch. Calm the beating of my heart so that I may hear the still silence. Awaken within me the lifeblood of desire for your words, your teaching and your very Presence. Steady my trembling knees so that I may walk beside you without fear. Remove the blocks from my mind that give birth to doubt and distrust, and flood my being with the fountain of your Light and

Love. For lo, the winter is truly past and the time for singing has come. My heart sings your praises with joy and delight. I am in you and you are in me, and there is no other. So it is.

June 11

"Then our mouth was filled with laughter, and our tongue with shouts of joy."

Psalm 126:2

How do you keep laughter and humor in your life? What happens when you lose your sense of humor?

"The more you praise and celebrate your life, the more there is to praise."

Oprah Winfrey

O God of Joy and Wonder, from the very beginning you have celebrated with your Creation. Remind us not to take our lives and our selves so seriously. Renew in us the innocent joy of a child so that we may love and laugh, play and dance. In the midst of the fiercest rainstorm you gift us with the beauty and promise of rainbows. Teach us to look for the good in all things no matter how dark the storm appears. We know you are always with us, and for that simple but incredible gift we offer you thanks and praise. Lift us above our everyday lives and circumstances, and show us the vision of the eagle so that we may soar on eagle's wings. So it is.

June 12

"Yeshua said: Many are standing by the door, but only those who are alone and simple can enter the bridal chamber."

Gospel of Thomas, Saying 75

Do you have challenges with the priorities in your life? What factors are important to you in creating your current priority list?

"Simplicity, clarity, singleness; these are the attributes that give our lives power and vividness and joy."

Richard Halloway

Loving Creator God, there is so much about our world that creates despair, fear and sadness. So much is difficult to understand and too complex to explain. Nothing seems simple in our lives yet we yearn for the clarity that comes with your Light and Truth. We pray for your Wisdom and Vision, O God. We pray that you would open our minds and hearts to a greater understanding and a greater joy. Teach us to allow and accept without judgment, to celebrate the glorious diversity of your Creation without prejudice and to forgive wrongs even when our hearts break. We are all one family and in you we find our strength and our song. So it is.

June 13

> *"Truly I tell you, just as you did it to one of the least of these who are members of my family, you did it to me."*
>
> **Matthew 25:40**

Have you ever been on the receiving end of God's goodness through others when you needed it most? How are you reaching out to those less fortunate than you are?

> "The world does not need tourists who ride by in a bus clucking their tongues. The world as it is needs those who will love it enough to change it, with what they have, where they are."
>
> **Robert Fulghum**

God of Mercy and Compassion, you love all your children with an everlasting Love. Teach us how to love like you, without judgment, without counting the cost. There are so many in your world needing love, care and compassion. Often they appear different from us. Often their values and beliefs are different from ours. Focus our attention on what we have in common. Open our hearts so that we may truly share your Love and Light that resides within us. May we share and celebrate our truth while we respect and honor the truth of others. With a smile, with an embrace, with a blanket, with a cup of water or a whole meal, we bring your Love to Earth and it lives through us. May we be your hands and feet, your Voice and heart in a hurting world. So it is.

June 14

"And why do you worry about clothing? Consider the lilies of the field, how they grow; they neither toil nor spin, yet I tell you, even Solomon in all his glory was not clothed like one of these."

Matthew 6:28-29

Where is the line for you between faith and hard reality? Are you able to trust in God's goodness, care and protection even when the evidence around you looks grim? What has been the result of such trust?

"Do not anticipate trouble, or worry about what may never happen. Keep in the sunlight."

Benjamin Franklin

Generous and Ever-loving God, we worry too much and believe too little. We often spend our days creating terrible scenarios of the future that will never happen. Gift us with the profound trust and knowledge that you will never forsake us. Even when our burdens seem too much for us to bear, we know and affirm that you are there beside us lifting those burdens and sharing them with us. May we reach out to others and do as you do for us, bringing hope in the midst of fear and despair, compassion in the midst of grief and loss. In the darkness shine through us, dear God, and light our world with your Love. So it is.

Rev. Maryesah Karelon, O.M.M.

June 15

"The kingdom of God is not coming with things that can be observed; not will they say, 'Look here it is!' or 'There it is!' For, in fact, the kingdom of God is among you."
Luke 17:20-21

How are you living the kingdom of God? How is it part of you and your life?

"I have never met a person whose greatest need was anything other than real, unconditional love. You can find it in a simple act of kindness toward someone who needs help. There is no mistaking love. You feel it in your heart. It is the common fiber of life, the flame that heats our soul, energizes our spirit and supplies passion to our lives. It is our connection to God and to each other."
Elizabeth Kubler-Ross

Wondrous God, you surround us with the magical and the mystical, but all too often we miss the forest and see only the trees. Open our inner eyes, expand our vision and kindle our imagination so that your kingdom may truly be born among us. We yearn for your Justice and Peace in our world, O God. May we become part of the manifestation of your kingdom, your reign among us. Teach us to journey to the sacred temple within our souls. There we will find you waiting for us, ready to spread the banquet table of the kingdom with unimagined Abundance. Your kingdom welcomes all your children Home and invites us all to celebrate at the banquet table as one family. Home is in the innermost chamber of our sacred heart. There you wait for us. We have come Home at last. So it is.

June 16

"Trust in him at all times, O people; pour out your heart before him; God is a refuge for us."

Psalm 62:8

What is necessary for you to trust someone? Compare a relationship where there is trust with one where there is no trust. What is the difference?

"It is better to be disliked for who you are than to be liked for who you are not. How much easier to be authentic than to pretend to be someone you are not. What a relief just to be. How clear and simple. How honest. How real. The only thing you really have to share with anyone, anyway, is your own state of being."

Judith Ann Parsons

O God of our Salvation, you reveal yourself to us and we learn what trust is through you. We learn that you will always be there for us, that we can share our innermost heart with you and you will honor our sacred trust. Show us how to reveal ourselves, walking honestly and freely without fear. We give you thanks and praise for showering us with your Love, your Peace and your Light. As we heal our hearts and minds from past hurts, may we become true reflections of you. In you we find our true Selves. In you we find the Self we can trust. In you we discover how to trust and embrace our neighbors and our world. Thank you, thank you, thank you. So it is.

June 17

"I have heard your prayer, I have seen your tears; indeed, I will heal you."
2 Kings 20:5

What is your understanding of healing? What needs healing in your life—physically, emotionally, spiritually?

"Every one of us alone has the power to direct the course of our lives by choosing what actions we will or won't take. While sometimes it's easier to believe you don't have a choice, the reality is that you always have a choice to behave differently."
Francine Ward from <u>Esteemable Acts: 10 Actions For Building Real Self Esteem</u>

O God of Wisdom and Truth, you bring your healing Power into our lives and baptize us with your Spirit of loving fire. We know that there can be no healing for us without our cooperation and participation. Remove the stumbling blocks we place on our path. Teach us the value of self-examination and honest evaluation of our words and actions. Remove the despair and lack of self-worth that would give up when the going gets tough. With you beside us, with you before us, with you behind us and above us we will always have another choice. May we choose well with your Guidance so that our path will be smooth and our direction clear. May that path be according to your Will and in Divine Order. The journey continues. So it is.

June 18

"You show me the path of life. In your presence there is fullness of joy; in your right hand are pleasures forevermore."

Psalm 16:11

Who have been your guides and teachers in your earthly life? How are you passing on that legacy to others?

"Many people spend a great deal of time complaining about the government, their parents, and the sorry state of affairs in the world, but in doing so they forget that we are the miracle. They blame God for the suffering that surrounds us saying 'How could a loving God allow such things to happen?' They behave like slaves who blame an overseer, forgetting that free will has given them the responsibility, so that the deeper issue has nothing to do with God or the government but rather with the fundamental shift that must occur in the human heart if peace is to become a reality. We think of responsibility as a burdensome obligation when in fact it is a gift."

Darren John Main from <u>Spiritual Journeys Along the Yellow Brick Road</u>

Holy One, so often we seek someone to blame out of our frustration and often the buck stops with you. We forget that we are reflections of you, that you gave us the oversight and responsibility of this beautiful world. Help us to seek your Wisdom and Guidance instead of blaming you for our challenges. We are not helpless children. We can learn to use the skills and talents you have given us to better our lives and our world. We can become teachers and loving guides for others as we journey together. We can all do our part, no matter how small, to re-create our Earth. For this we were born. For this we continue to live and breathe. May the breath of your Holy Spirit blow into us in Power and bless us in Strength. Our legacy awaits us. It is up to us to create in Goodness and Peace. So it is.

June 19

"For truly I tell you, if you have faith the size of a mustard seed, you will say to this mountain, 'Move from here to there,' and it will move; and nothing will be impossible for you."

Matthew 17:20

Reflect on a time in your life when you were asked to do the seemingly impossible. What was the result and what did you learn?

"One ought never to turn one's back on a threatened danger and try to run away from it. If you do that, you will double the danger. But if you meet it promptly and without flinching, you will reduce the danger by half. Never run away from anything. Never!"

Winston Churchill

Faithful God, you have promised to walk beside us wherever we go, no matter how dark the way. When our faith wavers and there appears to be no light ahead, even then your hand is there to steady and guide us. Strengthen our faith so that we may truly walk where angels fear to tread. Go before us as our Wayshower.

Teach us that what we believe we will truly see and manifest, so expand our imaginations to include the impossible. For we know that all is possible with your help and according to your Divine Purpose. Remove our fear, replace it with unshakeable faith and then prepare us for miracles! We praise and thank you for what you give through us and to us. May we truly be one with your Love and Light. So it is.

June 20

"If anyone is in Christ, there is a new creation; everything old has passed away; see, everything has become new!"

2 Corinthians 5:17

What are you currently birthing in your life?

"Every day, just as a tree grows, so do we as beings. As you change, observe how your beauty changes. Within change is the beauty of life's mysteries. The mysterious thing called life is not a mystery at all but a natural evolution toward perfection."

Ron Rathbun from *The Way is Within*

Mother of all Mysteries, in the long ago past you embraced us in the warmth of your womb. Now you call us to be reborn. Yet we carry so much baggage from the past. Surround us with your healing Presence and lift our burdens of guilt and regret. Release us from the chains of shame and blame. Cleanse our hearts and prepare us to receive your Fountain of Life. Holy Shekinah, we open the door of our sacred temple and welcome you. Come into us and birth us anew in the beauty and holiness of your Presence. We give you thanks and praise for your ever-present Love, Light and Protection that never fail us. May we always know that we are secure under the shadow of your wings. So it is.

June 21

"I will turn the darkness before them into light."

Isaiah 42:16

As we approach the Summer Solstice, reflect on the light and the dark in your life. What does it mean to you that soon we will once again begin our journey toward the darkness?

"Everything has its wonders, even darkness and silence, and I learn, whatever state I may be in, therein to be content."

Helen Keller

Holy Mother, as we celebrate your Light we begin our journey to darkness. We acknowledge the perfection of your Plan and your continued Presence in our world. Show us the good even in the darkness and teach us to reverence life as it manifests in all its glory before us. Remove our judgments and our assumptions, and open our hearts simply to allow and accept. May we walk gently upon your good Earth and live in harmony with all your creatures. Show us how to heal our wounds so that we may be called your children and your stewards. As we seek balance in our lives, we seek your Truth and Justice for all. In the light or in the dark, as male and female, we unite in your Love and Compassion. So it is.

June 22

"See, now is the acceptable time; see, now is the day of salvation!"

2 Corinthians 6:2

Reflect on the different meanings of time. How does time affect your life?

"When you are on a journey, it is certainly helpful to know where you are going or at least the general direction in which you are moving, but don't forget: the only thing that is ultimately real about your journey is the step that you are taking at this moment. That's all there ever is."

Eckhart Tolle from <u>*The Power Of Now*</u>

God of all Times and Places, so often we focus all our attention on the past or the future. You meet us in the here and now and remind us that this moment is all we truly have. Teach us how to make the most of the time you give to us. Protect us from fear of the future or regrets from the past. Allow us to journey onward knowing that every step we take is a step in the present and an investment in the future. May we chart our course by your Divine Will and Order knowing that the right time, the moment of your in-breaking Presence, happens when we least expect it. Thank you for the magical surprises of our lives that are always right on time, your time. So it is.

June 23

"Your will be done, on earth as it is in heaven."

Matthew 6:10

How do you experience God's Will in your life?

"If there is truly nothing you can do to change your here and now, and you can't remove yourself from the situation, then accept your here and now totally by dropping all inner resistance. The false, unhappy self that loves feeling miserable, resentful, or sorry for itself can then no longer survive. This is called surrender. Surrender is not weakness. There is great strength in it. Only a surrendered person has spiritual power. Through surrender you will be free internally of the situation. You may then find that the situation changes without any effort on your part. In any case, you are free."

Eckhart Tolle from *The Power Of Now*

Almighty God, you have placed before us a banquet of opportunity that surpasses anything we could imagine. You have placed your Image within us so that literally we are reflections of your Love and Light. We are not separate from you and you are not separate from us. Yet we often force that separation because we willfully want to be in control. With hard experience we encounter the awesomely difficult task of swimming upstream against the current, struggling to progress on our spiritual path. If we would just let go and allow your Will to guide us, we would find ourselves effortlessly floating in the stream of your powerful Love. Teach us to trust you, dear God, to place ourselves in your capable hands and let you navigate our way. With a deep breath, we surrender to your Will. So it is.

June 24

"Therefore let all who are faithful offer prayer to you; at a time of distress, the rush of mighty waters shall not reach them."

Psalm 32:6

Do you believe prayer is effective, and if so, how does it work? Reflect on times when your prayers have been answered.

"...first put your spiritual life in order, everything else falls into place. Once you align yourself with your Higher Self, this will lead you to find your own destiny...spend less time worrying about the everyday details and commit more time to unleashing your spiritual potential, then the solutions to your everyday problems will naturally emerge as flashes of intuition or realization. Prayer is the tool that helps you to do this and should be used as a first resort—a creative help to heal and guide you."

Chrissie Blaze and Gary Blaze from *Power Prayer*

Gentle God, you listen and hear our prayers even when we can only speak the words of our broken hearts. Teach us to wait patiently to see your answers, for often they come in surprising ways. Draw us ever closer to you so that our lives may become a living prayer. May we experience the joy of the sacred in everyday moments—doing laundry, cooking a meal, cutting the grass, hugging a child. When the rush of life becomes overwhelming, guide us to that quiet place away from it all where we may hear your still, small voice whispering to us. May you become a habit in our busy lives and may we grow in the depth of our love and knowledge of you. So it is.

June 25

"Yeshua said: I am the Light that shines on everyone. I am the All. The All came forth from me and the All came into me. Split wood and I am there. Turn over the stone, and there you will find me."

Gospel of Thomas, Saying 77

Have you ever asked God for something in prayer that wasn't fulfilled? Why do you think this happened and how did it affect your faith?

"Not to react, not to revise or embellish or expound, not even to respond, but simply to listen is a gift. When we are able to be truly silent, to truly listen, then God can speak. This is a discipline. Mother Teresa points out that what we have to say is never as essential as what God says to us and through us:

'All our words are useless if they do not come from within. Words that do not carry the light of Christ only increase the darkness.'"

Johan Christoph Arnold from <u>Seeking Peace</u>

Generous and Ever-Loving God, teach us how to ask for our heart's desire, knowing that it is always your good pleasure to give us what we truly need, what is for our highest good. Often we are afraid to dream; often we are scared to ask; often we fear we will be disappointed when nothing happens. Remove our fears and give us the courage to speak, for though you know us better than we know ourselves, you wait for us to ask. So we ask that you shower us with your miracles. We pray that you will open our hearts, our eyes and our ears to perceive them, for most likely they will come in surprising ways. May we see the wind of your Spirit in the trees and hear the flutter of angel wings. May we feel a flood of all-encompassing Love flowing into our hearts. Then we will know. Thank you for what already is and what is yet to be revealed. So it is.

June 26

"You have been my help, and in the shadow of your wings I sing for joy. My soul clings to you; your right hand upholds me."

Psalm 63:7-8

How would you define an angel? Have you ever experienced an angel's presence?

Rev. Maryesah Karelon, O.M.M.

"When your tasks seem a little heavy and over-whelming remember to do just one thing at a time quietly, and leave the rest because the rest is not your job. What you cannot get through you must hand back to God, and God will work it out for you."

White Eagle from *The Quiet Mind*

Holy Shekinah, you gather us under the shelter of your wings and cover us in the Glory of God. When the world is too much with us and our spirit is dragging, show us the way to our inner temple of joy. We seek you in the quiet stillness of our hearts even when around us there is chaos and turmoil. In this sacred space, we recognize the subtle messages of the angels and realize that we are never alone. On a crowded highway, beside the bed of a sick child or in the embrace of an old man in his twilight years, you wrap us in the warmth of your gentle yet powerful Love. Thank you, sweet Spirit, for all you do for us beyond our asking. So it is.

June 27

"You shall love the Lord your God with all your heart, and with all your soul, and with all your strength, and with all your mind; and your neighbor as yourself."

Luke 10:27

What do these two great commandments mean for your life? How do you love your neighbor as yourself?

"If love is an action, how do you express self-love? Self-love starts with having the courage to be who you are, regardless of what others might think. It is about having the courage to live your dreams, to do what makes you happy in life, so that one day you won't wake up saying, 'I wish I had.' Self-love is about self-care, making your health a priority. Self-love is revealed in your willingness to stay focused on the things you say are important. It's about having the courage to set boundaries and protect them."

Francine Ward

Holy One, you have given us your commandments not to burden us with law but to free us in Spirit and Truth. Teach us to truly live and embody what you would have us be. Show us the breadth and the depth of your Love that knows no boundaries and makes no distinctions. As we grow in knowledge of you, we expand and flower as your beloved children. We know in the deepest recesses of our souls that we can only be happy when we find rest in you. May we dream our dreams of Home and find you waiting on our doorstep with gifts so precious and rare. So it is.

June 28

"*Happy are those…whose hope is in the Lord their God.*"

Psalm 146:5

Are you happy at this moment in your life? What would you change to bring greater fulfillment and happiness?

"Happiness lies in the consciousness we have of it."

George Sand

O God of Joy and Gladness, you bring us the Joy of your Presence and the assurance that all good gifts come from you. What more could we ask? Teach us that true happiness and fulfillment lie not in how much we earn or how many things we collect but in the riches of a heart dedicated only to you. Keep our priorities simple and our motives pure. Remind us to appreciate our loved ones and never take them for granted. Show us the wisdom of the butterfly that will never be caught if chased but if we sit quietly, may land right on our shoulder. May our joyful hearts offer you thanksgiving with our lives and our voices. Happy are we when we remember who we truly are and celebrate our divine legacy. So it is.

June 29

"Beloved, I do not consider that I have made it my own; but this one thing I do: forgetting what lies behind and straining forward to what lies ahead, I press on toward the goal for the prize of the heavenly call of God in Christ Jesus."

Philippians 3:13-14

What are your current goals in life?

"Ideals are like stars; you will not succeed in touching them with your hands, but like the seafaring man on the desert of waters, you choose them as your guides, and following them, you reach your destiny."

Carl Schurz

Mother/Father God, we all have goals in our lives and sometimes we attain them, other times we fall short. Perhaps we are still climbing the long path up the mountain. Help us to discern our true and holy Purpose, and to make that our first priority. Then all the rest will fall into place and be offered to us. May we listen in the silence for your call and then find the courage to accept the challenges you lay before us. We know that it is in these challenges that we learn and grow, becoming the person we are meant to be. May we dream wondrous dreams and see visions filled with possibilities, and then build foundations under our clouds to bring your Love, your Peace and your Justice to Earth. So it is.

June 30

"More than all else, keep watch over your heart, since here are the wellsprings of life. Turn your back on the mouth that misleads, keep your distance from lips that deceive. Let your eyes be fixed ahead, your gaze be straight before you. Keep straight the path of your feet, and all your ways will be sure."

Proverbs 4:23-26

Reflect on the path that has brought you to this point in your life. What people, circumstances and conditions assisted you the most? Can you see God's hand working through your life?

"There are no little events in life, those we think of no consequence may be full of fate, and it is at our own risk if we neglect the acquaintances and opportunities that seem to be casually offered, and of small importance."
Amelia E. Barr

Holy God, as we continue quietly along our chosen paths, remind us to be aware of the chance encounters and the casual conversations that can bring your messages. We journey onward one step at a time. Sometimes the climb is steep and we need a helping hand. Sometimes we find ourselves in a beautiful meadow and we're tempted to stay and rest awhile. But always you call us onward even when we are not certain of the destination. Just as you have called so many before us out of their comfort zones, you call us and we answer, and we journey onward. We realize that the journey has become our home for this lifetime and this reality. May we learn our lessons along the Way until we finally reach our true Home. We give thanks for all those who have been guides and teachers along the Way. We give you thanks and praise for never giving up on us no matter how slowly we climb and how many detours we take. May we stay on the Path of your Truth and Light, knowing that the prize of your Love awaits us. So it is.

July

Find a balance for yourself
between freedom and discipline,
and live your life on that balance point.
Know that "the Lord is the Spirit,
and where the Spirit of the Lord is,
there is freedom." (2 Corinthians 3:17)
Therefore, seek always to spread your wings
as a gifted child of God, while remaining grounded
and humble as a fallible human.

Light in the Darkness

July 1

> "Let me hear what God the Lord will speak, for he will speak peace to his people, to his faithful, to those who turn to him in their hearts."
>
> **Psalm 85:8**

How is God speaking to you in your life?

> "The quieter you become, the more you can hear."
>
> **Ram Das**

Holy One, you speak to us in the quietness that is so rare in our busy lives. Teach us how to stop the rush of life and just breathe in the silence of your Presence. As we journey inward to the sacred temple of our heart, we find you waiting for us. In the security of your Love, we ask for your continued Guidance in our lives. You know our needs before we even speak them, but remind us how to ask so that we may be showered with your blessings. Thank you, thank you, thank you God. So it is.

July 2

> "I bless the Lord who gives me counsel; in the night also my heart instructs me. I keep the Lord always before me; because he is at my right hand, I shall not be moved."
>
> **Psalm 16:7-8**

How does your dream world connect you to God? Recall any significant dreams you have had recently that spoke to you of God.

"The most pathetic person in the world is someone who has sight but has no vision."

Helen Keller

Mother/Father God, in the watches of the night we hear your call. In the mists and visions of our dreams we see your Way for us. Open our minds and our hearts so that we may perceive the many and unusual methods that you may use to communicate your messages. Help us to translate the language of the sacred so that we clearly perceive your Will for our lives. We are open to your leading, dear God. Teach us how to follow your Way, resolutely, steadfastly, without fear though the path be narrow and dark. So it is.

July 3

"But truly God has listened; he has given heed to the words of my prayer."

Psalm 66:19

Reflect on how God has answered your prayers.

"Know beyond all doubt that God is love, and that all things work together for good for those who love God. See divine law operating in your own life and in the life of the whole of humanity. Look always for the good, look for God, and you will find that God's great love is working out a wise and beautiful purpose through human evolution."

White Eagle from *The Quiet Mind*

Gracious and Loving God, how often we face challenges in our lives that appear on the surface to be traumatic and disastrous. Show us how to rise above our all too human emotions and fears. Allow us to see from a higher perspective where we can expand our horizons and perceive the larger picture. On an act of faith, we affirm that all things work together for good. We may not see the evidence in front of us, but we trust in your everlasting Wisdom to show us the Way to your Truth. Teach us what we must know in our heart of hearts to walk gently on this Earth in Faith and Love. So it is.

July 4

"Likewise the Spirit helps us in our weakness, for we do not know how to pray as we ought, but that very Spirit intercedes with sighs too deep for words."

Romans 8:26

Recall a time when circumstances brought you literally or figuratively to your knees. What words did you use to communicate with God or were words unnecessary?

"Let your religion be less of a theory and more of a love affair."

Gilbert Keith Chesterton

Gracious Spirit, you come to us in those moments of life when there are no words that can express our pain and despair. You embrace us when we feel lost and alone. You lift us up when we have stumbled and are too weary to rise. You gift us with the sighs of our hearts, which are more precious in the sight of God then all the polished prayers we could pray. Remind us, Sweet Spirit, that prayer is not about "doing it right" but simply being open to doing it at all. If we open the door, God will walk through it. We can depend on that. Our job is to prepare the way, even if it is a path in the wilderness. Come Holy Spirit and fill us with your Love, Light and Peace. So it is.

July 5

"My house shall be called a house of prayer for all peoples."

Isaiah 56:7

What can you do to promote understanding and tolerance among the world's religious faiths?

"It is hard to let old beliefs go. They are familiar. We are comfortable with them and have spent years building systems and developing habits that depend on them. Like a man who has worn eyeglasses so long that he forgets he has them on, we forget that the world looks to us the way it does because we have become used to seeing it that way through a particular set of lenses. Today, however, we need new lenses. And we need to throw the old ones away."

Kenich Ohmae

Source of All Being, you spread your Light and Love over all the Earth, enfolding all peoples in your arms. We affirm the beauty and the unity of all our brothers and sisters. They may call upon you with other names, Yahweh, Allah and Buddha. They may worship you in ways that seem strange to us. But you are One, Most Holy God, and beyond all human names. Let not the names divide your children. May we come together and offer prayers of peace, justice and unity for your world. Come and make your dwelling with us. Let your glory, your Shekinah, hover over us. As our Father and our Mother, we praise and thank you for all the blessings you have showered upon us. We invite you to dwell in our hearts so that we may be One with you and be drawn ever closer to all your children, in the Oneness of your Light and Love. So it is.

July 6

"Now I appeal to you, brothers and sisters, by the name of our Lord Jesus Christ, that all of you be in agreement and that there be no divisions among you, but that you be united in the same mind and the same purpose."

1 Corinthians 1:10

As you look around our nation and our world, what do you believe is the cause of the violence and divisions that separate people?

"While we watch the storm clouds gather and prepare for the storm, let us never forget that the sun still shines behind those dark clouds, and may somehow break through before the storm descends. I see sunshine in the real desire for peace in the hearts of humanity, even though the human family gropes toward peace blindly, not knowing the way."

Peace Pilgrim from <u>Peace Pilgrim: Her Life and Work In Her Own Words</u>

O God of Peace and Compassion, all around us we see brokenness and the violence of hate. It is so hard to believe in your Love and your Peace when the world is crying for vengeance. Teach us to withhold our very human and often wrong judgments. Show us a better way, a gentler way, a more loving way to live on this precious Earth. Guide us back to the Wisdom of the heart which never lies and which embraces all when truly healed and whole. We ask and pray for that healing and wholeness that only you can bring to our lives, our hearts and our minds. As we learn to love and forgive, we become ever closer to your true Image and our true Selves. So it is.

July 7

"For if you forgive others their trespasses, your heavenly Father will also forgive you."

Matthew 6:14

Reflect on a person and/or circumstance in your life where forgiveness played a key role. Were you being asked to forgive or did you need to be forgiven? What was the ultimate outcome and how has that affected your relationship with God?

"The forgiving state of mind is a magnetic power for attracting good."

Catherine Ponder

Loving and Forgiving God, you have shown us by example how important forgiveness is. You also know how difficult it can be. Give us the strength and the courage to open ourselves to the river of forgiveness. Wash our hearts clean of anger, hurt, vindictiveness, guilt and despair. Cleanse us from the blame and shame that we so often heap upon ourselves. Open the door so that we may welcome the true Freedom you offer us as beloved children of the Most High. Enshrine in our hearts that no one can ever take your Love away from us. In grateful joy, we offer your Love and Forgiveness to all our brothers and sisters, even and most especially those who may have hurt us deeply. Praise God we are free! Thank you, thank you, thank you. So it is.

July 8

"*In your presence there is fullness of joy; in your right hand are pleasures forevermore.*"

Psalm 16:11

How do you experience the Joy of God's Presence in your life?

"Live ecstatically every day! Dance with God every day! In your spiritual journey follow the highest path you know."

Rita Benson

Playful God, often we take life so seriously and fail to find time to laugh, play and dance in your Joy. Free us from the worries and concerns of our lives that sap our strength for true living. Loosen our spirits and enliven us with your wondrous Spirit. Teach us to find happiness in little things and silver linings in our cloudy days. When we look at life as a glass half-full of water instead of half-empty, we are inviting you to come fill us to the brim with your effervescent Joy. We affirm that this Joy is your Will for our lives. We invite it into our hearts now and allow it to flow through every cell and organ, every vein and artery of our bodies. To know you, to experience your Love, is Joy unbounded. Come into us and dance with us. So it is.

July 9

"Ask, and it will be given you; search, and you will find; knock, and the door will be opened for you."

Matthew 7:7

What is the greatest gift that you have ever received?

"Jesus only healed those people who ASKED him to (or those for whom someone else asked on his or her behalf). Jesus said 'Ask and ye shall receive.' He did not say 'Make me guess.'"

Edwene Gaines

Gracious God, you offer us so many wondrous blessings, far beyond our imaginings. Yet you honor our free will and wait for us to open the door and allow your Goodness and Joy into our lives. Teach us how to ask and how to receive with grace and thankfulness. Show us how to give away what we have guarded so carefully. You are the treasure we seek and with you there is no lack. Our abundance is sure and certain within the shadow of your wings. So when we hear you knocking gently on the door of our hearts, let us quickly come to greet you and make room in our lives for your joyful and loving Presence. If we go seeking and searching for you, dear God, we know we have only to look within our most sacred temple and you will be there. So it is.

July 10

"Yeshua said: If you bring forth that which is within you, then that which is within you will save you. If you do not bring forth what is within you, then what you do not bring forth will destroy you."

Gospel of Thomas, Saying 70

What are you currently "bringing forth" in your life? Could this saying refer to bringing forth and releasing our blocks and our shadow? How is this happening for you?

"All the doors that lead inward to the sacred peace of the Most High are doors outwards—out of self, out of smallness, out of wrong."

George MacDonald

Holy Sophia, you come to dwell in the secret places of our hearts and bring your holy Wisdom into the deepest recesses of our being. Teach us to dive deep and surrender to your whispers of intuition. May we drink of your ever-flowing waters so that we need never again thirst for Divine Knowledge. It is all within our sacred heart of hearts. As we draw ever closer to you we will encounter our true Selves. Remove the fear and expand our wings. Teach us to fly and light your world with Love, Truth and Peace. So it is.

July 11

"For thus said the Lord God, the Holy One of Israel; in returning and rest you shall be saved; in quietness and in trust shall be your strength."

Isaiah 30:15

Who or what is in control of your life? Do you find it difficult to let go of control and simply allow and trust? What happens if you do?

"So often we try to gird ourselves to face a harsh and difficult world when we might instead gentle both ourselves and our world just by slowing down. We could take a cue from music here: 'Rest' is a musical term for a pause between flurries of notes. Without that tiny pause, the torrent of notes can be overwhelming. Without a rest in our lives, the torrent of our lives can be the same."

Julia Cameron from <u>Walking In This World</u>

O God of our Salvation, come and save us from ourselves and our addiction to being in control. Teach us how to truly let go and surrender to your Love and Care for us. We believe, dear God. Help our unbelief. We trust but with conditions and only so far. May we hear your Voice above the din of our own needs and worries, and above the voices that chatter all around us. May we follow where you lead even if it is out on a limb, where the very best fruit is waiting for us. We trust your Wisdom, we trust your timing, we trust your Divine Will and Order for our lives. So it is.

July 12

"But by the grace of God I am what I am, and his grace toward me has not been in vain."

1 Corinthians 15:10

How do you see Grace operating in your life?

"I always say I am a little pencil in God's hands. He does the thinking. He does the writing. He does everything and sometimes it is really hard because it is a broken pencil and He has to sharpen it a little more. Be a little instrument in His hands so that he can use you any time, anywhere. We have only to say 'yes' to God."

Mother Teresa of Calcutta from <u>*The Joy In Loving*</u>

Gracious God, there are so many grace-filled moments in our lives! Our hearts sing with thanksgiving and praise, acknowledging the abundant blessings that you shower upon us. Remind us to wake up each day and say "Good morning, God" instead of "Good God, it's morning!" Teach us to appreciate the little gifts you give to us through friends and family, through chance encounters and intense relationships. May your Grace be our constant companion throughout our days, for you promise us that it will be sufficient for all our needs. May we trust that promise and live in the Light of your Grace. So it is.

July 13

"I will heal them and reveal to them abundance of prosperity and security."

Jeremiah 33:6

In what ways are you able to share abundance with others?

"When we give cheerfully and accept gratefully, everyone is blessed."

Maya Angelou

O Source of All, so often we focus on the lack in our lives and forget to give thanks for all the good that surrounds and enfolds us. We see the glass as half-empty, when truly it is half-full. Teach us the gift of a grateful heart and the blessings that come to a cheerful giver. May we find ourselves in the abundant flow of your universe, watered by ever-flowing streams. May we pause to drink deeply so that we may be filled with your Spirit. We cannot give away what we do not have. When we are tired and overwhelmed, remind us to replenish our resources from your deep and refreshing well. And always, dear God, lead us back to you as our true Source and the Fountain of All Life. So it is.

July 14

"Awake, my soul! Awake, O harp and lyre! I will awake the dawn. I will give thanks to you, O Lord, among the peoples."

Psalm 57:8

Reflect on the blessings in your life. What fills your heart with thankfulness?

"If the only prayer you said in your whole life was, 'thank you,' that would suffice."

Meister Eckhart

Loving Creator, it is easy to say 'thank you' when everything is going smoothly in our lives. It is natural to count our blessings and be grateful for your good and beautiful Creation. It is much more difficult, dear God, to give thanks for the lessons and challenges you bring to us. But for these we are also grateful, for without them we would not learn and grow. Stretch our boundaries and our limitations so that we may truly know how wondrously we are made. Show us a mirror so that we may see our Selves clearly, brothers and sisters all, empowered by your Loving Spirit to do your work in the world. Filled with that Spirit, we say thank you, thank you, thank you God. So it is.

July 15

"Very truly, I tell you, the one who believes in me will also do the works that I do and, in fact, will do greater works than these, because I am going to the Father."

John 14:12

How are you being empowered to do the work of God's kingdom? Do you believe that human beings like yourself have the same potential that Jesus manifested?

"So keep on keeping on living the life which your inner voice directs, kindly, lovingly; giving help wherever you can, giving love and sustenance to this great work of illuminating all life...Your life is like a pebble dropped into a pool of water, creating ripples endlessly. You do not know the end of a word, a thought, an action."

White Eagle from *Beautiful Road Home*

Beloved One, you call us into your Presence with the promise that we have always been Home in your loving arms. We have never left. Our seeming separation is only an illusion. When we feel powerless and helpless, we are only seeing in the mirror dimly. Turn our hearts to your Truth. Turn our eyes to your Light. Open our minds to the infinite expanse of your Wisdom and Power. Our world is in great need of your Love and your Peace. There is no time for excuses, for cop-outs, for fears of failure or fears of success. We are needed at our full potential, NOW. We ask that you send Archangel Michael with his sword to empower us for Truth and Justice in your world. May we speak your words of Light. May we always walk on your pathway of Light. And may that Light illumine our darkened world. So it is.

July 16

"And all of us, with unveiled faces, seeing the glory of the Lord as though reflected in a mirror, are being transformed into the same image from one degree of glory to another; for this comes from the Lord, the Spirit."

2 Corinthians 3:18

What are the greatest changes that you need to make in yourself to come closer to your Divine Image?

"They always say time changes things, but you actually have to change them yourself."

Andy Warhol

Holy One, you call us forward in our lives and out of our comfort zones. We acknowledge that often we become stuck in our habits and the familiar. Unstick us that we may welcome freedom and change in our lives. Walk before us into the unknown. Remove our doubts and fears, and replace them with the faith and trust that we are secure and protected always as your beloved children. We walk by faith, not by sight, into your future which we co-create with you. May it manifest in Peace, Freedom and Justice for all our brothers and sisters. So it is.

July 17

"Agree with God, and be at peace; in this way good will come to you."

Job 22:21

Has your freedom ever come into conflict with someone else's freedom? How did you resolve the conflict? Where does your freedom end and that of your neighbor's begin?

"There is a peaceful state of consciousness, a powerful state of beingness, which dwells beyond the opposites. What are the opposites? Good/bad, happy/sad, love/hate, like/dislike...even male/female, in/out, hot/cold and even down/up! This is the 'middle way' spoken of by the Buddha, and it brings what Jesus called 'Peace, but not the peace that the world gives' and 'The peace that passes all understanding.' It is the sacred center within you. Jesus identified it as the key to the Kingdom of Heaven. You will find this center in the silence of your heart of hearts."

Greg Barrette

O God of Patience and Peace, how stubborn we sometimes become, insisting on having things our way when deep in our hearts we know your Way leads to Peace and Freedom. Teach us the paradox of surrender. When we allow you to have the remote control of our lives, everything that we could ever imagine and more is spread before us. Remind us what Jesus taught us about Freedom. He said that in saving our lives we would lose them, but if we surrender our lives to the Divine, we are saved; saved in Love and Light, saved for Peace and Freedom. Your Peace is not found in faster, bigger, better. Your Peace flows into the silence of our hearts and brings that inner knowing of Truth. We are One but we are only one. May we live in the middle of that balance point. So it is.

July 18

"A friend loves at all times."

Proverbs 17:17

What does friendship mean to you? What happens when you have a fight with a friend? Is God your friend?

"Always be a first-rate version of yourself, instead of a second-rate version of somebody else."

July Garland

Beloved of my Heart, in all times and places you are there. Through the darkest hours, I feel your arms holding me and surrounding me with your Love. When I dance for joy, I am never without a partner for you are there dancing with me. When human love fails me and betrays my trust, you dry my tears and soothe my aching heart. Teach me to seek your friendship first, within my innermost being, instead of looking outside myself for my answers and my source of companionship. Thank you for your Love, for your Gentleness and Compassion, for your Wisdom and Guidance. What more could I ask for in a friend? So it is.

July 19

"Though we stumble, we shall not fall headlong, for the Lord holds us by the hand."

Psalm 37:24

Reflect on a mistake that you have made in your life. What did you learn and what would you do differently next time?

"If God had wanted me otherwise, He would have created me otherwise."

Johann von Goethe

God of Mercy and Compassion, even though you call us to be perfect we know there are times we don't quite measure up to that standard. Remind us that your Love and Forgiveness are not based on how perfect we are. Teach us not to judge ourselves so harshly, to forgive our blunders and mistakes, pick ourselves up and move on. As you are gentle with us, teach us to be gentle with ourselves and with each other. You are not finished with us yet. The polishing of the diamond continues so that we may become ever closer to the perfect reflection of your Light and Love. So it is.

July 20

"Create in me a clean heart, O God, and put a new and right spirit within me."

Psalm 51:10

What qualities are asleep inside of you and how would you awaken them?

"Without change, something sleeps inside us, and seldom awakens. The sleeper must awaken."

Frank Herbert

O God of the Ages, you are unchanging and yet you bring constant change into our lives. You are the steady rock around which our chaotic Earth whirls. Be our touchstone and foundation. Cleanse our hearts and minds from fear, doubt and regret. Remove hurt, anger and frustration. Create us anew, dear God, and transform our lives so that we may reach out to transform our world. Empower us with your Spirit that blows wherever it will. With your Courage and Strength within us, we know we can face the storms of life. We welcome the rain that brings rainbows and new growth. We welcome the wind that blows away the debris and outworn habits of the past. We welcome the water that flows into us and around us, cleansing and filling us to overflowing with Love and Peace. We hear you call to us: "Sleeper, awake!" Awaken us in every fiber of our being so that we may truly remember who we are and why we are here. So it is.

July 21

"See, I am making all things new."

Revelation 21:5

What difference can your presence make in our world? How can you change it for the better?

"Seize this day, this moment. And if you choose to do the right thing now, if you just make a decision to try, then change begins. When the next moment comes, all you have to do is to repeat that decision, maintain the course, and perseverance will take root and grow."

Patrice Gaines from <u>Moments of Grace: Meeting the Challenge to Change</u>

O God of all Times and Places, you meet us in this moment of time and nudge us forward into the newness of your Creation. Teach us to seize this one tiny moment, precious as it is, and make it memorable. The past is finished and gone, and the future hasn't arrived. All we have is today. Stop us in our tracks as we madly rush through life. May we take time to say, "I love you." May we take time to hug and be hugged. May we take time to praise children and tell them they are beautiful. May we take time to make that phone call, take that vacation, to invest our time with those who are precious to us, for today will never come again. And may we pay less attention to our bank accounts and more to the Love, Peace and Joy that we can invest in and give away to our hurting world. Seize the day and live! So it is.

July 22

"Attachment to matter gives rise to passion against nature. Thus trouble arises in the whole body; this is why I tell you 'Be in harmony...' If you are out of balance, take inspiration from manifestations of your true nature. Those who have ears, let them hear."

Gospel of Mary Magdalene 8:1-10

What is out of balance in your life? What are the symptoms of this imbalance and how can balance be restored?

"Always remember that the real treasure is within."

Dan Millman from *The Journeys of Socrates*

Source of All Being, you created a world in balance and harmony, but looking around us that is not what we see. Be the anchor of our lives and bring us back to center point. Teach us how to work and play and love in partnership with our brothers and sisters. Show us how to balance our priorities so that we live according to your values. May we discover the treasures that lie within us and release our attachment to what lies all around us. You are the most important security in the storms of life, for only you can still those storms and keep our boat afloat. Thank you, dear God, for being our Anchor and our Protection when the surf gets rough. So it is.

July 23

"Be strong and of good courage, and act. Do not be afraid or dismayed; for the Lord God, my God, is with you. He will not fail you or forsake you."

1 Chronicles 28:20

What actions can you take in your life today to manifest the vision of sacred union and partnership?

"The union of flesh and spirit is not only possible but inevitable. The spiritual meaning of love is best measured by what it can do, which is many things. Love can heal. Love can renew. Love can make us safe. Love can inspire us with its power. Love can bring us closer to God."

Deepak Chopra from <u>The Mystery of Love</u>

Emmanuel, God with us, you invite us into partnership with our sacred Selves and with you. You invite us to wholeness within and without for in truth there is only Oneness. As we see the fear and separation around us, give us the wisdom and courage to act for transformation and change. Let us bring your healing and safety to our troubled world. Let us become your Love and so come ever closer to you. So it is.

July 24

"Do not be conformed to this world, but be transformed by the renewing of your minds, so that you may discern what is the will of God—what is good and acceptable and perfect."

Romans 12:2

How will you transform your life so that you may better serve God?

"There is no such thing as can't, only won't. If you're qualified, all it takes is a burning desire to accomplish, to make a change. Go forward, go backward. Whatever it takes! But you can't blame other people or society in general. It all comes from your mind."

Jan Ashford

Loving Creator God, you spoke our world into being and continue to speak to us today of new creation and transformation. As we move beyond our fear of the unknown, open our eyes and our hearts to the excitement of the opportunities you place before us. Create us anew, O God, and then send us out to plant new seeds in your garden. So it is.

July 25

"O you who dwell in the gardens, my companions are listening for your voice; let me hear it."
Song of Songs 8:13

What new leadership opportunities do you see blossoming for you?

"Journeys bring power and love back into you. If you can't go somewhere, move in the passageways of the self. They are like shafts of light, always changing, and you change when you explore them."
Rumi, Sufi Mystic Poet

Son of the Sun, you light our way as we journey into newness. Be our beacon and open the doors for us. As your messengers, give us your seeds of Justice, Truth and Hope to plant. Reveal to us the gifts that lie buried within our deepest Selves, the potential that only you can know because it is your seed within us. May we become ever brighter until we change into your true Image. So it is.

July 26

"God is our refuge and strength, a very present help in trouble. Therefore we will not fear, though the earth should change, though the mountains shake in the heart of the sea."

Psalm 46:1-2

How do you cope with the challenges in your life?

"You need not look for God either here or there. He is no farther away than the door of your heart: there He stands waiting till He finds you ready to open the door and let Him enter."

Meister Eckhart

Holy God, you are our rock and our refuge. Cover us with the gentle Power of your steadfast Love. Lift us above the chaos of our lives on the sureness of eagle's wings. Let us fly free as your beloved children, without fear or hesitation. Help us know beyond all doubt that you are always with us, closer than the very beat of our hearts. As we hear our heartbeat, let us remember to listen in the stillness for your Voice. So it is.

July 27

"Until now you have not asked for anything in my name. Ask and you will receive, so that your joy may be complete."

John 16:24

What would you ask for to complete your joy?

"You have to have the courage to claim that which is yours, dare to claim the good that God wants for you."

Edwene Gaines from *The Four Spiritual Laws of Prosperity*

O God of Joy and Wonder, you promise to gift us with all good things if we but ask. Teach us how to ask. You lay a banquet table before us, inviting us to come and enjoy your feast. Open our hearts that we may say "Yes" to your radical Abundance. In gratitude and in joy we give you thanks and praise. Remind us that your blessings are your Love made manifest for all your children. May we share our good fortune with those in need and those who are too afraid to ask and believe. So it is.

July 28

"The wind blows where it chooses, and you hear the sound of it, but you do not know where it comes from or where it goes. So it is with everyone who is born of the Spirit."
John 3:8

How do you encounter the presence of Spirit in your life?

"For my ally is the Force, and a powerful ally it is. Life creates it, makes it grow. Its energy surrounds us and binds us. Luminous beings are we, not this crude matter. You must feel the Force around you; here, between you, me, the tree, the rock, everywhere."

Master Yoda from *"Star Wars: The Empire Strikes Back"*

Gracious Holy Spirit, you come to us in power and gentleness. You dry our tears and flow into our hearts when they are filled with sadness. You strengthen us and infuse us with Courage when life's challenges seem too much for us. How can we thank you for never failing us, Our Comfort and Our Ever-Present Help? Lift us up on your wings, O Spirit, and allow us to fly ever closer to our God. So it is.

July 29

"*Do not judge by appearances, but judge with right judgement.*"

John 7:24

How do you balance the responsibilities of your every-day life with your spiritual growth? How do you prioritize for you, your family and God?

"The art of life is to live in the present moment, and to make that moment as perfect as we can by the realization that we are the instruments and expression of God."

Emmet Fox

O God of Time and Space, you challenge us to make room in our busy lives for you. There are so many choices, so many priorities. Help us to choose the highest and best for us and for our loved ones. Give us the courage and certainty so that our decisions are not affected by the opinions of others. May we choose our service wisely and know that whatever we choose, you go before us. Show us the way to grow closer to you as we learn who we truly are. So it is.

July 30

"A new heart I will give you, and a new spirit I will put within you; and I will remove from your body the heart of stone and give you a heart of flesh."

Ezekiel 36:26

What do you feel the prophet Ezekiel meant by comparing the heart of stone and the heart of flesh?

"God created each of us in His own image. He put a little of Himself—His love, His grace, His power—in each of us. Unfortunately, this is the last place most of us think to look to find it."

Walter Staples

Holy God, forgive us when we search for you in all the wrong places and worship the empty idols of our material lives. Create in us a clean heart and put a new spirit within us. Remind us always that we are reflections of your Love and your greatness. Help us to keep the mirror polished so that we may be true reflections of your Image within us. So it is.

July 31

"What are human beings that you are mindful of them, mortals that you care for them? Yet you have made them a little lower than God, and crowned them with glory and honor."

Psalm 8:4-5

How do you balance your "angelic" self with your human frailty? How do you manifest your true Divine Image without pride and ego?

"Remember for just one minute of the day, it would be best to try looking upon yourself more as God does, for She knows your true royal nature."

Hafiz of Persia

Holy Mother, you joined our Father in sacred partnership before time began and gave birth to the glories of Creation. We are your beloved children, molded as much in your Image as our Father's. Don't ever let us forget your Wisdom, your Compassion, your Strength and Courage. Remind us that these qualities are inside of us, just as you are. As a mother comforts her children, so you love and comfort us as we are sheltered under your wings. So it is.

August

Always remember that the soul needs rest
just as the body does.
Find time on a daily basis
for the restoring power of silence.
Turn off the world and retire to your own inner
temple and find your peace,
for "in returning and rest you shall be saved;
in quietness and in trust shall be your strength."
(Isaiah 30:15)

August 1

"But I, through the abundance of your steadfast love, will enter your house; I will bow down toward your holy temple in awe of you."

Psalm 5:7

Where do you find God's holy temple in your life?

> "I am Light itself, reflected in the heart of everyone; I am the treasure of the Divine Name, the shining Essence of all things. I am every light that shines; every ray that illumines the world. From the highest heavens to the bedrock of the earth All is but a shadow of my splendor."
>
> **Fakhruddin Araqui, Sufi Mystic and Poet**

Holy, Holy, Holy Lord;
God of Power and Might,
Heaven and Earth are full of your Glory,
Hosanna in the Highest!
Blessed is he who comes in the Name of the Lord,
Hosanna in the Highest!
So it is.

August 2

"If then your whole body is full of light, with no part of it in darkness, it will be as full of light as when a lamp gives you light with its rays."

Luke 11:36

How are you sharing your light with family, friends and neighbors? What is your response to darkness?

"There are two ways of spreading light: to be the candle or the mirror that reflects it."

Edith Wharton

O God of Light and Darkness, you shine in us in the midst of our doubt and fear. Remind us that we are indeed Light. Give us the courage to place our lamp on a lampstand so that we may light the Way in our troubled world. May we always speak words of Light. May our feet always walk on the Pathway of Light. May our hands reach out to bless all we touch with the Light of Peace and Love. So it is.

August 3

"Your statutes have been my songs wherever I make my home."

Psalm 119:54

How do you distinguish between God's Law and God's Spirit? Which is most important to you?

"For all of you who want to walk a spiritual path, I suggest you stop and take a look at all the things you think and all the assumptions that you make…before you speak. Try some discipline and see if you can for a whole week, just watch your thoughts."

Hinono

El Shaddai, O God of the Mountain, you gave your law to Moses and have covenanted with your people since that long ago day. We admit that the words "law" and "discipline" don't fit easily into our spiritual life. And yet it is through this ordered way of spiritual guidance that we come to know your Will for our lives; your Love, your Wisdom and your Truth. Remind us again and again that if we seek to be among the chosen, we only have to choose ourselves, as you continue always to choose us in your Love and Mercy. So it is.

August 4

"*Commit your work to the Lord, and your plans will be established.*"

Proverbs 16:3

How does your spiritual relationship with God affect your commitment to serve others?

"Service to others is the rent you pay for your room here on earth."

Muhammad Ali

O Lord of the Future, teach us how to dream dreams and see visions, knowing that this is how the future will manifest and become reality. Guide our thoughts and our steps, so that all we do may be your Divine Order. As we do your work in the world, may we know your Presence in our hearts, drawing us ever closer to our true Oneness with you. So it is.

August 5

"I delight to do your will, O my God; your law is within my heart."

Psalm 40:8

Has there ever been a time in your life when you felt you were not doing God's will or that it was a struggle? What did it feel like and how did you resolve the issue?

"Look beyond the moment. Send your thoughts out on a shaft of faith into tomorrow where the full meaning of today becomes apparent."

Jack Boland

Mother/Father God, you inspire us with such awesome possibilities to become greater than we ever conceived we could be. We are truly caterpillars, waiting to transform into butterflies without the conscious knowledge of our true identity. Teach us to fly. Show us the magnificent reality of our soul. Draw us into the deep well of our divinity and explode in us the miracle of true sacred union within. O Jesus our brother, light the Way for us to follow. So it is.

August 6

"Remember, I am with you always, to the end of the age."

Matthew 28:20

Do you believe that we are living in the "end times?" If we are, what is significance of this time?

"The time always was, is, and always will be now! Now is the time; the time is now."

Dan Millman

Source of All Being, we hear your still small voice. You whisper to us in the wind and the rustle of the leaves. You come to us in the little things of life and beg us to listen, wake up and experience your Presence in the every day. Help us to quiet the many voices that surround us so that we may hear you clearly and follow where you lead us. So it is.

August 7

"The disciples asked Yeshua: 'When will the Kingdom come?' Yeshua answered: It will not come by watching for it. No one will be saying, Look, here it is! or, Look, there it is! The Kingdom of the Father is spread out over the whole earth, and people do not see it."

Gospel of Thomas, Saying 113

Where do you see evidence of the kingdom of God in your life and the world around you?

"It is this belief in a power larger than myself and other than myself which allows me to venture into the unknown and even the unknowable."

Maya Angelou

Emmanuel, God-with-us, we see you in the wonderful miracles and fearful storms of our life. You are always near us even when we ignore your Presence. Teach us how to become more like you, to reach for the stars, to unlock the secret door of our divinity. Let us taste, if only briefly, the glory that awaits us as your daughters and sons. Our light is your Light. Our truth is your Truth. Our love is your Love. Let our Light, Truth and Love be manifest in our world, for the highest good of all. So it is.

August 8

"Jesus answered them, 'Have faith in God. Truly I tell you, if you say to this mountain, "Be taken up and thrown into the sea," and if you do not doubt in your heart, but believe that what you say will come to pass, it will be done for you.'"

Mark 11:22-23

How has faith in God worked miracles in your life?

"This is the first step toward understanding the process of real, lasting change: simply knowing with certainty that you can do whatever you need to do. This understanding has a dual edge: On the one hand, it increases your confidence and dignity. On the other hand, it places full responsibility on you if you fail to make the change you set out to make. But this is a good thing, not a guilt trip."

Bo Lozoff from <u>It's a Meaningful Life: It Just Takes Practice</u>

Faithful God, you have promised to increase our faith if we ask. I am asking. Erase the doubts and fears that come with being too much in the world. Help me to step "outside the box" of normal reality, to see with your eyes and know beyond a shadow of a doubt that all things are possible through your Love and Power. Let your Will be done, on Earth as in heaven. So it is.

August 9

"In fulfillment of his own purpose he gave us birth by the word of truth, so that we would become a kind of first fruits of his creatures."

James 1:18

What seeds are you bringing forth to manifest whom you truly are as a chosen one of God?

"I see you filled with the light of Spirit, capable of overcoming all things, rich, free, vigorous and enthusiastically joyous! I know for you that which the Christ of your being knows for itself already: that you are destined for greatness so let that bright light shine!"

Greg Barrette

God of all Creation, you set the stars to shine in the heavens, and gave us the sun to light our days and the moon to protect our nights. We praise and thank you for the security of your Plan that keeps our universe together even while it seems like our world is spinning apart. Allow us a vision of your future Hope and give us the Courage to become part of the solution instead of part of the problem. May we live in harmony as one family. May we plant seeds in good and fertile soil for the benefit of all the kingdoms of your Creation. So it is.

August 10

"Our heart is glad in the Lord our God, because we trust in his holy name. Let your steadfast love, O Lord, be upon us, even as we hope in you."

Psalm 33:21-22

Recall a time in your life when hope and faith were hard to find. What kept you going? How did you find your way out of the darkness?

"Our good nature and endearing qualities will not arouse the answers to our prayers. Rather, it is our mischievous, dishonest attributes that provide master keys to heaven. When we identify and work to transform our self-centered qualities and crooked characteristics, the key turns and the gates unlock. Blessings and good fortune are now free to rain down upon us."

Yehuda Berg

Gracious and Merciful God, you see our imperfections and yet you love us still. Teach us how to forgive as you forgive, to love as you love and to surrender our judgments to your Divine Wisdom and Mercy. Give us the Strength and the Courage to clean house of all the anger, frustration, petty hurts and jealousies that keep us from coming ever closer to you. At the sacred altar of our heart, we offer all that is unworthy of you and ask that you transform it with your Love. So it is.

August 11

"My brothers and sisters, whenever you face trials of any kind, consider it nothing but joy, because you know that the testing of your faith produces endurance; and let endurance have its full effect, so that you may be mature and complete, lacking in nothing."

James 1:2-4

Reflect on one of the most challenging times in your life. How did you come through it to where you are now and how was your faith in God strengthened?

"When you are full of problems, there is no room for anything new to enter, no room for a solution. So whenever you can, make some room, create some space, so that you find the life underneath your life situation."

Eckhart Tolle

God of Compassion, you lift us up in your loving arms when we have lost our strength. You carry us when we can walk no further. Remind us in the dark moments of our life that you are Light and you are Love. In your Light, there is no darkness. In your Love, there is no fear. So let us go forward and fear not. So it is.

August 12

"Live as children of light—for the fruit of the light is found in all that is good, and right and true."

Ephesians 5:8-9

Looking back on the last few months of your life, how would you evaluate your progress toward your spiritual goals? What new efforts would you like to manifest in the near future?

"To find truth you must experience it in your soul. You can read hundreds of books, or study the religions of all time, and find that all of them have one common point, one common denominator: and this is love—which is another word for light or soul illumination. To realize this soul illumination you have to shut away the clamor of the lower mind, to become humble, very simple."

White Eagle from *Beautiful Road Home*

Holy God, you chose us as your beloved children. Remind us to choose ourselves. Show us the narrow gate within to our sacred inner temple. There the noise of the world is stilled and we hear your Voice gently calling us Home. Overwhelmed by the demands and responsibilities of our lives, we seek a quiet space and Peace at last in your embrace. So it is.

August 13

"Give, and it will be given to you. A good measure, pressed down, shaken together, running over, will be put into your lap; for the measure you give will be the measure you get back."

Luke 6:38

Which is easier for you—to give or to receive? Why do you believe this is true?

"To love and be loved, we must know our brothers and sisters, for knowledge always leads to love, and love to service. Our work is only the expression of the love we have for God."

Mother Teresa of Calcutta from *The Joy of Loving*

Loving God, you have shown us your Love over and over again. Now you challenge us to become your Love in our world. May we be your gentle hands, your warm voice, your resolute feet that walk the path of service. Our work is before us. Show us the Way. So it is.

August 14

"*Pleasant words are like a honeycomb, sweetness to the soul and health to the body.*"

Proverbs 16:24

How have you experienced the positive and negative power of words and thoughts?

"Kindness is more important than wisdom, and the recognition of this is the beginning of wisdom."

Theodore Isaac Rubin

Holy Sophia, you come to us and remind us to be kind and gentle with your children and your beloved Earth. So often, we don't find the time. So often we don't engage our brains and hearts before opening our mouths. Teach us the power of thought and word so our world can evolve into a gentler, kinder place. It begins with us. Inspire us to practice random acts of kindness and magical works of love. So it is.

August 15

"To this end we always pray for you, asking that our God will make you worthy of his call and will fulfill by his power every good resolve and work of faith, so that the name of our Lord Jesus may be glorified in you, and you in him."

2 Thessalonians 1:11-12

What role does prayer play in your spiritual life?

"You pray by touching the deepest part of you that longs, that needs, that is. Let it speak in its own language, more often than not without words."

"Emmanuel" as compiled by Pat Rodegast and Judith Stanton

Holy One, you walk beside us through the cares of life. Hear the words of our hearts even when we are too busy or too overwhelmed to form the words. Remind us that it is in the stillness and the quiet that we hear your Voice. Give us the Courage to order our lives so that you become our first priority. Your Beloved Son taught us to seek first your kingdom and everything else would be given to us. So now we seek, dear Lord. We seek, we knock and we know we shall find you waiting. So it is.

August 16

"Seek the Lord and his strength; seek his presence continually. Remember the wonderful works he has done."

Psalm 105:4-5

What evidence can you give in your life for the power of answered prayer?

"There is a solitude which each and every one of us has always carried within. More inaccessible than the ice cold mountains, more profound than the midnight sea: the solitude of self."

Elizabeth Cady Stanton

O Lord my God, you call me to go within and discover the treasures that you have placed there. Lead me into the most profound depths of my soul that I may dig deep and immerse myself in your Wonder. Inside the well of my most sacred Self is my Holy Grail. Guide me on my quest for Truth, Wisdom, and Knowledge of you. So it is.

August 17

"We speak of these things in words not taught by human wisdom but taught by the Spirit, interpreting spiritual things to those who are spiritual."

1 Corinthians 2:13

Where is the boundary for you between what is spiritual and what is not? Is there a distinction or should there be?

"If we could see the miracle of a single flower clearly, our whole life would change."

Buddha

Almighty and Ever-Present God, you created such beauty all around us. Forgive us when we only see that which we call the negative in life. Guide us to a higher perspective so that we may live our lives as you see them, viewed from above. Remind us that we are but travelers on this delicate planet floating through space. Help us to love our Mother Earth and create justice for all her children. So it is.

August 18

"You are worthy, our Lord and God, to receive glory and honor and power, for you created all things, and by your will they existed and were created."

Revelation 4:11

How do you see yourself as part of God's creation? How is God's creative power working through you?

"The grand show is eternal. It is always sunrise somewhere; the dew is never dried all at once; a shower is forever falling; vapor is ever rising. Eternal sunrise, eternal dawn and gloaming, on sea and continents and islands, each in its turn, as the round earth rolls."

John Muir

Loving Creator, you have gifted us with eternity yet so often we cannot see beyond this instant, this day, this obstacle. When we seek your Presence, then our lives fall into place and we reframe our vision. Help us to be co-creators with you so that our world may benefit from our light and love, and the Justice and Truth that only your Wisdom can bring. So it is.

August 19

"Do you not know that your body is a temple of the Holy Spirit within you, which you have from God? Therefore glorify God in your body."

1 Corinthians 6:19-20

How do you perceive the Image of God in your physical body? What challenges do you find in treating your body as a temple of the Holy Spirit?

"There is a deep wisdom within our very flesh, if we can only come to our senses and feel it."

Elizabeth A. Behnke

Light of my life, I am your temple here on Earth. Teach me how to be a worthy reflection of your Glory, your Holy Light and your Holy Spirit. Give me the Courage to change whatever needs to be changed in my life so that I may be a clearer, stronger channel for your Love, your Light and your Truth. So it is.

August 20

"You will know the truth, and the truth will make you free."

John 8:32

What does freedom mean to you, politically and religiously? How do you manifest freedom in your life?

"We create a tremendous amount of suffering for ourselves because we are not willing to get off our position of needing to control everything. But until we can see we are doing this, we will just keep doing it in more and more sophisticated ways. Prayer gives us the chance to pause long enough to blow the whistle on our own strategies."

Regina Sara Ryan from <u>Praying Dangerously: Radical Reliance On God</u>

Ever-Patient One, you see our detours and our determined attempts to live our lives in our own way. Teach us how to surrender to your Way, dear God. Teach us that surrender is not giving up and not weakness but simply asking for a Strength far beyond our own. When we let go and let God, we have unlimited resources to draw on. Thy will be done, on Earth as in heaven. So it is.

August 21

"I came that they may have life, and have it abundantly."

John 10:10

How would you define an "abundant life?"

"To know God is the beginning of wisdom. The nearer we live to the source the more we receive of that which comes from the source. The mind that is not consciously living with God may have intellect and mental capacity, but the wisdom that knows can come only to that mind that is walking with God every moment of conscious existence. The mind that does not know God thinks in the darkness; the mind that does know God thinks in the light."

Christian D. Larson from *The Pathway of Roses*

All-Knowing and Ever-Loving God, you search us and know us to the depths of our souls. Teach us how to truly know you so that we may discover within ourselves the fountain of abundant life.

As we drink from this fountain, we know we shall never thirst again. May this water spring up in us and flow freely to water the parched lives around us. So it is.

August 22

"He has sent me to bring good news to the oppressed, to bind up the brokenhearted, to proclaim liberty to the captives, and release to the prisoners."

Isaiah 61:1

How are you fulfilling this commission in your daily life?

"Be the change you wish to see in the world."

Mahatma Ghandi

O God of our Salvation, you are our lighthouse in the midst of the storm. Keep our gaze fixed on your Light as turmoil and chaos swirl around us. Be our beacon in the darkness. We remember that we are called to let your Light shine through us, to be your heart and hands in the world. You are the seed of Hope in our hearts. May we become the Light of Hope for others. So it is.

August 23

"As God's chosen ones, holy and beloved, clothe yourselves with compassion, kindness, humility, meekness, and patience. Bear with one another and, if anyone has a complaint against another, forgive each other."

Colossians 3:12-13

What are the most important spiritual gifts? Which ones do you feel are your strengths and which are weaker?

"The eye by which I see God is the same as the eye by which God sees me. My eye and God's eye are one and the same—one in seeing, one in knowing, and one in loving."

Meister Eckhart

God of Wisdom and Truth, you guide our footsteps and light our way. You have written your Truth upon our hearts; a covenant of everlasting Love and Mercy. Forgive us when we fail to recognize that Truth and dim our light and sparkle. Teach us to shine for you and for what is right and true. So it is.

August 24

"The kingdom of God is as if someone would scatter seed on the ground, and would sleep and rise night and day, and the seed would sprout and grow, he does not know how."

Mark 4:26-27

Reflect on what you remember about your birth and earliest years. How have the seeds sown then affected your life and your spiritual path?

"Every thought is a seed. If you plant crab apples, don't count on harvesting Golden Delicious."

Bill Meyer

Creator God, you gave birth to us and planted us as seeds in your beautiful universe. We give thanks for the opportunities you give us to grow and develop, becoming more than we ever dreamed we could be. Remind us to always keep you before us as our mirror so that we will grow ever closer to your Image of us which is planted in our hearts and souls. Keep us faithful to your teaching and never let us be parted from you. So it is.

August 25

"Now faith is the assurance of things hoped for, the conviction of things not seen."

Hebrews 11:1

What is the difference between faith and hope?

"There is no waiting for something to happen, no point in the future to get to. All you have ever longed for is here in this moment, right now."

Oriah Mountain Dreamer

Lord of the Past, the Present and the Future, you guide us and protect us as we journey. When we doubt our direction, give us faith to walk in your Way. When we lose hope in the present, show us a glimpse of your future of Hope and Brilliance. Teach us the Patience of the eternal Now moment so that we may truly experience your Presence, not remembered in the past or dreamed of for the future, but now in this very moment of our daily lives. Thank you, God. So it is.

August 26

"Jesus said to her, 'Everyone who drinks of this water will be thirsty again, but those who drink of the water that I will give them will never be thirsty. The water that I will give will become in them a spring of water gushing up to eternal life.'"

John 4:13-14

What is the secret to prosperity?

"Life is a gift and it offers us the privilege, opportunity and responsibility to give something back by becoming more."

Tony Robbins

God of Wonder, you shower us with every blessing we could imagine and many we never even conceived of. Help us to receive with thankful hearts and remember our connection to the Vine, our Source of all Goodness. Remind us always that as branches of your Vine, we wither and die disconnected from you.

May we reach out to others in loving service and give as we have received. So it is.

August 27

"Take my yoke upon you, and learn from me; for I am gentle and humble in heart, and you will find rest for your souls."

Matthew 11:29

Do you have a quiet place in your life to talk to God? Is this a challenge at times? What are the benefits?

"We need to find God, and He cannot be found in noise and restlessness. God is a friend of silence. The more we engage in silent prayer, the more we can give in our active life. The essential thing is not what we say but what God says to us and what He says through us."

Mother Teresa of Calcutta

Gentle God, you spoke to Elijah in that still, small voice. Quiet the voices in our minds and in our world so that we may listen for your whisper. As we seek your shalom, your Peace that passes all our understanding, may we remember the secret place within us where you always abide. So it is.

August 28

"My people will abide in a peaceful habitation, in secure dwellings, and in quiet resting places."

Isaiah 32:18

What is the connection for you between spiritual peace within and world peace without?

"We are not channels, we are instruments. Channels give nothing of their own; they just let water run through them. In our action, we are instruments in God's hand and He writes beautifully."

Mother Teresa of Calcutta

Abba, you have taught us how to love you. You have taught us that to love our neighbor is also to love you. Somehow the message has fallen on deaf ears. We look around us at the war and bloodshed, the pain and turmoil and we wonder if there can ever be peace. From our peaceful sacred space within, guide us to acts of Justice and Love on behalf of your children everywhere. May we truly bind the wounds of the brokenhearted and set the captives free. So it is.

August 29

"Keep on doing the things that you have learned and received and heard and seen in me, and the God of peace will be with you."

Philippians 4:9

Rev. Maryesah Karelon, O.M.M.

What can you do as one person and as part of the family of God to promote world peace?

"Go forth into the busy world and love it. Interest yourself in its life; mingle with its joys and sorrows."

Ralph Waldo Emerson

Holy Shekinah, you have promised to pitch your tent in the midst of your human children, no matter how wayward and rebellious we become. We invite your Power and your Presence to be among us now. We need your Wisdom and your Guidance more than ever. Show us how to love the unlovable and forgive the unforgivable. Save us from self-righteousness and the arrogance of our blind conceit. Remind us that we are all one family though we may call you by different names. Help us to focus on what we have in common rather than what pulls us apart. Gather us all under the shelter of your wings and protect us all our days. So it is.

August 30

"Yeshua said: When you make the two into One, you will be a Son of Man. And when you say: Mountain move! It will move."

Gospel of Thomas, Saying 106

How does your sense of wholeness and balance affect your faith?

"God became a human being in order that human beings might become God."

Iranaeus, Second Century Christian Bishop

Holy God, we hear your call to us just as you called to the prophets of old. You ask us to once again walk among your people and speak your words of Truth. Give us the Faith to follow where you lead. Give us the voice of Courage to face the winds of doubt and fear. Give us the heart of Compassion to reach out and embrace those who are hurting and hating. We know love is the answer but it needs to be powered by your Divine Love. We cannot stand alone. Strengthen our hearts when they grow faint and our backbones when we're pushed to the brink. May we truly write your love letter to the world. So it is.

August 31

"If I take the wings of the morning and settle in the farthest limits of the sea, even there your hand shall lead me, and your right hand shall hold me fast."

Psalm 139:9-10

Have you ever tried to run from God? What were the circumstances in your life that caused you to attempt this and what were the results?

"It makes no difference how deeply seated may be the trouble, how hopeless the outlook, how muddled the tangle, how great the mistake. A sufficient realization of love will dissolve it all."

Emmet Fox

Loving and Merciful God, so often we are like Jonah, running away from your Voice and your Will, not realizing that you will follow us and be with us wherever we run to. Heal our fear and our need to be in control. Teach us the beauty of surrender to your Will. Allow your Divine Love and Light to flow into our hearts and our lives so that we may become true channels of your Peace to the world. So it is.

September

Cultivate a life filled with joy and laughter,
for joy truly manifests the Presence of God
and humor is the best medicine
when life becomes too serious and intense.
Take time to appreciate a rainbow,
to smell newly-cut grass,
to hear the happy voices of children playing,
to touch the velvety petals of a rose.
Allow God's immanence to come near you
and you will never be alone.

Light in the Darkness

September 1

"Yeshua said: The Kingdom of the Father is like the woman who carried a jar of flour. After she walked a long way, the handle of the jar broke, and the flour began to spill behind her along the road. Heedless, she noticed nothing. When she arrived, she set down the jar and found it empty."

Gospel of Thomas, Saying 97

What signs or messages are you ignoring in your life? What may be the consequences?

"Put your ear down close to your soul and listen hard."

Anne Sexton

Gracious God, we acknowledge that often we are running so fast through life that we fail to notice the little things that are so important in our work for you. Open our eyes and our ears so that we truly perceive the signs of your Presence in our world. Slow us down, Lord, so that we may walk gently on your good Earth. Your kingdom is spread all around us. You call us to be its messengers. Deepen our awareness of your Truth so that we won't lose what's most important in our lives. So it is.

September 2

"Six days shall work be done; but the seventh day is a sabbath of complete rest, a holy convocation; you shall do no work."

Leviticus 23:3

How do you keep the Sabbath Day holy? Is it important for you to do so?

"Wherever you've been, wherever you are on your spiritual journey, you are on a path that can connect you with being at home in the consciousness of God where all things are possible."

Mary Masters

Holy God, you are Lord of the Sabbath and Lord of the entire universe. We give honor and praise to your Name. Remind us that we are created in your Image as stewards of your wonderful kingdom. As we grow closer and closer to our divinity within we grow ever closer to you, and all things become possible for those who believe. May we always remember who we are and why we are here. So it is.

September 3

"My steadfast love shall not depart from you, and my covenant of peace shall not be removed, says the Lord, who has compassion on you."

Isaiah 54:10

What is the relevance of this promise for us today?

"Love is in you. Go inward. Play with the Creator. The Creator is waiting for you with Love."
Chalanda Sai Ma

Playful God, you danced Creation into being with your Love and Light. Forgive us when we become so bogged down in our mundane lives that we forget how to laugh, play and enjoy living. Teach us the Joy of being a child again and the innocent, carefree happiness that comes when we trust in your Love and Care. Remind us that the doors of your kingdom open easily to the child within us. So it is.

September 4

"*Therefore, since we are receiving a kingdom that cannot be shaken, let us give thanks, by which we offer to God an acceptable worship with reverence and awe.*"
Hebrews 12:28

What are the blessings in your life and how do you give God thanks for them?

"Even within the seemingly most unacceptable and painful situation is concealed a deeper good, and within every disaster is contained the seed of grace."
Eckhart Tolle from <u>Stillness Speaks</u>

Father/Mother God, how often we forget to count our blessings. Instead we focus on what we do not have; what has gone wrong in our lives; our faults and our failures. Teach us to be happy for today with what we have instead of comparing ourselves with others. For the breath of life in your beautiful world, we give you thanks. For work to do and people to love, we give you thanks. For your Presence and all encompassing Love, we give you thanks. May we never become too busy to stop and remember to say "Thank you, God." So it is.

September 5

"A pleasant vineyard, sing about it! I, the Lord, am its keeper; every moment I water it. I guard it night and day."

Isaiah 27:2-3

Reflect on the meaning of the "Vine." What does this symbol mean to you?

"Life is not a random event. It has purpose and provides for the unfoldment of a divine plan with opportunities to make choices and decisions in every moment."

Colin C. Tipping from <u>Radical Forgiveness</u>

Holy Sophia, you are abundant Wisdom and Love. We seek to know you. Gift us with the fruits of your Presence. Shower us with your generous, life-giving Mercy and Compassion. Graft us onto your Vine so that we may always receive your nourishment.

Plant our roots firmly in your good Earth so that we may truly experience you as our Mother and the source of our protection and care. As you gather us under your wings, may we gather a rich and abundant harvest to your Honor and Glory. So it is.

September 6

"And God is able to provide you with every blessing in abundance, so that by always having enough of everything, you may share abundantly in every good work."
2 Corinthians 9:8

As you have faced challenges of abundance in life, how have they brought you closer to trusting in God's eternal Abundance and Care?

"What we really want to do is what we are really meant to do. When we do what we are meant to do, money comes to us, doors open for us, we feel useful, and the work we do feels like play to us."
Julia Cameron

God of All That Is, you created this wonderful and abundant universe and danced with delight when men and women crowned your Creation. You planted us here on Earth to be stewards of your Abundance and to enjoy and play in your garden. How often we have strayed from that original Wonder and Grace. Lead us back to your Joy and your Peace so that we may always rest in your abundant blessings. So it is.

September 7

"Do not worry about anything, but in everything by prayer and supplication with thanksgiving let your requests be made known to God."

Philippians 4:6

How is worry the opposite of faith and trust? What happens in our lives when we worry?

"Faith does not rely on knowing anything with certainty. It requires only the courage to accept that whatever happens is for the highest good."

Dan Millman from <u>The Journeys Of Socrates</u>

God of all Time, you call us to live in this moment, trusting that the past is finished and gone, and the future has yet to arrive. Remove the pain and anxiety of worry from our lives. Teach us to believe in your Goodness. Support us all the day long and into the night, when all we can say is "Lord, I believe. Help my unbelief." As our trust grows, so will our lives expand and blossom. So it is.

September 8

"The spirit of God has made me, and the breath of the Almighty gives me life."

Job 33:4

When was the first time that you felt God's presence? Reflect on how this Presence has affected your life.

"Take your needle, my child, and work at your pattern. It will come out a rose by and by. Life is like that, one stitch at a time taken patiently, and the pattern will come out all right, like embroidery."
Oliver Wendell Holmes

Holy Mother God, we see in you the compassionate heart and the merciful Love of the Divine. Gather us under the shelter of your wings when we are feeling lost. Dry our tears when we are discouraged. Teach us how to believe in ourselves because you never stop believing in our goodness. We, your children, honor you and praise you and thank you. Be near to us in the simple tasks of our daily lives. May your Presence make each moment holy and sacred. So it is.

September 9

"You shall eat the fruit of the labor of your hands; you shall be happy, and it shall go well with you."
Psalm 128:2

How would you define happiness?

"It is not selfish to be happy. It is your highest purpose. Your joy is the greatest contribution you can make to life on the planet. A heart at peace with its owner blesses everyone it touches."
Alan Cohen

O God of Joy and Gladness, you created us for the joy of living and loving. Forgive us when we become too busy in our lives to celebrate life itself. Remind us that being happy, content and at peace is our birthright, no matter the outer evidence of our world. Teach us that Joy is the infallible sign of your Presence and show us how to manifest that Joy from the Light within our inner sacred heart. So it is.

September 10

"For you shall go out in joy, and be led back in peace; the mountains and the hills before you shall burst into song."

Isaiah 55:12

What is the connection between our having personal joy and what we experience in the world?

"When you say, I enjoy doing this or that, it is really a misperception. It makes it appear that the joy comes from what you do, but that is not the case. Joy does not come from what you do, it flows into what you do and thus into the world from deep within you."

Eckhart Tolle from *A New Earth*

Lord of the Dance, we know you hold our future in your hands. We also acknowledge that you have given us the commission to heal our broken world. Be the Light of Joy and Love within us. Give us the strength and courage to walk in Faith and Joy in the face of chaos and turmoil. Teach us that the deepest inner joy is not created or affected by the outer world or material circumstance. Your Joy and your Peace spring from within us. We invite you now to be that ever-flowing fountain of eternal life in our hearts. So it is.

September 11

"The Lord is my shepherd, I shall not want. He makes me lie down in green pastures; he leads me beside still waters; he restores my soul. He leads me in right paths for his name's sake. Even though I walk through the darkest valley, I fear no evil, for you are with me; your rod and your staff—they comfort me. You anoint my head with oil; my cup overflows."

Psalm 23:1-5

What new insights have you gained since the attacks of 2001 and how are you implementing them in your life?

"You gain strength, courage and confidence by every experience in which you really stop to look fear in the face. You are able to say to yourself, 'I have lived through this horror. I can take the next thing that comes along.' You must do the thing you think you cannot do."

Eleanor Roosevelt

Mother/Father God, today we remember and we give thanks for the lives of those who died and the lives of those who survived, scarred but alive. We know we are in your Care even when there is chaos and turmoil all around us. Help us to embrace the changes in our lives without fear. Help us to embrace all people without judgment and condemnation. We are all your children. Teach us how to love and forgive and how to live as one family. So it is.

September 12

"Love your enemies and pray for those who persecute you, so that you may be children of your Father in heaven."

Matthew 5:44-45

Reflect on the power of forgiveness and the events of 9/11. What are the possible lessons that you are learning and that we are learning as a nation?

"If we could all hear one another's prayers, God might be relieved of some of his burdens."

Ashleigh Brilliant

Holy God, we acknowledge our interconnectedness with all your children. Gift us with the understanding of what it truly means to be one family. Remove the greed and the arrogance that has strained our relationships with other peoples around the world. If Spaceship Earth is to survive, we need the talents and the efforts of all of us. If that means letting go of some of our privileges, then so be it. For the love of the world's children, let Justice flow like a never-ending stream. So it is.

Rev. Maryesah Karelon, O.M.M.

September 13

"Put things in order, listen to my appeal, agree with one another, live in peace; and the God of love and peace will be with you. Greet one another with a holy kiss."

2 Corinthians 13:11-12

Is there someone in your life with whom you are currently in conflict? Reflect on ways to reconcile with them.

"If we truly believed that love is eternal, we would heal our relationships rather than kill the perceived enemy. We would eliminate the desire to attack ourselves or anyone else when difficult issues surface. We would understand that unless we heal through love, the same problems will keep reemerging."

Aeeshah Ababio-Clottey & Kokomon Clottey from
<u>Beyond Fear: Twelve Spiritual Keys to Racial Healing</u>

O God, some of our brothers and sisters call you Allah, some Jehovah, others the Christed One. Teach us that you are but one God and we are but one people. Heal our division and our separation. May we learn the wisdom of the eagle—from above there are no boundaries. So it is.

September 14

"I will instruct you and teach you the way you should go; I will counsel you with my eye upon you."

Psalm 32:8

What lessons has God taught you recently? Were they easy or difficult? How have they affected your life?

"The practice of meditation takes us on a fabulous journey into the gap between our thoughts, where all the advantages of a peaceful, stress-free, healthier, fatigue-free life are available, but are simply side benefits. The paramount reason for doing this soul-nourishing meditation practice is to get in the gap between our thoughts and make conscious contact with the creative energy of life itself."

Wayne W. Dyer from <u>Getting in the Gap</u>

Abba, we come to you as our loving Parent, knowing that we don't always live up to our own standards, let alone yours. Surround us with loving Justice and discipline so that we may learn to listen to your Voice of instruction, grow beyond our limitations and become your Vision of us as children of Light and Love. Teach us gently with Love. So it is.

September 15

"He destined us for adoption as his children through Jesus Christ...to the praise of his glorious grace that he freely bestowed on us."

Ephesians 1:5-6

Who would you become if you had no human limits? What needs to happen for you to manifest beyond these limits?

"Be proud. You are not the momentary whim of a carefree creator experimenting in the laboratory of life. You are not a slave of forces that you cannot comprehend. You are a free manifestation of no force, but mine, of no love but mine. You were made with a purpose. Feel my hand. Hear my words. You need me...I need you. We have a world to rebuild...and if it requires a miracle what is that to us? We are both miracles and now we have each other."

Og Mandino from *The Greatest Miracle in the World*

Creator God, empower us to become our true Selves. Stretch our vision to journey beyond our human limitations. Allow us to imagine and manifest the miracles that you have destined for us. May we work as your partners to heal and restore our beautiful planet. We have work to do and it is your work. Let us go forward together as One. So it is.

September 16

"Jesus looked at them and said, 'For mortals it is impossible, but not for God; for God all things are possible.'"

Mark 10:27

Recall a time in your life when something "impossible" manifested. How did you feel? Did you attribute the manifestation to God?

"Only those who dare to fail greatly can ever achieve greatly."

Robert F. Kennedy

Holy One, you call us from our comfort zones and promise to support us as we walk the high wire of risk. Teach us to swallow our fear and trust in your never-failing Guidance. Explode in us new opportunities and possibilities. May the Light of your Love flood through us and empower us, healing our doubts and fears, removing the blocks and barriers. Walk with us on our quest for our true Selves. When we reach that Holy Grail we will find you waiting for us, longing for us to return Home. So it is.

September 17

"Then your light shall break forth like the dawn, and your healing shall spring up quickly."

Isaiah 58:8

What elements in your life are in need of healing or change? How could this be accomplished?

"Change. It has the power to uplift, to heal, to stimulate, surprise, open new doors, bring fresh experience and create excitement in life. Certainly it is worth the risk."

Leo Buscaglia

Almighty God, you are the unchanging center of our universe. All about us we experience a center that will not hold. Only by staying grounded in your Love and Light can we hope to maintain our balance in the winds of our existence. Give us Courage to face these winds without fear, to walk into the night with only your Light to guide us. Let us truly let go and let your Divine

Rev. Maryesah Karelon, O.M.M.

Order rule our lives, for that is the only certainty. Mold us and remake us according to your Will. So it is.

September 18

"Teach me to do your will, for you are my God. Let your good spirit lead me on a level path."

Psalm 143:10

Has there ever been a time in your life when you have wrestled with God and what you perceived as God's will for your life? What was the outcome?

"To some people, surrender may have negative connotations, implying defeat, giving up, failing to rise to the challenges of life, becoming lethargic, and so on. True surrender, however, is something entirely different. It does not mean to passively put up with whatever situation you find yourself in and to do nothing about it. Nor does it mean to cease making plans or initiating positive action. Surrender is the simple but profound wisdom of yielding to rather than opposing the flow of life."

Eckhart Tolle from *The Power Of Now*

Holy One, we praise your Name and give thanks for all the blessings you have showered upon us. Forgive our stubborn need to be in control of our lives when in reality everything would flow so much more smoothly if we would just let you take over the driving. Teach us how to "go with the flow" of your sweet Spirit. Help us take a long, deep breath and relax into your gentle embrace, knowing that all is well. So it is.

September 19

"Even the sparrow finds a home, and the swallow a nest for herself…at your altars, O Lord of Hosts, my King and my God."

Psalm 84:3

Where do you feel most at home? Is there ever a struggle between your material, physical home and your spiritual home?

"We are not valuable because we are a member of a certain group or because we call God by a certain name. We are not valuable because we follow a guru or observe a certain diet. We are valuable because we are a spark of the divine. And the only thing gurus, priests, rabbis and elders can do for us is point us back in the direction of home, and home is, of course, within."

Darren John Main from <u>Spiritual Journeys Along the Yellow Brick Road</u>

Source of All Being, you call us Home to the center of our souls; to our heart center and to you. So often we become attached to our material home and forget that we are spiritual beings having a physical experience. Remind us again and again that our true Home is with you and that we will be restless until we arrive there. No material fix will do, no matter how enticing. Our only true destination must be to return to your loving embrace through the doorway of our sacred hearts. So it is.

September 20

"By day the Lord commands his steadfast love, and at night his song is with me, a prayer to the God of my life."
                                                                Psalm 42:8

Reflect back on the last few weeks. What were the high points and low points of your life? What lessons did you learn?

"We have a will toward mystery, a yearning, greater even than our will to live. And lucky, too, because our will to live, our grasping at life, is killing us. The will toward mystery is our homesickness for God."
                                                                Stephen Levine

Mother/Father God, you teach us that the journey is our home. And you have promised to walk the path with us, wherever it may take us; the valleys as well as the mountaintops. We give you thanks and praise for your Guidance and Support, your Love and Care. Teach us to seek the treasures that lie within our own inner temple. Remind us to invite you to join us there, often. May this journey become our true Home and our secret to rest and renewal. So it is.

September 21

"I am the real vine, and my Father is the gardener. Every barren branch of mine he cuts away; and every fruiting branch he cleans, to make it more fruitful still. You have already been cleansed by the word that I spoke to you. Dwell in me, as I in you. No branch can bear fruit by itself, but only if it remains united with the vine; no more can you bear fruit, unless you remain united with me."

John 15:1-4

Have you ever felt disconnected from the Source? What was the cause of this illusion?

"The first step to be taken in anything we wish to do is to seek divine assistance. To ask God to go with us and work with us, and to enter into such perfect spiritual harmony with God that we can feel His supreme power through and through—that is first and most important, be it work pertaining to body, mind or soul."

Christian D. Larson

Source of All Being, you teach us that our life-force and our very life flows from you. Help us to stay entwined with your life-giving Vine so that our branches may bear good and plentiful fruit. May our harvest be one of Joy, Abundance and Peace. So it is.

September 22

"Let us love, not in word or speech, but in truth and action."

1 John 3:18

How do you put God's Love into action in your life?

"There is no limit, because God is love and love is God. And so you are really in love with God, and God's love is infinite. And that's why it's not how much you do, but how much love you put into the action."

Mother Teresa of Calcutta from <u>The Joy of Loving</u>

Mother/Father God, we look around our world and we see so much need, so many people who go unloved and believe that they are unlovable. Yet you challenge us to embrace those that are hurting and bind up the wounds of heart and body. We hear your call, O God, but we are overwhelmed by the desperation of our world. How can one person make a difference? Remind us that it is always better to light one candle than to stumble in the darkness. We can always share a little love, do a small random act of kindness, and that makes our world a little brighter. We are only one person but when we are One with you, dear God, we become so much more. So it is.

September 23

"Yeshua said: The Kingdom of the Father is like the man who had some good seed. His enemy came at night and sowed weeds among the good seed. The man would not allow them to pull up the weeds, saying, 'I fear you might pull up the wheat as well.' Indeed, at harvesttime the weeds will be conspicuous. They will be pulled up and burned."

Gospel of Thomas, Saying 57

What weeds can you identify in your life? How do you intend to deal with them?

"It's but little good you'll do a-watering the last year's crops."

George Eliot

God of the Seasons and all the Circling Years, we trust in you. You created the heavens and the earth, the sea and the dry land, the day and the night, man and woman; and so you brought balance into being. We ask that you bring our lives into a healthy harmony and lead us out of duality into the blessed balance of sacred union. So it is.

September 24

"The earth is the Lord's and all that is in it, the world, and those who live in it."

Psalm 24:1

How do you celebrate the beauty of nature and God's Creation?

"You may call this thought by whatever fancy words you wish—psychology, theology, sociology, or philosophy—but you must think of Mother Earth as a living being. Think of your fellow men and women as holy people who were put here by the Great Spirit. Think of being related of all things!"

Ed McGaa from *Mother Earth Spirituality*

Creator God, you spoke our universe into being and called it good. All around us we see violence and bloodshed and it is difficult to remember the goodness of your original Creation. Teach us to look for the simple beauty of a rose; to appreciate a glorious rainbow; to stand in a warm summer rain and laugh. We have forgotten how to love your Creation, dear Mother, and she calls out to us in pain. May we become better stewards and active apostles of Love and Light to a world in darkness. So it is.

September 25

"The creation itself will be set free from its bondage to decay and will obtain the freedom of the glory of the children of God."

Romans 8:21

When you reflect on all the recent natural disasters—hurricanes, floods, fires, tidal waves, etc.—how do you see these relating to Mother Earth as a living being? Why is she in so much pain and how can we help her?

"It is not God's function to create, or uncreate, the circumstances or conditions of your life. God created you, in the image and likeness of God. You have created the rest, through the power God has given you. God created the process of life and life itself as you know it. Yet God gave you free choice, to do with life as you will."

Neale Donald Walsch from <u>*Conversations With God, Book 1*</u>

Holy Lord, we acknowledge that much of what we have created in your beautiful universe is ugly and violent. We have brought pain and bloodshed to many of your children. Heal us, O God, and help us to heal our world. We know that we cannot be free as long as our Earth is in bondage. While many are enslaved by structures that threaten their very survival, we are slaves to our appetites. We pray for balance and Wisdom. Show us the way, even if it is difficult, to love our neighbors as ourselves. So it is.

September 26

"Now the Lord is the Spirit, and where the Spirit of the Lord is, there is freedom."

2 Corinthians 3:17

How does the presence of the Holy Spirit bring freedom to your life?

"Do not seek after what you yearn for, seek the source of the yearning itself."

Adyshanti

Sweet Spirit, you come to us on the breath of the wind and in the power of fire, whispering of a Freedom we have never known. Come into our hearts and our minds. Melt the doubts and the fears until our human limitations crumble to dust. Empower us with the Knowledge of our true power and destiny, but let us never forget from whence we came—children of the Earth born to be angels of the stars. Gift us with the remembering of our true Purpose and we shall be free indeed. So it is.

September 27

"Take off the sandals from your feet, for the place where you are standing is holy ground."

Acts of the Apostles 7:33

How would you define the meaning of "holy?"

"Confidence, like art, never comes from having all the answers; it comes from being open to all the questions."

Earl Gray Stevens

Holy Shekinah, we have beheld your Glory in those mountaintop experiences of our lives. Most of the time, we choose to live in the valleys. We need a reminder of the holiness of everyday life. It is the little things that are truly sacred, from a shared meal with friends and loved ones to a child's first step. Help us to invite the sacred into our daily lives. Never let us forget that it is in the questions and the unknown that we find holy miracles. Thank you, dear God, for always surprising us. So it is.

September 28

"Do not be afraid, for I have redeemed you; I have called you by your name, you are mine. Should you pass through the sea, I will be with you; or through rivers, they will not swallow you up. Should you walk through the fire, you will not be scorched and the flames will not burn you. For I am Yahweh, your God, the Holy One of Israel, your savior."

Isaiah 43:1-3

Reflect on the times of great distress in your life when God has answered your prayers. What have these experiences taught you?

"Walk in peace. Be undisturbed and unperturbed: all is in God's plan. Never doubt this. Bring God into your life, and you will see miracles."

White Eagle

Almighty and Ever-Present God, we are called to walk by faith not by sight. All around us we see visions of terror and fear. Teach us to be fire walkers. Gift us with the Courage of commitment and inner knowing. Standing on the precipice, we step out in faith and we fly. So it is.

September 29

"Now to him who by the power at work within us is able to accomplish abundantly far more than all we can ask or imagine, to him be glory."

Ephesians 3:20-21

Do you believe that angels walk among us? Have you ever met one?

"You have to learn to seek first the kingdom of heaven, the place of stillness and quiet at the highest level of which you are capable, and then the heavenly influences can pour into you, recreate you and use you for the salvation of all human kind."

White Eagle

O Michael our Protector, Gabriel our Divine Messenger, Raphael our Healer and Uriel our Light: surround us now with the Power of your glorious wings. We feel your Presence near us. We know you will never leave us. Strengthen our trust in that which we cannot physically see. Open our ears to hear divine messages. Allow our minds to seek your Wisdom. Flood our hearts with your Love and Light so that we will know beyond the shadow of a doubt that we will never be alone. Thank you, thank you, thank you. So it is.

September 30

"I am the vine, and you the branches. He who dwells in me, as I dwell in him, bears much fruit; for apart from me you can do nothing...If you dwell in me, and my words dwell in you, ask what you will, and you shall have it."

John 15:5, 7

If you knew you could ask anything of God and receive it, what would it be?

"Practice following your intuition in everyday things, trusting your gut feelings moment by moment and acting on them as best you can. As you learn to trust yourself in smaller matters, you will build power and confidence to take bigger risks and deal with the larger issues in your life successfully."

Shakti Gawain from <u>Reflections In the Light</u>

Mother/Father God, you offer us so much more than we can comprehend. All we need do is ask yet often that is the most difficult of all. Even when you know what we need, what is in our most sacred and secret heart space, still you will not violate our free will. You will not force us to do or be anything. You simply wait patiently for us to realize the incredible and unimaginable riches that are waiting for us. Open our hearts to receive, dear God, and open our eyes to believe in magic. So it is.

October

Devote yourself to study
of the spiritual masters and the teachings of Love, for
as you absorb them into your being
you shall become ever closer
to the spiritual perfection you seek.
Let your "mouth speak wisdom:
the meditation of [your] heart
shall be understanding." (Psalm 49:3)

October 1

"Guard me as the apple of your eye; hide me in the shadow of your wings."

Psalm 17:8

How have you experienced divine protection in your life?

"Hope is a Rainbow, shining through every cloud and every storm."

Erin Parzen

Faithful God, you promise us your Love and Care no matter where we are. When the clouds and the rains come into our lives, remind us that the sun is still shining though we cannot see it. Show us the gift of your Rainbow. Wrap it around our shoulders and caress us with your never-ending Love. Shelter us from the storms of life and inspire us to journey onward knowing that we are never alone. So it is.

October 2

"I will establish my covenant between me and you, and your offspring after you throughout their generations, for an everlasting covenant, to be God to you and to your offspring after you."

Genesis 17:7

What does God's covenant mean to you? How do you define it and see evidence of it in your life?

"In the seamless stitching together of life, work and art, the thread of divine order is woven."

Sarah Ban Breathnach

Holy One, in you we trust. In you we live, move and have our being. Teach us your Truth so that we may walk in your Way. Write your covenant upon our hearts, and engrave your commandments in our minds so that we walk your path in Love and Light for the good of all your children. We acknowledge our responsibility as the agents of your covenant of Love in our world. May we let our light shine in the darkness without fear, knowing you will never fail us. So it is.

October 3

"Lead me in your truth, and teach me."

Psalm 25:5

What is God's Truth for you? How do you find that Truth?

"The Divine Mind ever seeks the good of the whole. Therefore, in all your earthly problems, seek not for the purely personal solution, but for underlying principles. If you can lay your problem beside a principle; or, in other words, if you can lay it beside the Master's thought, you will always find a true solution to it."

White Eagle from *The Quiet Mind*

O God of Wisdom and Truth, open our minds and our hearts so that we may hear your Voice. May we thirst for your Wisdom as though we were in a desert wasteland. Your Truth is the river of Life that nourishes our body, our mind and our spirit. Without you we cannot truly live. May we feed on you in our hearts, creating a fountain of ever-flowing Joy. We are one with your Truth. We are one with your Light. We are one with your Love. We are one with you. So it is.

October 4

"*Light and darkness, life and death, right and left, are brothers and sisters. They are inseparable. This is why goodness is not always good, violence not always violent, life not always enlivening, death not always deadly...*"

Gospel of Philip, Verse 10

How do you balance the dualities of your life? Can you recall a personal example that fits the above description?

"In life, stress happens when you resist what arises."

Dan Millman from *The Journeys of Socrates*

Gentle God, you whisper to us in the silence of our hearts. Teach us to still the noise of our lives and quiet our minds so that we may truly hear you. In quietness and peace, we find our answers and our destination. Thank you, sweet Spirit, for never giving up on us. Show us the path ahead and give us the Courage to follow where you lead. Your Divine Order is our Way, our Truth, and our Life. So it is.

October 5

"From there you will seek the Lord your God, and you will find him if you search after him with all your heart and soul."

Deuteronomy 4:29

Where and how does God manifest in your life? How do you talk to God?

"There is no glimpse of the light without walking the path. You can't get it from anyone else, nor can you give it to anyone. Just take whatever steps seem easiest for you, and as you take a few steps it will be easier for you to take a few more."

Peace Pilgrim from *Peace Pilgrim: Her Life and Work in Her Own Words*

Generous and Ever-Loving God, too often we come to you as a last resort when nothing else seems to be working. Teach us how to ask for your Help and your Guidance first, to release control of our lives into your hands. Teach us how to trust in your Wisdom even when it cuts against the grain of the world's wisdom. Teach us to talk to you from our heart and soul, knowing that you will hear us, listen to our pain and our doubt, and then show us the way Home. Thank you for never giving up on us. So it is.

October 6

"Then the Lord answered me and said: 'There is still a vision for the appointed time...If it seems to tarry, wait for it; it will surely come, it will not delay."

Habakkuk 2:2-3

What has been the most difficult time of waiting that you have experienced? What was the result?

"Do not be discouraged because the 'means whereby' to bring about the accomplishment of your dreams may not be apparent. In other words, you do not have to know how this will happen. You only have to know that it will happen."

Jack Boland from <u>And That's the Way It Really Is</u>

O God of all Ages, how often our time frame runs counter to your reality. We desire everything yesterday and cannot imagine waiting patiently for what you have promised. Slow us down, Lord, and teach us that the race is not always won by speed, but often by persistence and determination. Teach us to trust in your Divine timing and your vision for our lives. May we learn to breathe with your Holy Spirit and walk with that powerful and loving Spirit as our guide. So it is.

October 7

"Wait for the Lord; be strong, and let your heart take courage; wait for the Lord!"

Psalm 27:14

Reflect on a time in your life that required a great deal of courage. What were the circumstances and what was the result?

"Adversity does not build character; it reveals it."

Author Unknown

Gracious and Loving God, you inspire us with your Spirit to move forward with courage and faith when our vision grows dim. We admit that often we see our way only in part and we stumble when we trust only our own knowledge. Teach us to dive deep into our hearts where you wait for us. Show us the Courage that is born of your never-failing Love and wrap your arms around us. May we always walk on the Pathway of Light and Love. May we always speak words of Light and Love. May we always know that we are One with you in Light and Love. So it is.

October 8

"I will pour water on the thirsty land, and streams on the dry ground; I will pour my spirit upon your descendants, and my blessing on your offspring."

Isaiah 44:3

How do you see God's spirit working in your life?

"Grace is the wonderful spirit that imbues every fiber of our being when we practice the fruits of the spirit: kindness, patience, understanding, forgiveness, love, gentleness, fellowship and endurance."

Edgar Cayce

Loving Creative Spirit, we are thirsty for the living water only you can give. Fill us and in-spirit us. May our lives blossom with the fruit your nourishment can bring forth. Send us out into our hurting world to be your gardeners. As you shower us with more blessings than we could ever imagine, may we respond by showering our families, our neighbors and our world with kindness, gentleness, forgiveness and love. Let each of us become an oasis of compassion in the desert wasteland of our world. So it is.

October 9

"I will turn their mourning into joy, I will comfort them, and give them gladness for sorrow."

Jeremiah 31:13

Can you feel joy in the midst of turmoil and sadness? What is the source of that joy?

"Sometimes your joy is the source of your smile, but sometimes your smile can be the source of your joy."

Thich Nhat Hanh

O God of Joy and Wonder, remind us that our long dark nights of the soul can give birth to joy in the morning. You gift us with a Joy that is rooted deep in our heart and soul, that cannot be taken away by the pain and turmoil of the world around us. May we dive deeply to encounter that Joy and drink of the fountain within us. Keep before our eyes the image of the glass that is half-full, not half-empty. We move forward in faith and trust, knowing that your Love can transform any challenge into a joyful rebirth. So it is.

October 10

"*I sought the Lord, and he answered me, and delivered me from all my fears.*"

Psalm 34:4

What is your greatest fear? How do you intend to overcome it?

"I am only one, but I am one. I cannot do everything, but I can do something. And I will not let what I cannot do interfere with what I can do."

Edward Everett Hale

Loving and Merciful God, we know that most of our fears are of future happenings that will never come to pass. Teach us how to live in the Now so that we may focus our powerful minds on what is, not what could be. Deliver us from worry, guilt and fear. Expand our horizons so that we see through your eyes and experience your Vision of our limitless possibilities. Inspire us to become who you created us to be—your true child with a Self and a Soul reflecting your Image. As we touch the Divine within us, draw us ever closer to your Divine Will. May we see your kingdom spread out before us as a gift and a blessing to all humanity. So it is.

October 11

"Eye has not seen, not ear heard, nor have entered into the heart of humanity the things which God has prepared for those who love him."

1 Corinthians 2:9

What are your greatest gifts? How are you manifesting them in your life?

"Believe in yourself! Have faith in your abilities! Without a humble, but reasonable confidence in your own powers you can not be successful or happy."

Norman Vincent Peale

Source of All Being, you spread before us a table of Abundance and opportunity. Give us the courage to sit at your table and enjoy your banquet. We give thanks for all the gifts and blessings that you shower upon us. Inspire us to use what you have given in the best possible way and according to your Will for our lives. Remind us again and again that you created us to be much more than we can ever imagine. Open our eyes so that we may truly see our own magnificence. Thank you, thank you, thank you. So it is.

October 12

"By the glory of the Father, we walk in newness of life."

Romans 6:4

What is new in your life? What unfulfilled potential would you like to manifest?

"If we would have new knowledge, we must get a whole world of new questions."

Susanne K. Langer

O Creative Spirit, as we were created in your Image, create in us a desire to live in your Love. Create in us the vision of what we yet may become. Create in us a new heart and a willing spirit to be co-creators with you. Fill us with your Wisdom and Truth so that we may go out into your world and share that Truth, Love and Wisdom with all we meet. May we become your beacons in the darkness. May our light, which is your Light, shine before all. So it is.

October 13

"For the Lord gives wisdom; from his mouth come knowledge and understanding."

Proverbs 2:6

What are the sources of wisdom and knowledge in your life? How do you discern what is true and what is false for you?

"We demand instant communication, instant coverage of world events, instant gratification, instant wealth, and even instant relationships. Ultimately, even fast food isn't fast enough—we want instant food. What is lost in our fast-paced society is depth. What is lost is not only the chance to reflect on our stories, but even the thoughts that we should want to reflect on them. In turn what is lost is wisdom."

Earnie Larsen from *Destination Joy*

O God of Wisdom and Truth, there are so many "truths" in our world that we are overwhelmed by the world's wisdom. Give us the Courage to stop for a moment, slow our lives down to a crawl and take a deep breath so that we may hear the whisper of your Voice. So often we even forget to listen because listening takes time and peace and quiet. None of these do we have in abundance and so we substitute our version of the truth for Divine Wisdom. But inside, in the deepest recesses of our hearts, we know something is missing. May we seek you, your Word and your Way, for when we ask, you have promised that we will receive. When we seek, we shall surely find. So it is.

October 14

"When Jesus had said this, he breathed on them and said to them, 'Receive the Holy Spirit.'"

John 20:22

What is the connection between the breath and the Spirit?

"Divine guidance gingerly invites you to cross the frontiers of what you already know into the unknown."

Sharon Connors from <u>Adventures in Prayer</u>

Holy Shekinah, long ago you chose to make your home with humanity and established your dwelling here on Earth. Ever since, your breath has enlivened our lives and whispered to us of the Divine Presence and Power. Breathe on us once again, O

Breath of God, and fill our lungs with your sweet Spirit. We long for you with a hunger that no material comfort will satisfy. Lead us into the true unknown, the unexplored frontier of our inner souls. With your Guidance may we delve deeply and drink of the fountain of Knowledge that wells up within us. You are as near to us as our very breath. As you are One with the Divine, may we become One with you. So it is.

October 15

"As a deer longs for flowing streams, so my soul longs for you, O God. My soul thirsts for God."

Psalm 42:1-2

Define the desires of your heart. What part does God play in these desires and their manifestation?

"The best way to write your story is with love. Love is the material that comes directly from your integrity, from what you really are."

Don Miguel Ruiz from *The Voice of Knowledge*

Beloved of my Heart, I do indeed long for you as a young doe searches out a pool of refreshing water. You are the Source of my life. You cleanse me with your healing fountain of Love. You fill me with all good things and remove the emptiness that threatens to overwhelm me. You wrap your arms around me when nothing else in my life seems to work. Hold me in the palm of your hand and shelter me with your wings that I may dwell in your Presence always. So it is.

October 16

"Neither the one who plants nor the one who waters is anything, but only God who gives the growth."

1 Corinthians 3:7

How are weeds interfering with the growth of your spiritual garden?

"To be aware of a single shortcoming in oneself is more useful than to be aware of a thousand in someone else."

The Dalai Lama from *The Path To Enlightenment*

Loving and Forgiving God, we know that often the gardens of our lives become clogged with weeds and careless, discarded trash. Teach us how to care gently and patiently for our souls as we would our most precious children. Teach us how to feed and nurture our soul's growth, to water it with your living and cleansing Truth. May we learn to practice non-judgment and forgiveness for ourselves and for our neighbors, as we trust in your Mercy and Forgiveness for us. We are not perfect, dear God, and we know that you are not finished with us yet. Guide us as we polish the Image that you have placed within us. May we bloom beautifully wherever you plant us! So it is.

October 17

"Yeshua said: Once a sower went out and sowed a handful of seeds. Some fell on the road, and were eaten by birds. Some fell among the thorns, which smothered their growth, and the worms devoured them. Some fell among the rocks, and could not take root. Others fell on fertile ground, and their fruits grew up toward heaven. They produced sixty and one hundred-twenty units per measure."
Gospel of Thomas, Saying 9

What seeds have you planted in your life? Did you plant them in good soil?

"Our ordinary mind always tries to persuade us that we are nothing but acorns and that our greatest happiness will be to become bigger, fatter, shinier acorns; but that is of interest only to pigs. Our faith gives us knowledge of something better: that we can become oak trees."
E. F. Schumacher

O God of the Seasons and all the Circling Years, you bless our Earth and our lives with change. You bless us with the abundance and the overflowing goodness of your harvest. Teach us to bring forth our own harvest of abundance and joy. Teach us to walk gently on your good Earth and work for justice among all the kingdoms of this world. Show us the promise that grows from moving forward and leaving the familiar. We grow as we mature. We transform as we let go of the old. We become ever brighter lights of your Love as we open to your Presence among us. So it is.

October 18

"Do not pronounce judgment before the time, before the Lord comes, who will bring to light the things now hidden in darkness and will disclose the purposes of the heart."

1 Corinthians 4:5

What in your life is coming out of the darkness into the light? How is this change affecting you and your loved ones?

"Look at your feet. If you do not like where you are standing, MOVE!"

Ray Rathbun from *The Way Is Within*

Almighty and Ever-Loving God, you call us forward even when we dig in our heels and say "NO" to change. You shine light into our dark and shadowy closets that are often the hiding places of our fears. We thank you for your Wisdom, Love and Light that push us to become, grow and change. We acknowledge the effort and hard work that this requires. Give us the strength and determination to stay the course even when the going gets tough. You have promised us the desires of our heart if only we focus on your Purpose and Will for our lives. May you grant us the serenity to accept that which we cannot change, courage to change what we can and the wisdom to know the difference. So it is.

October 19

"Therefore be imitators of God, as beloved children, and live in love, as Christ loved us."

Ephesians 5:1-2

What does it mean to live your life "from the heart?"

"If I create from the heart, nearly everything works; if from the head, almost nothing."

Marc Chagall

Mother/Father God, in our scientific world we worship technology and live in our heads. We often believe that all our answers will be found in the mind and intellect. Remind us that you speak most eloquently and urgently through the whispers of our heart and soul. Teach us to listen and act on our intuitions and the murmuring of our inner Self even when logic says otherwise. May we lead with our hearts and walk in your Love, knowing that we are reflecting that Love to all we meet. Create in us a clean heart, O God, and put a right and willing spirit within us. So it is.

October 20

"For the earth brings forth fruit of herself; first the blade, then the ear, after that the full corn in the ear."

Mark 4:28

What are you currently harvesting in your life? Are you pleased with your harvest?

"To you the earth yields her fruit and you shall not want if you but know how to fill your hands. It is in exchanging the gifts of the earth that you shall find abundance and be satisfied. Yet unless the exchange be in love and kindly justice, it will lead some to greed and others to hunger."

Kahlil Gibran from *The Prophet*

O Lord of Change and Truth, we seek your Guidance in these times of great uncertainty. We seek your Truth for our families, ourselves and our world. Teach us to stand strong for your kingdom and your Purpose. Walk beside us as we hesitantly step forward through fog and darkness. Light our way and help us when we stumble. As we lift our souls to you, may we become open to your Wisdom, your Light and your Truth. The time is NOW. Show us your Way and we will follow wherever the path may take us. So it is.

October 21

"Open my eyes, so that I may behold wondrous things out of your law."

Psalm 119:18

How do you see God's law operating in your life?

"Keep your eyes open and your ears tuned for evidence of God's will working on your behalf. Especially in a moment of indecision, when someone unexpectedly or unknowingly pierces your consciousness with a bit of advice that rings true, recognize that God is speaking by proxy. If you are discerning, miracles can happen."

Albert Clayton Gaulden from *Signs and Wonders*

El Shaddai, O God of the Mountain, we see your Glory and hear your call. You come to us in fire and smoke to gift us with your holy Law. Open our hearts that we may receive what you have enshrined in us. Engrave your commandments on our hearts so that we may walk in your Way always. Teach us your Will for our lives and your Truth for our minds. As your children, may we follow where you lead us no matter how difficult or how narrow the path. So it is.

October 22

"You shall love the Lord your God with all your heart, and with all your soul, and with all your mind. This is the greatest and first commandment. And a second is like it. You shall love your neighbor as yourself."

Matthew 22:37-39

Which of these commandments is most difficult for you to manifest in your life and why?

"I sought to hear the voice of God and climbed the topmost steeple, but God declared: 'Go down again—I dwell among the people.'"

John Henry Newman

Almighty God, we know that we often fail to honor the Law that you have given to us. How different our world would be if we were truly to keep your commandments. Show us the Way of Love and remind us that you dwell within the secret places of our hearts. Show us there is no place we can go that you are not there. As we trust in your Love, may we learn how to live and share that Love. As you love us, may we love you and become One with you in Love. So it is.

October 23

"It will be a healing for your flesh and a refreshment for your body."

Proverbs 3:8

Pause to take inventory of your mental, emotional, physical and spiritual bodies. What needs healing in your life? What do you need to do to open to this healing?

"If I keep a green bough in my heart, the singing bird will come."

Chinese Proverb

Gracious and Loving God, you bring Strength, Healing and Comfort in our time of need. Whether it is broken limbs or broken hearts, we praise and thank you as the Great Physician. When we are harried and hurried, slow us down and lead us to your fountain of refreshment. May we drink and breathe deeply, feeling the power of your healing Love in every cell and organ of our bodies. Flow through our veins and arteries with your energy of living Light that our hearts may truly sing your praise. So it is.

October 24

"First clean the inside of the cup, so that the outside also may become clean."

Matthew 23:26

Reflect on the meaning of these words of Jesus for your life.

"Great souls are they who see that spiritual is stronger than material force, that thoughts rule the world."

Ralph Waldo Emerson

Gentle and Merciful Father, there are many times that we focus on the outside when the solution to the challenges in our lives lies within. Our attitudes, our thoughts, our inner feelings all create the reality that surrounds us. Lead us within, O God, and cleanse the error of our minds and hearts. Focus our attention on your eternal Truth and those things that endure. Remove our foolish obsession with the material and the physical, for we know that ultimately they will both pass away. Teach us that we truly are spirit inhabiting a physical form, not a material body with an inner spirit. Reorder our priorities so that we may become clean vessels for your precious Spirit. So it is.

October 25

"A word fitly spoken is like apples of gold in a setting of silver."

Proverbs 25:11

Recall a time in your life when your words healed and encouraged someone close to you and then recall a time when words spoken in haste or without thought harmed another. What did you learn from each of these encounters?

"The strongest and sweetest songs yet remain to be sung."

Walt Whitman

O God of Light and Darkness, you spoke the creation into being and called it "good." Your Word comes into us in many and varied ways. We are inspired by you to speak. Teach us to listen first for your gentle Wisdom before words utter from our mouths. May we know the creative power of the words we speak. May we remember that we share with you the power to heal and to harm. May our words be gifts of kindness and compassion, teaching and healing in your Name, and with your Blessing and Power. So it is.

October 26

"If then there is any encouragement in Christ, any consolation from love, any sharing in the Spirit, any compassion and sympathy, make my joy complete: be of the same mind, having the same love, being in full accord and of one mind."

Philippians 2:1-2

What gives you joy in your life today?

"Joy does not simply happen to us. We have to choose joy and keep choosing it every day. It is a choice based on the knowledge that we belong to God and have found in God our refuge and our safety and that nothing, not even death, can take God away from us. Joy is the experience of knowing that you are unconditionally loved and that nothing—sickness, failure, emotional distress, oppression, war, or even death—can take that love away."

Henri Nouwen

O God of Joy and Wonder, you created us for Joy and Gladness and intended us to live in Harmony and Peace. Yet when we look at the world around us, we perceive sorrow and pain, despair and separation. It is difficult to live in joy when so many of your children live in need. Teach us that your true Joy is not based on the illusions of our world but flows from the spring of living water within us. As we allow that ever-flowing spring to bubble up from within, we are watered, nourished and inspired to share that living water with a thirsty world. Open our eyes to the true Joy and Wonder that is still alive here on planet Earth. One with you and all of creation, we praise and thank you for the showers of blessings that we receive every day. May we count those blessings and see the glass of our lives as half-full, not half-empty. So it is.

October 27

"So shall my word be that goes out from my mouth; it shall not return to me empty, but it shall accomplish that which I purpose, and succeed in the thing for which I sent it."

Isaiah 55:11

What is the connection between an intention and a purpose manifested on the physical plane?

"The vision that you glorify in your mind, the ideal that you enthrone in your heart—this you will build your life by, and this you will become."

James Lane Allen

O God of all Creation, you spoke and your Word manifested. We are one of those manifestations and your divine spark, your holy intent, dwells within each of us. Teach us to be aware of the power of our thoughts and our words. As reflections of your divine Love and Truth, as co-creators with you in our world, may we create in Wisdom and Love. May your Intention and Purpose be fulfilled in us and through us. As we think, so shall we be. So it is.

October 28

"O send out your light and your truth; let them lead me."

Psalm 43:3

How does God light your way?

"When I dare to be powerful, to use my strength in the service of my vision, then it becomes less and less important whether I am afraid."

Audre Lorde

Light of my life, you bring light into my darkest hours and shine your unfailing Truth into the shadows of my life. I give you thanks and praise for the assurance of your Presence in all times and places. I thank you for leading me out of doubt and fear into the Light of your new day. Gift me with the courage to walk my chosen path. Strengthen my resolve when I doubt the way. May I always walk in the Light. May I always speak words of Light and Truth and seal the door where evil may dwell in my life. So it is.

October 29

"Do not worry beforehand about what you are to say; but say whatever is given you at that time, for it is not you who speak, but the Holy Spirit."

Mark 13:11

Recall a time in your life that you were aware of the power of Spirit speaking through you. What was the result and what did you learn?

"When we realize that the strength of the Infinite is our strength and that the strength of the Infinite is limitless, we must come to the conclusion that we are capable of doing anything that the living of a great life may demand."

Christian D. Larson from <u>The Pathway of Roses</u>

Sweet Spirit, fill us with your Love and your Wisdom. Remove the blocks in us that insist on being in control and help us to allow you to guide us. We acknowledge our stubborn determination that so often stands in the way of your Will. Teach us how to surrender, not by giving up but by simply turning over to you what we cannot control anyway. Remind us that life becomes much easier and calmer with you in the driver's seat. Transform our lives as we open to the flow of your Power and Love. May we become willing to lose control in order to become your hands, your eyes, your ears, your voice and your heart in a hurting world. So it is.

October 30

"As shepherds seek out their flocks when they are among their scattered sheep, so I will seek out my sheep. I will rescue them from all the places to which they have been scattered."

Ezekiel 34:12

In what ways do you lead and serve others in your life today?

"I may never meet you or know what you do for a living, but I know this about you; unless you choose a life of love and service, you will never be happy."
Albert Schweitzer

Gentle God, you come to us as the Good Shepherd and seek us when go astray. You promise that you will never desert us or give up on us no matter where our journey may take us. Thank you for that unconditional promise of Love. As you seek the lost of your flock, teach us to be good shepherds here on Earth. May we seek out those who are lost and in need, and minister to them in your Name. We offer ourselves in Love and Compassion, in quiet service to our brothers and sisters. When you call and say, "Who will go for me?" let us respond with, "Here I am, Lord. Send me." So it is.

October 31

"On that day you will know that I am in my Father, and you in me, and I in you."
John 14:20

What does it mean to be One with God? Have you ever come close to experiencing it?

"The best way to find yourself is to lose yourself in the service of others."

Mahatma Gandhi

Source of All Being, in our quiet moments and even in our mad rush through life, we yearn for Oneness with you. Often we go searching for you in books and classes, in retreats and techniques, when you are nearer to us than our very breath. Teach us to seek you in the depths of our heart and soul; in the stillness of a morning sunrise; in the tenderness of a baby's tiny hand. All your exquisite and abundant Creation celebrates your nearness. How could we ever be lost? There is no place we could go to escape your Love and Care. We are so grateful. We acknowledge your call on our lives and pledge that we will walk the Path of loving service. Our brothers and sisters call out to us. They desperately need a gentle and compassionate shepherd. May we say "Yes" and seek them out in your Name. So it is.

November

Greet each new day with a prayer of thanksgiving
and a heart filled with praise,
for from such moments
come the blessings of a lifetime.
Choose to sow in abundance and joy
and you will reap a bountiful harvest.

November 1

"I pray that you may have the power to comprehend, with all the saints, what is the breadth and length and height and depth, and to know the love of Christ that surpasses knowledge, so that you may be filled with all the holiness of God."

Ephesians 3:18-19

How would you define a "saint" in 21st century America? Do you believe it's possible to receive guidance and support from spiritual teachers on the "other side?" Has this ever happened in your life?

"For me holiness is not a state or a condition, like a special badge or suit of clothes I may wear. It's not like a graduate degree or certificate that I earn through study. It's not even an 'energy' or a charismatic presence. It is certainly not spiritual celebrity hood. Holiness instead emerges from relationship. It's dynamic. It's a manifestation of what is happening between me and another in the moment. Was Mother Teresa a holy person treating the poor and the ill in Calcutta, or was she a person who was holy while treating the poor and the ill in Calcutta?"

David Spangler from <u>*Blessing: The Art and the Practice*</u>

O God, our Help in ages past, our Hope for years to come; we thank you for touching the lives of so many of your children and inspiring them to lead lives of love and service in your Name. Remind us that there are still saints walking among us, perhaps those we would least expect. May we aspire to walk in their footsteps, offering a caring touch, a hot meal or a warm blanket to those in need. Teach us that it is the little things we do that often matter most. Keep our light burning brightly when we are overwhelmed by the darkness and chaos all around us. It is indeed better to light one candle than to stumble in the dark. So it is.

November 2

"Let all that you do be done in love."

1 Corinthians 16:14

What is the most loving action that you can take to make a difference for your family, neighborhood and our planet?

"It is easy to love people far away, very easy to think of the hungry people in India. You must see first that there is love at home and at your next-door neighbors and in the street you live in, in the town you live in and only then outside."

Mother Teresa of Calcutta from <u>The Joy of Loving</u>

Loving and Compassionate God, you embrace us with loving arms and gentle words. You lift us up when we stumble and fall. You walk beside us even in our most lonely hours. Teach us how to do the same for our brothers and sisters. Random acts of kindness can plant seeds of Love and Peace in our world. Remind us that holiness is not about how perfectly good we are but how much good we offer others, however imperfectly. May we become the very best we can be and may we inspire all those we meet to do the same. Change begins one person at a time, one seed at a time, one small action at a time. So we take a deep breath, step back from being overwhelmed and know that you will never give us more than we can handle. We give you thanks and praise for your blessed Presence. As you never give up on us, may we never give up on each other and our world. So it is.

November 3

"I give thanks to you, O Lord my God, with my whole heart, and I will glorify your name forever. For great is your steadfast love toward me."

Psalm 86:12-13

How does your faith in God assist you in staying positive and hopeful about your life and our world?

"We must be ever thankful for small miracles, and ever hopeful for receiving greater ones."

Elmer Shultz

Source of All Being, you shower us with blessing upon blessing. We have so much to thank you for, yet often we focus our attention on lack and misfortune. It is easy to forget the goodness of life given the pain and tragedy in our world. Yet you created us to live in Joy and Abundance. Show us how to manifest these as realities in our lives. Fill our minds and our hearts with your Love and Joy. Surround us with your miracles and open our eyes to perceive them. We know that our very life is a miracle. May we rise each morning and greet the new day with a song of thanksgiving. Thank you, thank you, thank you, God. So it is.

November 4

"I will give them a heart to know that I am the Lord; and they shall be my people and I will be their God, for they shall return to me with their whole heart."

Jeremiah 24:7

What are the most important priorities in your life? What criteria do you use to determine your priorities?

"For man, autumn is a time of harvest, of gathering together. For nature, it is a time of sowing, of scattering abroad."

Edwin Way Teale

God of All Times and Seasons, you are a God of order and simplicity. Your Creation follows this law of order and yields its harvest in due season. If good seed has been planted in fertile soil and is nourished by sun and rain, then abundance and plenty will spring forth. We acknowledge the goodness of your Divine Order and commit ourselves to place our hearts and our souls in your Care. Only by serving your Divine Will may we open ourselves to your wondrous bounty. Still the ego voices within us that insist on being in control. Show us the ultimate paradox of surrendering so that we may receive everything we can imagine and more. May we follow where you gently lead us and celebrate with the feast that you have prepared. We are indeed your people and your commandments are engraved upon our hearts. May they become our ultimate concern. So it is.

Rev. Maryesah Karelon, O.M.M.

November 5

"For where your treasure is, there your heart will be also."

Matthew 6:21

How does your current financial circumstance affect your life and your faith in God?

"The voice in your head is like a wild horse taking you wherever it wants to go...When the voice in your head finally stops talking, you experience inner peace."

Don Miguel Ruiz from <u>The Voice of Knowledge</u>

Gracious God, we know and affirm that you gift us with everything that we need for an abundant life. Often what we want may not be what we truly need. Just as often what you give us as a blessing and a gift we perceive as a lack or a misfortune. Raise us above the smallness of our everyday lives and teach us, O Lord, to view our reality from your higher perspective. In small steps, may we learn to trust in your wonderful Providence and release the stranglehold that worry has on us. We thank you and praise you that as your beloved children you care for us so much that only the very best is waiting as our inheritance. We affirm: Only good comes to us, only good goes from us. Thank you, God. So it is.

November 6

"I am the good shepherd. I know my own and my own know me, just as the Father knows me and I know the Father. And I lay down my life for the sheep."

John 10:14-15

How are you living as a "good shepherd" in your life?

"Our neighbor is anyone who needs assistance, whether friend or stranger. We cannot expect to correct all the ills of the world but we can help the people with whom we come in contact. This is our spiritual service."

Elizabeth Sand Turner

O Shepherd of the Lost, you come searching for us when we wander from the Path. You seek us out when we are too busy or too preoccupied to seek you. Teach us how to still the many voices of the world and the many voices inside our minds so that we may hear your still, small voice as you call our name. Lead us onto the Path of Love, Light and service to others. Inspire us with your Compassion and your Justice so that we may reach out to our brothers and sisters and become good shepherds in your Name. We hear your call. We choose to follow your Way of Light and Truth. Our world desperately needs more shepherds of Love and Peace. As your instruments, may we sow only Love where there is hatred; only Forgiveness where there is injury; only Faith where there is doubt; and only Joy where there is sadness. So it is.

Rev. Maryesah Karelon, O.M.M.

November 7

"Let your steadfast love become my comfort according to your promise to your servant."

Psalm 119:76

Recall a time in your life when you were in need of comfort. Where did this comfort and support come from? How was God present to you in this difficult time?

"In our deepest hour of need, the Creator asks for no credentials."

Eulogy of Horace Harris

Loving Mother/Father God, in our darkest hours you are there with us. You dry our tears and gather us into your arms. You become our shelter from the storm of life and in you, we find safety at last. Remind us to breathe deeply of your Love and Light so that Peace may flow to every cell and organ of our bodies. When we discover our Oneness with you, nothing in all of Creation can disturb or unsettle us. Thank you, Beloved One, for always being our Light in the darkness. Kindle a fire of your Light within us so that we may light our world. May we bring Comfort and Hope to all whom we meet, trusting in your Divine Order for our lives and our precious Mother Earth. So it is.

November 8

"For I am convinced that neither death, nor life, nor angels, nor rulers, nor things present, nor things to come, nor powers, nor height, nor depth, nor anything else in all creation, will be able to separate us from the love of God."
Romans 8:38-39

Reflect on a time when you felt separated from God. What evidence of this separation did you see in your life? How did you repair the damage and return to fellowship with the Divine?

"Learn to get in touch with the silence within yourself, and know that everything in life has purpose. There are no mistakes, no coincidences, all events are blessings given to us to learn from."
Elizabeth Kubler-Ross

Faithful and Ever-Loving God, in the dark nights of our soul you speak to us in Love. When we hide from you in our caves of despair and remorse, you seek us out to bring us Home once more. Remind us, dear God, that you never leave us, ever. It is we who leave you and feel the pain of a separation that is only of our own making. We know in our heart of hearts that we can never be separated from your Love and Care yet there are moments when panic and fear overwhelm us. Teach us to trust and surrender. Teach us to walk by faith in the darkness with our eyes focused on that tiny candle ahead. The darkness is as light to you, and with your Guidance we will soon be showered with the rays of the sun. You have given us the rainbow as your Promise of Hope in a storm. Thank you, thank you, thank you, God, for always being there. So it is.

Rev. Maryesah Karelon, O.M.M.

November 9

"That which is, already has been; that which is to be, already is."

Ecclesiastes 3:15

How do you define time and how does it affect your life? Is it linear or cyclical, or both?

"You cannot find yourself in the past or future. The only place where you can find yourself is in the Now."

Eckhart Tolle from *Stillness Speaks*

O God of all Times and Places, you come to us in each present moment, but so often we are focused on the past or the future and we miss the special time of your Now. Teach us how to live in the present and cherish each second that you give to us. The past is truly finished and gone. You have created everything, including us, fresh and new. Our future has yet to be written. What we have is today. May we spend it wisely walking your sacred Path in the company of those we love. In this way, we will create a future filled with Peace, Abundance and Joy. Thank you for each breath we take and each beat of our heart. May we treasure your Now and celebrate your Presence in each and every moment. So it is.

November 10

"Now may the Lord of peace himself give you peace at all times in all ways."

2 Thessalonians 3:16

How do you find inner peace in your everyday life?

"Don't let yesterday use up too much of today"

Cherokee Proverb

O God of Mercy and Peace, we look around our world and see violence and war. Peace seems a far away dream as your children struggle in conflict and misunderstanding. Create in us pure hearts that will open to your Love for each and every one of your children. Create in us a way to understand differences within unity, diversity within Oneness. It is your Peace we seek, not a dream but a reality in our heart and soul. Teach us to befriend our neighbor and the stranger we do not know. When we discover that they are simply friends that we have yet to meet, we will be on the path to Peace. May we always walk on the pathway of Light. May we speak words of Light, Truth and Peace. May your Peace dwell in our hearts and keep us from all harm as we become peacemakers for our troubled world. So it is.

Rev. Maryesah Karelon, O.M.M.

November 11

"The light shines in the darkness, and the darkness did not overcome it."

John 1:5

Do you believe that good will ultimately triumph and light will overcome darkness in our world? How can you assist this in manifesting?

"I am a child of the Light. I love the Light. I serve the Light. I live in the Light. I am protected, illumined, supplied and sustained by the Light and I bless the Light."

St. Germain

O Lord of Light and Darkness, you created the sun, moon and stars to penetrate the darkness of the void. You are all Light and all Goodness, and in you there can be no darkness. Increase our faith so that we may truly trust in your promises and live by your Light. Embrace us with your Love and remind us that in your Love there is no fear. May we go forward into the darkness of the void and fear not, for we know you walk beside us to guide our steps and light our way. We give you thanks and praise, Holy One, for the candle you keep burning for us. May we spread that Light wherever we go. So it is.

November 12

"Have unity of spirit, sympathy, love for one another, a tender heart, and a humble mind."

1 Peter 3:8

What does it mean to you to be humble? Is this a positive or a negative quality?

"When you are content to be simply yourself and don't compare or compete, everybody will respect you."

Lao-Tzu

O God of All That Is, it is easy to feel small and insignificant when we look upward into the heavens of your Creation. When we interact with our brothers and sisters, it is too easy to insist on our own way. Remind us to "play well with others" in the school of life. Life is not a competition to be won at all costs but a journey to be shared. Teach us to go within for a standard of comparison instead of focusing on external role models. You created each one of us to be unique and precious. May we learn to affirm our true worth as your beloved children while remembering our place in your immense and glorious universe. We give you thanks and praise for the beauty and perfection of this balance and harmony. So it is.

November 13

> "It is for this that you were called—that you might inherit a blessing."
>
> 1 Peter 3:9

How does your calling bring blessings to your life?

> "Stop trying to be ordinary. There is nothing special or desirable about being ordinary. In fact, it is totally unacceptable. You are an extra-ordinary being who must go into motion, into movement so that you will draw to yourself the equivalent of yourself. You have become an energy field that magnetically draws you to that which you are."
>
> Jack Boland

Beloved One of my Heart, you have called me by name. In your mirror of Light, I see the glimmer of my own potential and the person I truly can become. Still the loud voices of the world around me so that I may hear your call in the silence of my heart. Teach me to follow where you lead, trusting in your perfect Wisdom. When my life does not unfold as I plan, remind me that your Divine Order is still in effect. May I surrender to your Will knowing that many and unimaginable blessings are waiting for me. I ask that your Spirit flow through my life, and empower my body, mind and spirit to create and transform as you will. So it is.

November 14

"If we live by the Spirit, let us also be guided by the Spirit."

Galatians 5:25

What changes do you feel that the Spirit is bringing into your life?

"The only way to change your story is to change what you believe about yourself...Every time you change the main character of your story, the whole story changes to adapt to the new main character."

Don Miguel Ruiz from *The Voice of Knowledge*

Loving Creative Spirit, you flow into us and around us bringing change to our dull, everyday lives. We thank you for the Power and Inspiration of your Presence. Unstick us from our comfort zones and move us forward to meet our destiny as beloved children of the One. Show us how to transform our doubts and fears into confident trust. Infuse us with your creative challenges. May we welcome the transitions of our lives and know that your guiding, protecting wings will always be there to lift us above the turmoil of change. We affirm that out of chaos comes wondrous creation and blessings beyond imagining. So it is.

Rev. Maryesah Karelon, O.M.M.

November 15

"Devote yourselves to prayer, keeping alert in it with thanksgiving."

Colossians 1:11-12

What role does prayer play in your life? What blessings does it bring to you?

"The sovereign cure for worry is prayer."

William James

Wondrous God, you surround us with your Love and Light and whisper softly in our ear in our darkest hours. Remind us to stop our mad rush through our busy days and listen to your gentle Voice. We give you thanks and praise for walking beside us and filling us with the assurance of your Love. Open our hearts so that we may feel the rush of your ever-flowing Light that fills every cell, every organ, every vein and artery of our body. Wrap us in a cocoon of your Light energy so that every dark thought, every worry, every fear or doubt, will find no home in our minds. Draw us ever closer to you so that we may learn and experience the true Joy of Oneness. As we place you on the top of our priority list, every other challenge in our lives will fall into place. We let go and let you be in control. So it is.

November 16

"The Blessed One greeted them all, saying: 'Peace be with you—may my peace arise and be fulfilled within you! Be vigilant, and allow no one to mislead you by saying: 'Here it is!' or 'There it is!' For it is within you that the Son of Man dwells. Go to him, for those who seek him, find him. Walk forth and announce the gospel of the Kingdom."

Gospel of Mary Magdalene 8:11-24

How are you spreading the "good news," the gospel of the Kingdom?

"If you want to lift yourself up, lift up somebody else."

Booker T. Washington

Beloved One, you come to us in the stillness and whisper of the wind of Spirit. You remind us that we, too, are spirit. You created us to be true reflections of your Truth and your Light. Draw us ever closer to you. Open our hearts and minds so that we may seek your Truth for our lives. We know that the wisdom and truth of the world is foolishness compared to what you can teach us. Guided by Spirit, we seek a higher Truth and a higher Justice. Show us how we may communicate your spiritual Wisdom to a culture that believes in the god of materialism. In Spirit and Truth, we come before you in praise, in worship, in thanksgiving. So it is.

Rev. Maryesah Karelon, O.M.M.

November 17

"Listen to advice and accept instruction, that you may gain wisdom for the future."

Proverbs 19:20

From whom do you seek advice and why do you believe it is trustworthy? Does some of this advice come from the spiritual plane and if so, how do you discern its validity?

"The best test for the guidance we receive is elegantly simple. Ask, Is it divine? Is it loving, kind, generous, compassionate, peaceable, forgiving, truthful? If it is, you can be confident that it is coming from Spirit."

Sharon Connors

Holy Sophia, we open ourselves to your Divine Wisdom and Guidance. Too often we seek your counsel and advice only when things go radically wrong in our lives. Teach us to come to you as our first and most honored Teacher, not our Guide of last resort. We acknowledge that it is hard to let go of the steering wheel of our lives. We desire to do it all, to navigate even when we have no clue where we are going. Thank you for your patience with our stubbornness. Thank you for your willingness to be there whenever we are ready to listen and understand your words of Life. Gift us with the humility to ask for directions when we feel lost and to seek counsel when the going gets rough. We affirm that you have destined us for Joy, Happiness and Abundance always and in all ways. May we gratefully and openly accept your loving legacy. So it is.

November 18

"Let love be genuine; hate what is evil, hold fast to what is good; love one another with mutual affection; outdo one another in showing honor."

Romans 12:9-10

Recall a time when you felt you were greatly disrespected and a time when you were gifted with honor and respect. Compare your feelings and the circumstances that evoked them. What did you learn in both instances?

"Respect is one of the greatest expressions of love."

Don Miguel Ruiz from *The Voice of Knowledge*

Gracious and Merciful God, you show us so much Love and Compassion yet we have such a difficult time doing the same for each other, and particularly for ourselves. Teach us how to love, respect and honor our true Self that carries your Divine Image. Help us to carry that knowledge of our divinity into the everyday sameness of our lives. As we honor the Christ within our own heart, we will be able to look into the eyes of our brothers and sisters and see the Christ in them as well. We are all One in your Goodness and Love. How can we wrong another part of our own body that deserves only honor and respect? We will bring Peace and Love to our planet only when we finally learn to love ourselves. Teach us how special and worthy we are. Show us who we truly are and who we are to become. So it is.

November 19

"For we are what he has made us, created in Christ Jesus for good works, which God prepared beforehand to be our way of life."

Ephesians 2:10

How do you prioritize between the spiritual and the material?

"Love all God's creation, both the whole and every grain of sand. Love every leaf, every ray of light. Love the animals, love the plants, love each separate thing. If you love each thing, you will perceive the mystery of God in all; and once you perceive this, you will from that time on grow every day to a fuller understanding of it until you come at last to love the whole world with a love that will then be all-embracing and universal."

Fyodor Dostoyevsky from *The Brothers Karamazov*

Holy One, you molded us in your Divine Image and called us by name. Then you breathed into us the breath of your Spirit and sent us out to do your work in the world. Remind us that this planet is more than a schoolroom. This life that we are living is much more than a dreary round to no purpose. We are here for a reason and you have given us work to do. May we have the strength and the courage to seek out our destiny and then to unfold the wings of the butterfly that we are. Thank you, dear God, for all the many gifts and blessings that you shower upon us. Help us to remember that there are no mistakes and no coincidences even when we don't fully understand your Purposes. Each event in our lives is given as a gift to ultimately teach us how to love. May we continue to learn and grow and work in your beloved world. So it is.

November 20

"You shall bring in the table, and arrange its setting; and you shall bring in the lampstand, and set up its lamps."

Exodus 40:4

How do you prepare for Thanksgiving?

"Nothing has the power to create stress."

David Hawkins from *Power vs. Force*

Gentle God, as we rush and worry about all the little preparations for food and family, remind us to stop, breathe and remember you. Show us how to step back and let you take charge, and then watch our stress melt away. There is always enough of everything we need; enough time, enough patience, enough love. When we get to the end of our rope, teach us to tie a knot and hang on tight, for you are always there for us. In all the preparations for Thanksgiving Day, let us remember to give thanks in the midst of it all and let go. Stress is not on the menu for our Thanksgiving and we give you thanks for that. So it is.

November 21

"Welcome one another, therefore, just as Christ has welcomed you, for the glory of God."

Romans 15:7

Reflect on how your faith in God and your spiritual life affects your interpersonal relationships.

"Ironically, the people who seem to upset us the most are those who, at the soul level, love and support us the most."

Colin C. Tipping from <u>Radical Forgiveness</u>

Almighty God, you have indeed welcomed us into your divine fellowship and surrounded us with an everlasting Love. Remind us that there are no favorites in your fellowship. All humanity are your beloved children. It is we who create division and separation with our judgments and prejudices. Cleanse our minds of the erroneous assumption that we are better, smarter or in any way above anyone else. Remove the competition and the comparison with others, and allow us to come together as equal sisters and brothers. Show us how to be patient and kind with one another for our world is so lacking in these qualities. Inspire us to random acts of kindness without thought of being thanked or repaid. May we walk as Christed ones in our world, creating blessed and sacred encounters as we walk. So it is.

November 22

"*Love is from God; everyone who loves is born of God and knows God.*"

1 John 4:7

What happens when we serve others but without love? Is it possible to truly love without reaching out to others?

"It is not how much you do, but how much Love you put into the doing that matters."

Mother Teresa of Calcutta

Loving Mother/Father God, we love because you first loved us and created us from that Divine Love. Yet we have changed the meaning of love and placed so many conditions upon giving it away. We want to be certain our love is returned. We want love if it is properly packaged and marketed. We will risk giving ourselves away in love only if we feel safe and secure. Our safety, our security is with you. If we listen, our inner Divine Knowing will tell us what is true and what is false. Teach us how to be vulnerable and share our innermost Selves while we listen for that voice that will warn us when it is not safe. You are our Protector and our Lover; our best Friend and our trusted Guide. Your Love embraces us no matter what, drying our tears and hugging away our fears. May we learn to love as you love us, without conditions, without counting the cost, without strings attached. Our world desperately needs the Power of that Love. So it is.

November 23

"The Lord is my light and my salvation...The Lord is the stronghold of my life."

Psalm 27:1

Recall a time of challenge and difficulty in your life. How did your faith in God assist you through the darkness? What was the ultimate result?

"There is a time for departure even when there's no certain place to go."

Robert Frost

Abba, you have promised never to desert us even when we forget and desert you. We give you thanks and praise for your faithful and steadfast Love. When the storms of life threaten to capsize our boats, you are there for us, the lighthouse in the storm. As we face the unpredictable winds of life, give us the strength and courage to trust in your Care and cast out all fear and doubt. We are never alone as long as our hope is in you. Still the storms and calm the seas of our turbulent times, for we know and affirm that your Will for us is Peace, Serenity, Abundance and Joy. For your Love and Light that light our way, we give your thanks and praise. So it is.

November 24

"My soul is satisfied with a rich feast, and my mouth praises you with joyful lips."

Psalm 63:5

What satisfies your heart and feeds your soul? Are your heart and soul in harmony?

"Happiness is when what you think, what you say, and what you do are in harmony."

Mahatma Gandhi

Source of All Being, you give us everything that is good, a feast beyond our imagining; forgive us when we desire more and more and more. Stop us in our tracks in our mad rush for the latest, the greatest and the most expensive. What satisfies our soul is far more important, for this is the source of our divine connection with you. When we are hungry for the material things of life, remind us there is a hunger that material things will never satisfy. Show us how to seek for that which is truly good for us; a healthy, spiritual diet that will nourish our yearning for something beyond money, sex, power and Ipods. May we keep you at the top of our priority list so that as we journey onward you will walk beside us as our Guide, our Protector and our Teacher. Thank you for filling us to overflowing with a rich and wonderful feast indeed. So it is.

November 25

"*Return, O my soul, to your rest, for the Lord has dealt bountifully with you.*"

Psalm 116:7

How do you find rest, physically and spiritually?

"Look at a tree, a flower, a plant. Let your awareness rest upon it. How still they are, how deeply rooted in Being. Allow nature to teach you stillness."

Eckhart Tolle from <u>Stillness Speaks</u>

God of all Creation, you surround us with so much beauty and so much bounty. This time of year we revel in the bright colors of leaves and the abundance of harvest. We peer into the glorious petals of a golden chrysanthemum and see a mandala of your perfection. Teach us to open our eyes and our hearts to the Glory of your Creation that surrounds us. Speak to us in the deepest level of our soul and bring us to the fountain of refreshment that is flowing within. As we are cleansed and healed by this everflowing stream we enter the stillness of your Presence. The noise and busyness of the world is no more. Here our soul can be fed from your table and nourished by your Light and Love. We are so grateful and so richly blessed. In the silence we hear you say to us "Be still, be still, and know that I AM." So it is.

November 26

"If there is a physical body, there is also a spiritual body."

1 Corinthians 15:44

Is there a "you" that exists beyond your physical body? How would you describe this non-physical part of your being?

"Beauty tells me that I am ugly. Purity tells me that I am impure. Sincerity tells me that I am insincere. I ask my sweet Lord if it is all true. My Lord says, 'How can you be ugly, My child, when My own Light is your body? How can you be impure, My child, when My Divinity is your heart's birthright? How can you be insincere, My child, when I, Myself, use your soul to speak through your mouth?'"

Sri Chinmoy from *Songs of the Soul*

Source of All Being, we are much more than we know or comprehend; too often we live in the shadows. Too often we create a laundry list of excuses to prevent us from being who you created us to be. Expand our vision, dear God, and open us to wonder and mystery. For indeed that is what we truly are—a wonder and a mystery. In the quiet stillness, we reach out and sense a universe beyond our imagination. Soon we will be living in this universe of wonders and Light. May we open to the healing, harmonizing, balancing potentials of our new Home. So it is.

November 27

"And you became imitators of us and of the Lord—so that you became an example to all the believers."

1 Thessalonians 1:6-7

What kind of example are you living out for your family, your friends and everyone you encounter? Can you say that you are "walking your talk?"

"Seek and reverence the light in the heart of every soul you meet. Remember the light shining in the heart of the simplest earth child; reverence that, and help that light in your brother-sister to shine. So, gradually, the light will spread throughout the world, and the new age of brotherhood will truly dawn."

White Eagle from <u>The Book of Star Light</u>

Light of the World, you came to us to bring Light into our darkness. Now you call us to do the same for one another. Fill us with your Light so that we may truly shine. Teach us how to see past the differences and judgments that separate us from one another. May we truly become your reflection and bring the Christ Light wherever we walk. As examples of your Love and Light, we now commit ourselves to reverence and honor for all humankind. We commit ourselves to Love and Compassion for the have-nots of our world. We commit ourselves to work for Justice and Truth for the forgotten ones who have no power or opportunity to speak for themselves. We are your hands, your voice, your loving arms and we embrace our brothers and sisters in your Name. So it is.

November 28

"Yeshua said: Whoever lives the interpretation of these words will no longer taste death."
Gospel of Thomas, Saying 1

Reflect on the possible meaning of these words since none of us can claim yet to be beyond physical death.

"All I have seen teaches me to trust the Creator for all I have not seen."
Ralph Waldo Emerson

Great Mystery, you are far beyond what our human minds can comprehend yet we are made in your Image and Likeness. Holy

One, there is so much that we do not understand and so much potential that lies dormant within us. Teach us to spread our wings like a butterfly emerging from a cocoon. Expand our vision and our reality beyond the flesh, blood and bone of our physical form. Your Universe is so much more. May we dare to cross that threshold and truly step beyond death and beyond human limitation. So it is.

November 29

"And you will have confidence, because there is hope; you will be protected and take your rest in safety."

Job 11:18

How will you keep the spiritual in the busyness of this season?

"Resist pessimism and negative thinking both in private and national life. Think only good. 'Think God.' Whatever your trouble, put God, and thoughts of God in place of that trouble. Think godly things. Even if he or she does not appear to be doing so, see that your brother-sister is striving towards God. See the world developing and growing more spiritual."

White Eagle from <u>*The Quiet Mind*</u>

O God of Hope and Promise, sometimes it so easy to lose hope. We are overwhelmed by the stress of everyone's demands on us. Life isn't always what we might wish or expect. Our lives are a combination of joy and sadness, pleasure and pain, serenity and turmoil. This is how you have designed our lessons for us. We ask for your Guidance and Patience as we struggle to learn, to trust, to walk in faith even when the path is dark and difficult. As holiday and family priorities descend upon us, teach us to let go of the past, close the door and move on to better things and greater joy. We affirm and know that in your Love and Protection the best is yet to be. We also know that it is much harder to see the good that is right in front of us if we're looking behind us. So we let go and let it be. So it is.

November 30

"The Lord will be your confidence and will keep your foot from being caught."

Proverbs 3:26

Recall a time in your life when you felt stuck and change seemed impossible or too risky. How did you resolve the situation?

"If you can't go somewhere, move in the passageways of the self. They are like shafts of light, always changing, and you change when you explore them."

Rumi, Sufi Mystic Poet

O God of the Morning Dawn, so often we keep our eyes closed and then wonder why we see only darkness. Give us the strength and the courage to open our eyes fully to the glory of your dawning day. Fill us with your confident Spirit that we may go forward to meet our Destiny and Purpose. Remind us that when change comes, as it inevitably will, your Love remains unchanging. As everything seems to whirl around us, as rugs are pulled out from under our feet, may we turn our gaze and put our trust in you. Be the center of our lives and we know that we will stay on course. Without fear, we ask you to transform us, remold us and make us into your Divine Image. This is our inheritance and our legacy. We accept it with grateful hearts as we trust in your Love and Light. So it is.

Rev. Maryesah Karelon, O.M.M.

December

Practice tolerance and understanding
of your fellow brothers and sisters,
for there are a variety of gifts in the body
and many differences.
Celebrate this richness created by God and
seek your place in the tapestry of creation.
Never lose sight of the ultimate paradox—
we are all One but we are only one.

Light in the Darkness

December 1

"Please accept my gift that is brought to you, because God has dealt graciously with me, and because I have everything I want."

Genesis 33:11

In this season of giving and receiving, how do you keep the two in balance?

"Give God the glory for what you have and you will receive more. Be grateful for the measure that is coming to you and that measure will increase perpetually. This is the law and it will never fail unless you fail to do to others what God is doing to you. Giving and receiving must be equal in your life. We must give something for everything we receive; nothing is free; the universe is not built in that manner; but giving does not imply the gift of things. True giving and true being are one and the same in real life."

Christian D. Larson

Generous and Ever-loving God, you shower us with blessings beyond our imagining and gift us with opportunities too many for us to count. Teach us how to say "Thank you" for what you have given by giving your Love away to others. Show us how to balance the giving and receiving in our lives so that we journey through this special season with an attitude of gratitude and an open heart. May we focus our attention on needs, not wants, for ourselves and those around us. As we wait in Hope for your coming may we be inspired by your Presence within us to be a gift to your precious world. So it is.

December 2

"I will thank you forever, because of what you have done. In the presence of the faithful I will praise your name, for it is good."

Psalm 52:9

Reflect on the reasons that you have to praise God and the ways that you can express that gratitude and praise in your life.

"We are very near to greatness; one step and we are safe; can we not take the leap?"

Ralph Waldo Emerson

O God of Wonder and Love, you have given us so much and so often we are like little children with new toys. We have no idea what to do with your wondrous giftings. We need instruction manuals. Teach us how to expand our horizons and become more than we ever dreamed we could be. You have planted the seeds within us and we are grateful. Now it is up to us to nurture those seeds and tend the garden well. Lead us within to encounter our true Self that is waiting to be our guide. Give us the courage to take that irrevocable step off the precipice knowing that we will be safe because you have given us wings to fly. We praise and thank you, dear God, for the opportunity to be who we are meant to be and see the universe through your eyes and Vision. Thank you, thank you, thank you. So it is.

December 3

"I will strengthen you, I will help you, I will uphold you with my victorious right hand."

Isaiah 41:10

What are the greatest needs in your life right now? How will the needs be met? Whom will you ask to help you?

"Faith is power. When we obsess about our problems and the things we lack, that is what will manifest in our reality. By imagining the possibilities—our positive intentions—clearly, then letting them go and having faith in the benevolence of the Universe, we remove the barriers of our limited thoughts and open the path for wonderful things to come our way."

Kathy Cordova from <u>Let Go Let Miracles Happen: The Art of Spiritual Surrender</u>

Gracious Holy One, 'tis the season to make lists and check them at least twice. We always seem to have a wish list of things that we want, perhaps even need. Teach us how to ask you for our true needs even though you already know what is in our hearts. In asking, we learn to trust and have faith. In letting go, we learn how to release our control and surrender to your loving Wisdom. In this season of miracles, may we trust in your miraculous Love for each and every one of your children. May we ask, knowing we will receive from your bounty. May we give, knowing that we can create miracles in someone else's life. May blessings of Love, Joy, Peace and Abundance multiply around the world in your Name and to your Glory. So it is.

December 4

"Whatever house you enter, first say, 'Peace to this house!'"

Luke 10:5

How do you plan to spread spiritual "holiday cheer" to friends and family? How can you make a difference in the many casual encounters of your day?

"The next time you find yourself stuck in a long line at an ATM machine, traffic jam, or supermarket checkout counter, resist your urge to react. Do not get frustrated. Do not become impatient. Do not get angry. The line is there to test you, and to give you an opportunity not to react. But if you do react, the situation controls you. The situation becomes the cause and you the effect."

Yehuda Berg from *The Power of Kabbalah*

O God of Peace and Harmony, too often we celebrate this season of Peace, Love and Joy by immersing ourselves in anger and frustration. We snap at our loved ones and lose our cool with clerks trying to be helpful. Slow us down, Lord. Remind us to take a deep breath, count to ten when the going gets rough and stash an extra supply of humor for our journey through Advent to Christmas. May we become your ambassadors of Love and Peace, and examples of what it means to embody that Love and Peace in our lives. May we know that you are always with us and within us. Thank you, Emmanuel. So it is.

December 5

"Surely there is a future, and your hope will not be cut off."
Proverbs 23:18

How do you view the future for yourself, your family, our nation and our planet?

"We must learn to live together as brothers or we are going to perish together as fools."
Martin Luther King Jr.

O Lord of the Future, we pray that you will be our Light and our Guide as we walk forward into the darkness. We need to live in Hope and Faith, and that is possible only if we focus on you. Teach us to believe in your positive possibilities, and allow us to let go of our fears and limitations. May we reach out and embrace our brothers and sisters knowing that the hope of our future depends on unity across our diverse world. As different as we may be, show us how much we have in common. We affirm that our future lies in the truth of our Oneness in you. Purge our minds of doubt and unite our hearts in Love. So it is.

December 6

"The path of the righteous is like the light of dawn, which shines brighter and brighter until full day."
Proverbs 4:18

Reflect on how you are affected by the darkness and the lack of daylight. What are the positives and negatives for you in this season of the year?

"We must enjoy each day—one at a time. We are here on a short visit. Be sure to smell the flowers."

Alfred A. Montapert

O God of Light and Darkness, as the days grow ever shorter we know this is your way of rest and renewal. Lead us into the darkness without fear. Be our Guide and our ever-present Light. Warm our souls when the gathering gloom becomes too cold. Remind us that the brightness of your Sun still shines and will return to us once again. Fill our hearts with Hope and Trust so that we may walk with Courage even though we do not know the Way. May we treasure the dark as we do the night, for it has secrets to tell and much to teach us. We pause, we rest, we reflect and we are renewed with your Love and your Spirit. So it is.

December 7

"For you were called to freedom, brothers and sisters; only do not use your freedom as an opportunity for self-indulgence."

Galatians 5:13

In what ways are you free and in what ways do you feel you are limited?

"The only limits to our realization of tomorrow will be our doubts of today. Let us move forward with strong and active faith."

Franklin D. Roosevelt

Source of All Being, you go before us into the future and wait for us there. You gift us with the Power of your Strength and Courage to move beyond our limitations and create our dreams. May those dreams be informed by your Light and Love so that we may become true partners with you, bringing Goodness, Truth and Justice into your world. We acknowledge that our freedom depends upon the awareness we have for all your children. If we wish to be truly free, the welfare and well-being of others must be our highest concern. Free us from the slavery of self-indulgence and the blindness of ignorance that focuses only on our own concerns. We are residents of a global village. May we live as responsible and aware citizens of the world. In that will be our freedom. So it is.

December 8

"And Mary said, 'My soul magnifies the Lord, and my spirit rejoices in God my Savior.'"

Luke 1:46-47

How have you experienced the special surprise of God's Presence in your life? How has it changed you?

"My will for you is not harsh or unpleasant. It is gentle and perfectly tailored to your unique needs. Do not fear my direction. I am your heart's happiest guide."

Julia Cameron from <u>Answered Prayers: Love Letters from the Divine</u>

Loving Mother/Father God, you knock on the door of our hearts when we least expect it. You bring challenges and opportunities combined with the blanket of your all-embracing Love. May we trust in that Love as young Mary trusted when she was told she would birth the child Jesus. Guide our footsteps along the Path that you have chosen for us. Open our hearts to the whisper of your gentle words of Wisdom and teach us how to face the shadows with strength and courage. We seek to follow where you lead us, traveling onward without a map, knowing only that your Way is our way. May we journey in Joy, for our soul can find rest only at Home in your Love. So it is.

December 9

"Yeshua said: You see the sliver in your brother's eye, but you do not see the log in your own eye. When you remove the log from your eye, then you will see clearly enough to remove the sliver from your brother's eye."

Gospel of Thomas, Saying 26

Reflect on the meaning of these words for your life and our world today. In what ways do you judge others without seeing your own faults?

"All we see of someone at any moment is a snapshot of their life; they're in riches or poverty, in joy or despair. Snapshots don't show the million decisions that led to that moment."

Richard Bach

Gracious God, you come to us when we are frustrated and disappointed with ourselves and our human family, reminding us not to judge, not to presume and assume, not to be self-righteous. We know we are not perfect and that it is our own insecurity and fear that insists to the world that we know it all. Gift us with the humility to understand our place in your great tapestry of the universe, yet show us the Truth of how precious we truly are. May we find the balance and walk gently and kindly on your good Earth and among our brothers and sisters. So it is.

December 10

"See that you complete the task that you have received in the Lord."

Colossians 4:17

Have you ever been tempted to quit in the midst of a difficult job or situation? What was the result of your decision?

"It's been proven that the only effective way to deal with fear is to walk through it, through the pain that accompanies doing something you're afraid to do. It takes courage to fulfill your commitments, courage to stay on track, courage to follow your dreams, courage to reach your goals, and courage to walk through your fear. Remember, reaching goals is not so much about doing big things when the feeling hits you; it's more about doing little things every day that move you toward your dream. It's about staying steady and on course."

Francine Ward from <u>Esteemable Acts: 10 Actions for Building Real Self-Esteem</u>

Gracious God, you knew us before we were born and called us by name for a special Purpose. Reveal to us that Purpose and give us the Courage to live it out in our life. Encourage us to keep on keeping on when we are tempted to give up. Pick us up when we stumble and fall. Walk beside us when we have mountains to climb. Speak to us in the lonely nights when doubt and fear crowd the shadows of our mind. Teach us how to believe in your miracles. Expand our vision and lift us above the limits of the world we can see. Show us the grandeur and beauty that await us as we become what you intend us to be. May our minds stay focused, our hearts stay true and our feet complete the journey you have set before us. Go before us to show the Way, walk beside us to be our Protection and walk behind us so we will never walk alone. So it is.

December 11

"What is my strength, that I should wait? And what is my end, that I should be patient?"

Job 6:11

Reflect on a time in your life when patience was difficult. How did you learn to wait and what was the result?

"Slow down and everything you are chasing will come around and catch you."

John De Paola

Abba, you are our Strength and Shield, our ever-present help in times of challenge. Teach us how to trust in your Strength and to wait patiently for the help that will not forsake us. Slow us down, dear Lord, and remind us that the race is not always to the swift. As Mary waited those long nine months for the birth of her child, may we wait patiently for your coming, knowing that the result is never in doubt. Show us how to learn and grow from our experience of waiting and watching. Keep us awake and aware so that we may be among the first to greet the Sacred Bridegroom when he comes. In patience, in anticipation, in trust and faith we wait, O Lord, for you. So it is.

December 12

"I lift up my eyes to the hills—from where will my help come? My help comes from the Lord, who made heaven and earth."

Psalm 121:1-2

Recall a time when you felt deserted by God. What did you learn from this experience?

"Be so strong that nothing can disturb your peace of mind. Talk health, happiness, and prosperity to every person you meet. Make all your friends feel there is something in them. Look at the sunny side of everything. Think only of the best, work only for the best, and expect only the best. Be as enthusiastic about the success of others as you are about your own. Forget the mistakes of the past and press on to the greater achievements of the future. Give everyone a smile. Spend so much time improving yourself that you have no time left to criticize others. Be too big for worry and too noble for anger."

Christian D. Larson

Faithful God, we admit that there are times when we forget to take time for you. When we feel a lack of Divine connection, when we feel deserted and alone, remind us that you have never, and will never, abandon us. We have simply deserted you. In the noisy busyness of this season, show us how to take a deep breath and go within to the inner silence of our hearts. There we will find you waiting for us, ready to re-energize us and encourage us to continue the journey. So it is.

December 13

"Ever since the creation of the world his eternal power and divine nature, invisible though they are, have been understood and seen through the things he has made."

Romans 1:20

How is God present for you in this season? Does God get lost in all the parties and presents, all the shopping and expectations?

"Great minds have purposes, little minds have wishes."

Washington Irving

Wondrous God, we are surrounded by so much glitz and glamour this time of year. You do not need an Ipod or a video game to communicate your message. You know how to keep it simple and say it with Love from the heart. Help us to step away from the dollar signs and the demands. The most precious treasures do not have price tags and cannot be bought or sold. Teach us to give of ourselves and hug a child; to say 'I love you' to an aging parent; to reach out with a tender touch when exhaustion overwhelms. May we re-discover the wonder of this wondrous season and see your magic reflected in the wide eyes of a child. Just for one little instant, let us become that child and be overcome once again with your Joy and Delight. So it is.

December 14

"But for you who revere my name the sun of righteousness shall rise, with healing in its wings."

Malachi 4:2

What needs to be healed in your life? How can you assist this to happen?

"...The greatest suffering is being lonely, feeling unloved, having no one. I have come more and more to realize that it is being unwanted that is the worst disease that any human being can ever experience."

Mother Teresa of Calcutta from *The Joy in Loving*

Loving Mother/Father God, you reach out to embrace each one of your children with your Love. Forgive us when we fail to do the same. Remind us how lonely this beautiful season can be for those who have lost loved ones, for those who exist on the fringes of life, even for those who have so much and yet yearn for the gift of your gentle Love. Teach us to show your Love to the lost, the frightened, the lonely and the alienated. Teach us to shine your Light into the dark shadows that crowd in upon us. It is so easy to be overwhelmed by the needs and wants of the world, but we can start with the needs of our neighbors, our family and friends; those down the street who have little and ask for less. We can share Hope, Love and Light even when we have limited resources ourselves. Your Abundance is our source of strength and we give you thanks and praise for the showers of gifts and blessings that we receive from you. Thank you, thank you, thank you, God. So it is.

December 15

"Like good stewards of the manifold grace of God, serve one another with whatever gift each of you have received."

1 Peter 4:10

If you were coming to Bethlehem to greet the Christ child, what gifts would you have to offer to him? How can you share these gifts with others in your life?

"Awakened souls strengthen and encourage each other by their friendships and interchange of thoughts and revealments. They create a network of light over the planet and spin threads of mutual upliftment and inspiration."

Vida Reed Stone

Sweet Spirit, you inspire us to work in joy and faith for Justice and Truth in your world. You gift us with so many opportunities to share, to love, to teach and heal. As we become more and more aware of the Christ presence within us, open our eyes and our hearts to the wondrous blessings that we can share. In humbleness and gentleness, may we let our light shine in service to our world and to our brothers and sisters. Help us to be a transformative presence in your Name for Peace, Love and Healing. So it is.

December 16

"Beloved, I pray that all may go well with you and that you may be in good health, just as it is well with your soul."

3 John 1:2

How do you keep your soul in good health? Is it well with your soul?

"The simplification of life is one of the steps to inner peace. A persistent simplification will create an inner and outer well-being that places harmony in one's life."

Peace Pilgrim

Holy One, in this material world it is so easy to get caught up in the tinsel and trappings of the commercial Christmas season. Show us how to go deeper and seek the child waiting to be born in each one of us. There are so many riches waiting for our discovery; so many wonderful gifts that you have given to us and hidden in the depths of our soul. May we take time to encounter our souls this Christmas. In quietness, in gentleness, without the hype and the bright lights, may we travel to our own manger and discover there the Christ waiting to be born within each one of us. May our soul be transformed and may the brightness of that birth shine forth as a light in the darkness. So it is

December 17

"And after he had dismissed the crowds, he went up the mountain by himself to pray. When evening came, he was there alone."

Matthew 14:23

Do you find private time to meditate, pray and connect with the Divine during this hectic time of the year? How do you prioritize with God?

"What we usually pray to God is not that His will be done, but that He approve ours."

Helga Bergold Gross

Gracious Holy Spirit, you come to us in the quietness and whisper in the silence. You surround us with your Light and Protection even when we're too busy to notice. Still our hurried pace and gift us with a moment of silence. May we open to your eternal Presence that is always near us and within us. Guide our steps and help us sort out our priorities. Remind us why we are shopping, writing cards and baking cookies. May we enfold your Love into each bow we tie, each cookie we bake and each card we write. Love is the reason for the season and Love is your Will for our lives. Love is at the top of our wish list along with Peace. May our prayers be for your Love and Peace to prevail on Earth as in heaven. So it is.

December 18

"But you are not in the flesh; you are in the Spirit, since the Spirit of God dwells in you."

Romans 8:9

What does it mean to live "in the Spirit" rather than "in the flesh?"

"And the Grinch, with his Grinch-feet ice cold in the snow, stood puzzling and puzzling, how could it be so? It came without ribbons. It came without tags. It came without packages, boxes or bags. And he puzzled and puzzled 'til his puzzler was sore. Then the Grinch thought of something he hadn't thought of before. What if Christmas, he thought, doesn't come from a store? What if Christmas, perhaps, means a little bit more?"

Dr. Seuss (Theodor Seuss Geisel) from *How the Grinch Stole Christmas!*

Holy Shekinah, we invite you to come dwell with us this Christmas time. Come pitch your tent in our hearts and fill us with your Power and your Joy. Journey with us as we seek a deeper meaning to all the bustle and busyness. Breathe into us a Spirit of Peace and contentment even as the time grows short and the to-do lists grow long. Remind us that in the end it is not how much we spend, how many boxes are under the tree, how many parties we attend, but how much room we have in our hearts for Love. As we pause for a deep breath, we breathe in your wondrous Light and Peace and all is well. So it is.

December 19

"God's temple is holy, and you are that temple."

1 Corinthians 3:17

What difference would it make in your life if you lived believing you are God's temple?

"God, why do I storm heaven for answers that are already in my heart? Every grace I need has already been given me. Oh, lead me to the Beyond within."

Macrina Wiederkehr

Almighty God, you have created us in holiness and in your Image to live out our lives as reflections of you. So often we lose sight of who we are and what our purpose is. Remind us, dear God, that you dwell within us, that our answers lie within us and not in some external authority. May we cherish who we are as physical, mental, emotional and spiritual temples of your Love and Light. May we bring that Love and Light to our world, seeing all our brothers and sisters as your Divine temples. We call you to unite us in Love and Peace and teach us to live as one family, for so we are. May we all come in Joy to your holy temple and celebrate as the family of God. We are One. So it is.

December 20

"Therefore I tell you, do not worry about your life, what you will eat or what you will drink, or about your body, what you will wear. Is not life more than food, and the body more than clothing?"

Matthew 6:25

Recall a time in your life when you were concerned for survival needs. How were these concerns resolved? What gave you the courage to move forward in the face of hardship?

"We take no step unpartnered...The Great Creator is an artist and he/she/it is an artist in partnership with other artists. The moment we open ourselves to making art, we simultaneously open ourselves to our maker. We are automatically partnered."

> Julia Cameron from *Walking in This World: The Practical Art of Creativity*

Creator of All, you are the artist and our lives are your canvas. Yet we know that you can inspire and empower us to become artists of our own lives. Create in us the fountain of Love and Truth that will overflow into our lives and the lives of all whom we meet. Make our life your masterpiece and plant in us the desire to be all that we were created to be. As we are transformed by your Love, we come ever closer to being true partners with you, working as one for the healing of our world. May the brush strokes be gentle, the colors bright and the painting a joy to behold. So it is.

December 21

"Those who sow in winter reap in summer; winter is this world, summer is the world of Openness. Let us sow in the world, so as to harvest in summer. To pray is not to prevent winter, but to allow summer. Winter is not a time of harvest, but of labor. Without seeds the earth bears no fruit."

> **Gospel of Philip, Verses 7-8**

How do you utilize this time of year for reflection and the incubation of new ideas?

"The first fall of snow is not only an event, it is a magical event. You go to bed in one kind of a world and wake up in another quite different, and if this is not enchantment then where is it to be found?"

J. B. Priestley

O Light of the World, in these long nights of darkness it is so easy to forget that your Light will always return. Teach us how to cherish the darkness. Remind us that just as plants must quietly germinate in order to grow, so we too have the opportunity to move into a quiet space of contemplation, reflection and inner growth. There is always a positive purpose for your cycles. May we use this time to full advantage so that we may be ready for the dawning of your springtime. Go with us into the darkness and be our Light and our Guide as we delve into the depths of our hearts and souls. So it is.

December 22

"What has come into being in him was life, and the life was the light of all people. The light shines in the darkness, and the darkness did not overcome it."

John 1:3-5

'Tis the season for less and less daylight and long, dark nights, but it also is the turning point when the light begins to grow and the day's become longer. Is the glass half-empty or half-full for you right now?

"Everything in our visible world has a beginning and an end; each beginning is a birth, each ending a death."

Robert Brumet

O God of Light and Darkness, we look around us and all we see is darkness. But the truth is that the light is coming, your Light that brings Hope to the world. Help us to trust in what we do not see. Help us to have faith in your great Plan that keeps everything in perfect balance. Remind us that we see only dimly with partial understanding. Expand our vision so that we may truly comprehend the Grace and Perfection of your universe. As we experience this turning point of the year, may we also experience it as a turning point in our lives towards transformation and your Light. Shine through us, O wondrous star, and create an unquenchable fire within for your Love, your Truth and your Way of Peace on Earth. So it is.

December 23

"Those who drink of the water that I will give them will never be thirsty. The water that I will give will become in them a spring of water gushing up to eternal life."

John 4:14

What is your concept of the afterlife and how does your belief affect how you live?

Rev. Maryesah Karelon, O.M.M.

"Yesterday is history. Tomorrow is a mystery. And today? Today is a gift. That's why we call it the present."

Babatunde Olatunji

O God of the Morning Dawn, we hunger and thirst for your Wisdom and your Truth. Come to us and flow into us, nourishing, cleansing and creating us anew. So often we seek Life where there is only death. We seek Truth and find falsehood. We seek Wisdom and find foolishness. Keep us focused in the present, in the Now, for Now is all we have. Teach us to go deeper than the superficial answers of the world. As we seek the fountain of your Wisdom, we know that it will never run dry. Transform our lives and gift us with the Peace of your Presence, for you are Life to us. May we drink deeply and live fully. So it is.

December 24

"It is more blessed to give than to receive."

Acts of the Apostles 20:35

What is the most precious gift that you can give to your loved ones?

"Many persons have a wrong idea of what constitutes true happiness. It is not attained through self-gratification but through fidelity to a worthy purpose."

Helen Keller

Generous and Ever-Loving God, we know we can never outgive you. You are our model of unconditional Love and generosity; sometimes we feel that we can never live up to your standards. Help us to realize that we don't have to be perfect and we don't have to have a large bank account to give as you give to us. In your Wisdom, show us that it is the little things that matter most. Reaching out to someone with a hug or even a simple smile may make their day. Giving our time to those who need it most has no price tag. Sharing our love and wisdom as a mentor to a child will bring rewards to all. Remember, it's not how much you paid for a gift that matters most. It's the love and compassion in your heart that is the best wrapping paper ever, so wrap your gifts well and give them with joy and delight. So it is.

December 25

"This will be a sign for you; you will find a child wrapped in bands of cloth and lying in a manger."

Luke 2:12

What lessons do you find for your life in the traditional Christmas story?

"People are often unreasonable, illogical and self-centered; forgive them anyway. If you are kind, people may accuse you of selfish, ulterior motives; be kind anyway. If you are successful, you will win some false friends and true enemies; succeed anyway. If you are honest and frank, people may cheat you; be honest anyway. What you spend years building, someone could destroy overnight; build anyway. If you find serenity and happiness, they may be jealous; be happy anyway. The good you do today, people will often forget tomorrow; do good anyway. Give the world the best you have, and it may never be enough; give the world the best you've got anyway. You see, in the final analysis, it is between you and God; it was never between you and them anyway."

Mother Teresa of Calcutta

Loving Mother/Father God, in one moment of time so long ago you embraced humanity with a Love we still have difficulty comprehending. We affirm that this was but one more example of your great Plan for your beloved children, a Plan that continues to unfold even now. We pray for your Presence among us, dear Lord, now as in the past. Show us how to weave your tapestry of Grace. Walk beside us as our Guide as we work for your Divine Order here on Earth. In quietness and peace, we seek your Wisdom and Truth, for we know the wisdom of the world is folly and illusion. May we go within to find you waiting for us in the stillness of our hearts. Thank you, Loving God, for your precious gifts to us. May we give to others as we have received from your bountiful Goodness. So it is.

December 26

"Arise, shine; for your light has come, and the glory of the Lord has risen upon you."

Isaiah 60:1

What are the possible stumbling blocks in your life to fully opening to the birth of the Christ within? How can the blocks be removed?

"Awakening is not a single event in time; it is a river endlessly flowing in this moment now."

Arjuna Ardagh

O God of Love and Compassion, often we are hardest on ourselves. We live for years with old resentments, old guilts, old anger and frustration. Now it is time to clean house. Heal us at the very depth of our souls. May we release the old baggage that we have carried for so long. Remove the blocks that build walls against loving and being loved. There is so much that we can do here in your world if we have the strength and the courage to walk forward, vulnerable and unafraid. Be our Protection, dear God. May your Light always surround us. May your Love always enfold us. May your Power always protect us, and may your Presence always watch over us. Wherever we journey, you go before us. Thank you, thank you, thank you, God. Alleluia. So it is.

December 27

"Then I saw a new heaven and a new earth; for the first heaven and the first earth had passed away, and the sea was no more...I heard a loud voice call from the throne, 'Look, here God lives among humanity. He will make his home among them; they will be his people and he will be their God, God-

with-them. He will wipe away all tears from their eyes; there will be no more death, and no more mourning or sadness or pain. The world of the past has gone."

Revelation 21:1, 3-4

What is your belief regarding changes for our planet in the next few years? Do you see the potential for these changes as positive or negative?

"The outcome of the world, the gates of the future, the entry into the super-human—these are not thrown open to a few of the privileged nor to one chosen people to the exclusion of all others. They will open only to an advance of all together, in a direction in which all together can join and find completion in a spiritual renovation of the earth…"

Pierre Teilhard De Chardin

O God of All Ages, we trust in your gracious Power and Mercy to bring change into our lives in a positive, transformative way. Remove our fears of the future and focus our attention on the Now, where we can make a difference in our life and the lives of those around us. Open our eyes to new possibilities and free us from old limitations, so that when the changes come we will bend with the winds but not break. Keep us flexible and strong in our faith so we may walk into the future with anticipation, not fear. So it is.

December 28

"Your life will be brighter than the noonday...And you will have confidence because there is hope."

Job 11:17-18

Where do you find hope as you experience your life today and the world around you?

"The day will come when after harnessing space, the winds, the tides and gravitation, we shall harness for God the energies of Love. And on that day, for the second time in the history of the world, we shall have discovered fire."

Pierre Teilhard De Chardin

Eternal and Loving God, it is your Love and Light that bring Hope into our darkness. Embrace us in your loving arms and bring us Comfort when sadness and pain come into our lives. Remind us that we are never alone. Teach us how to reach out to our brothers and sisters in need, knowing that it is the little things that make a difference; a gentle hug, a warm smile, an understanding arm to lean on. May we learn to listen and not judge; comfort and not count the cost. May we be your Light of Hope in a hurting world. So it is.

December 29

"You who live in the shelter of the Most High, who abide in the shadow of the Almighty, will say to the Lord, 'My refuge and my fortress; my God in whom I trust."

Psalm 91:1-2

What specifically can you do in the coming year to make someone's life better and brighter? How can you be a beacon of hope to others?

"Too often we underestimate the power of a touch, a smile, a kind word, a listening ear, an honest compliment, or the smallest act of caring, all of which have the potential to turn a life around."

Leo Buscaglia

Almighty God, you have given us so many blessings and opportunities, far beyond our expectations. You gift us with air to breathe and life itself. You gift us with families and friends who support and share and care. You gift us with trees, flowers, sunsets and sunrises, and all your creatures great and small. Remind us to pause and give you thanks for your gracious generosity. Teach us to share that generosity in small and large ways, from giving of our financial resources to sharing a hug or a smile. We can make a difference and that difference can change a life. So it is.

December 30

"Everything is for your sake, so that grace, as it extends to more and more people, may increase thanksgiving, to the glory of God."

2 Corinthians 4:15

What is the connection between grace, love and thanksgiving?

"Blessed is the season which engages the whole world in a conspiracy of love!"

Hamilton Wright Mable

Gracious and Loving God, you surprise us so often with unexpected wonders. We are amazed and grateful. Sometimes your Grace comes to us as a major miracle, an answer to prayer or an unexplainable synchronicity. Other times your Grace is more subtle and less obvious. A baby's first steps, a long-anticipated homecoming, a quiet sunset shared: these, too, speak of your Caring and Compassion for all your children. Great and small, you teach us that we are all worthy, all loved and all equal in your eyes. No matter where we go or what we do your Grace surrounds us, protects us and blesses us. May we remember to be gracious to our friends, family and neighbors in return, and may we always remember to give you praise and thanksgiving. So it is.

Rev. Maryesah Karelon, O.M.M.

December 31

"Thanks be to God for his indescribable gift!"

2 Corinthians 9:15

Reflect on the past year of your life. What have been the blessings and the challenges? Are there memories you are ready to heal and release? What new parts of yourself and your life do you want to focus on in this coming year?

"I have always looked at life as a voyage, mostly wonderful, sometimes frightening. In my family and friends I have discovered treasure more valuable than gold."

Jimmy Buffet

O God, our Help in ages past, our Hope for years to come, our Shelter from the stormy blast and our eternal Home; you go before us into the future. Steady our steps and comfort us in our uncertainty and fear. We thank you for this past year of gifts and lessons, of joys and sorrows, of wondrous surprises and sad goodbyes. We have grown from each event in our precious life. We are stronger, with greater Love and deeper Faith, not just another year older. May we remember the good times, release the bad and learn from both. May we cherish our friends and family knowing that time is precious and eternity only exists beyond the physical veil. As we walk forward into this New Year, we walk with you in Peace, in Love, in Joy and in Hope for our beloved Mother Earth. May we all come to know that we are one family in your Love. So it is.

Special Days

Walk fearlessly in the world
and speak your truth
as a disciple of the Risen Christos,
who confronted the powerful
and lifted up the weak;
who spoke out against injustice
and fed the hungry with more than bread.

Light in the Darkness

Ash Wednesday

"Then Jesus was led by the Spirit out into the desert to be put to the test by the devil. He fasted for forty days and forty nights, after which he was hungry, and the tester came and said to him, 'If you are Son of God, tell these stones to turn into loaves.' But Jesus replied, 'Scripture says: Human beings live not on bread alone but on every word that comes from the mouth of God.' The devil then took him to the holy city and set him on the parapet of the Temple. 'If you are Son of God,' he said, 'throw yourself down; for Scripture says: He has given his angels orders about you, and they will carry you in their arms in case you trip over a stone.' Jesus said to him, 'Scripture also says: Do not put the Lord your God to the test.' Next, taking him to a very high mountain, the devil showed him all the kingdoms of the world and their splendor. And he said to him, 'I will give you all these, if you fall at my feet and do me homage.' Then Jesus replied, 'Away with you, Satan! For Scripture says: The Lord your God is the one to whom you must do homage, him alone you must serve.' Then the devil left him, and suddenly angels appeared and looked after him."

Matthew 4:1-11

What does the season of Lent mean to you? What tests and challenges have you experienced in your life and what were the results?

"The outer path we take is public knowledge, but the path with heart is an inner one. The two come together when who we are that is seen in the world coincides with who we deeply are. As we grow wiser, we become aware that the important forks in the road are usually not about choices that will show up on any public record; they are decisions and struggles to do with choosing love or fear; anger or forgiveness; pride or humility. They are soul-shaping choices."

Jean Shinoda Bolen from <u>Crones Don't Whine</u>

Eternal and Ever-Loving God, you come to us when our lives are in ashes and remind us that you will never forsake us even in the tough times when the challenges threaten to overwhelm us. Forgive our doubts and our stumbles for we know you test us like metal in a refiner's fire. May we face our fires with the Strength and Courage of your Love in our hearts. May we emerge from these trials stripped to our core. That core is of finest gold; the purity of your Divine Image seeded within us as our conscience and integrity. May we stand for your Truth and your Principles in a material world that would buy us, tempt us and seduce us with fear. May we always walk on the Pathway of Light. May we always speak words of Light and Truth, and seal the door where evil may dwell in our lives. So it is.

Palm Sunday

"The crowds that went ahead of him and that followed were shouting, 'Hosanna to the Son of David! Blessed is the one who comes in the name of the Lord! Hosanna in the highest heaven!"

Matthew 21:9

Recall a time in your life when you were expectantly waiting for someone to arrive. What were the circumstances and who was "the expected one?" Did their arrival fulfill your expectations? What happens when expectations are not fulfilled?

"God never fails the children of earth. Do not seek for things to work according to your desires; or for your circumstances to be arranged according to your earthly will. But have faith that God is leading you on the path to ultimate happiness."

White Eagle from *The Quiet Mind*

Mother/Father God, today we stand in the crowds waving palm fronds to welcome a chosen Son of David. We shout the Hosannas but still wonder. "Who is this Expected One, who comes in your Name?" Teach us to let go of expectations and be filled with the wonder of your Presence. Remind us that we are all your chosen ones, sons and daughters of the Most High. May we follow in the footsteps of our Wayshower Jesus, even when those footsteps lead us through the darkest valleys. We will not be afraid for you are with us always. So it is.

Holy Thursday

"I have said this to you, so that in me you may have peace... Take courage; I have conquered the world."

John 16:33

Has a close friend or associate ever betrayed you? Recall the circumstances and the feelings. Do you now understand why it happened? Have you been able to forgive that person?

"Life is an adventure in forgiveness."

Norman Cousins

Gracious and Merciful God, how often have we betrayed your Love for us and denied your Presence in our lives? Forgive us for failing to live up to your Image that shines within us. Restore us to your fellowship and your banquet table. We know the invitation is always extended. May we say "Yes" to your gracious gifts and abundant bounty, trusting that when darkness falls we will never be alone. Teach us to serve each other in love as you have loved and served us. So it is.

Good Friday

"Then Jesus, crying with a loud voice, said, 'Father, into your hands I commend my spirit.'"

Luke 23:46

Have you ever had to face your own mortality? What lessons did you learn from walking through that experience? Where was God for you during that time?

"Surrender is the key that unlocks the door to grace."

Cheryl Richardson from <u>The Unmistakable Touch of Grace</u>

Abba Father, your Son called out to you in his torment just as we call to you in the crises of our lives. Remind us that you will never abandon us no matter how dark the night. May we listen carefully for your Voice and understand your message, even when it is difficult and different then what we might choose. Hold us in the palm of your hand and protect us until the dawn comes.

Then we know we will sing in the Joy of your Presence, now and forever more. So it is

Easter Sunday

"Open to me the gates of victory; I will enter by them and praise the Lord. This is the gate of the Lord; the victors shall make their entry through it. I will praise thee, for thou hast answered and hast become my deliverer. The stone which the builders rejected has become the chief corner-stone. This is the Lord's doing; it is marvelous in our eyes. This is the day that the Lord has made; let us rejoice and be glad in it."

Psalm 118:19-24

What do you believe about the resurrection of Jesus? What is resurrection and do you believe that anybody can be resurrected? When could or will this happen?

"The most beautiful thing we can experience is the mysterious. It is the source of all true art and science. He to whom the emotion is a stranger, who can no longer pause and stand wrapped in awe, is as good as dead. His eyes are closed."

Albert Einstein

Mighty and All-Powerful God, in the stillness before dawn you overwhelm us with Love. Our minds cannot comprehend what happened two thousand years ago. However, our hearts know the Truth. Open to us the doors of salvation so that we may understand the joys and opportunities that await us. Birth us anew into the Light of your consciousness, which is our inheritance. May we truly be raised on high with him who is our Brother and Wayshower. He awaits us at the wedding banquet. Come, let us go forward in Joy, Light and Love. So it is.

Pentecost

"When Pentecost day came round, they had all met together, when suddenly there came from heaven a sound as of a violent wind which filled the entire house in which they were sitting; and there appeared to them tongues as of fire; these separated and came to rest on the head of each of them. They were all filled with the Holy Spirit and began to speak different languages as the Spirit gave them power to express themselves."

Acts of the Apostles 2:1-4

What is the significance today of this giving of the Holy Spirit to humanity?

"Only as high as I reach can I grow. Only as far as I seek can I go. Only as deep as I look can I see. Only as much as I dream can I be."

Karen Raven

Great Spirit, in the Power of your Presence we celebrate your coming to us. In remembrance of that long ago day, we pledge ourselves to unity and tolerance of all your people. As we acknowledge your gifts to us, we seek to dream the dreams and see the visions of your new heaven come to Earth. May we become partners with your gracious Power to transform and rebirth our world. May we see with new eyes, hear with new ears, understand with minds transformed and feel with hearts wide open. Remold us and make us like you, divine as we are destined to be. As the wind of change blows through our lives, anchor us firmly in your Truth and Love. We give you praise and thanksgiving for the Hope you create for our Earth. So it is.

First Sunday of Advent

"'And they shall name him Emmanuel,' which means, 'God is with us.'"

Matthew 1:23

What is the Hope that Emmanuel brings to our world and to each one of us?

"All changes, even the most longed for, have their melancholy; for what we leave behind is part of ourselves; we must die to one life before we can enter into another."

Anatole France

Holy Emmanuel, you come to us in the beauty of this season and remind us that you are always with us, ever-present in our daily lives. Teach us to pause in the rush of shopping, parties and to-do lists to remember the reason for the season. In your coming, we have our Hope of renewal and rebirth. In your Light, we see through the darkness. O come, O come, Emmanuel. Come to us, come into us, come through us and birth us anew. So it is.

Second Sunday of Advent

"And suddenly there was with the angel a multitude of the heavenly host, praising God and saying, 'Glory to God in the highest heaven, and on earth peace among those whom he favors!'"

Luke 2:13-14

What are you doing to bring peace to our planet?

"It's possible to mend our world only by finding the courage to mend ourselves."

Sonya Friedman

Loving and Merciful God, you call us to live in peace with our brothers and sisters. You call us to do what is right, to love mercy and to walk humbly in your Way. Yet all around us we see violence and bloodshed, brother against brother. Teach us your Truth that we are one family born of the Love of one Divine Creator. May we beat our swords into ploughshares and reach out in Love to embrace each other. There is so much need and heartache across our planet. We must become part of the solution, not the problem. Let there be Peace on Earth, let this be our solemn vow, to take each moment and live each moment in Peace eternally. Let there be Peace on Earth and let it begin with me. So it is.

Third Sunday of Advent

"You have turned my mourning into dancing; you have taken off my sackcloth and clothed me with joy."

Psalm 30:11

How can you bring joy to someone else this holiday season?

"What does it take for your soul to dance with God? An eager spirit, a flexible heart and a willingness to let God take the lead in the dance!"

Greg Barrette

O God of Joy and Gladness, you come to us in Joy to lead us forth in Peace. Remove our doubts and fears and lift our tired spirits. Set our feet dancing with the music of the spheres that we hear in the silence of our hearts. As the bells ring out and the carols are sung, may our hearts sing with gratitude. May we prepare a place for the coming of the Christ within our souls; then we truly will sing with Mary, "My soul magnifies the Lord and my spirit rejoices in God my Savior." So it is.

Fourth Sunday of Advent

"Those who love me will keep my word, and my Father will love them, and we will come to them and make our home with them."

John 14:23

Rev. Maryesah Karelon, O.M.M.

How are you preparing a dwelling place for the Christ in your heart and home?

"Love is in you. Go inward. Play with the Creator. The Creator is waiting for you with Love."

Chalanda Sai Ma

Loving Creator God, you created us out of your desire and your Love. As reflections of you, may we truly mirror that Love and seek to see that Love all around us. In the darkest corners, some light is shining. In the dullest morns, there is always the hope of dawn. Teach us to have faith and hope. Open our eyes to the reality of your Presence all around us and in us. Remind us that we are never alone, never without hope and never lost in the darkness. Your Light and Love are always surrounding and protecting us from harm. Thank you, dear God, for the assurance of your ever-present Love. We rest in that Faith and Knowledge, and our hearts are at peace. So it is.

Christmas Eve

"And she gave birth to her firstborn son…and laid him in a manger, because there was no place for them in the inn."

Luke 2:7

What does the birth of the Christ child mean to you?

"Christmas is not a time nor a season, but a state of mind."

Calvin Coolidge

O God of Love, you have come into our darkness as a tiny child, defenseless and dependent on human love and care. Help us to learn this great lesson as we tell this story over and over again. Teach us how to respond to your wondrous gift with open hearts and loving arms. On this one night, may we embrace our hurting world. May we forget all our differences, all our perceived hatreds, all our jealousy and selfishness. For one night, Loving God, may we return your Love, for if we can love each other for one night, even one moment, we can walk arm-in-arm into the future. It only takes this one moment of Love to transform our world. Let us begin now. It is time. So it is.

Christmas Day

"But Mary treasured all these words and pondered them in her heart. The shepherds returned, glorifying and praising God for all they had heard and seen, as it had been told them."

Luke 2:19-20

As you ponder the meaning of the Christ birth in your own heart, reflect on how you can be more of a Christ in the year ahead. How can you birth the Christ within you?

"This is Christmas: not the tinsel, not the giving and receiving, not even the carols, but the humble heart that receives anew the wondrous gift, the Christ."

Frank McKibben

Beloved of my Heart, as Mary pondered the meaning of this Christ birth in her heart, may we ponder today the significance of your coming to us, not two thousand years ago but today here and now. Touch our lives with the miracle of your Presence. May we invite you into the inn of our hearts. May you be born in us and through us so that we may shine your Light into our dark world. Teach us to love and trust you as Mary did so long ago. From the mouths of babes great Wisdom is born. Open our ears, our minds and our eyes to the wondrous Knowledge that you bring to us. Fill us with your Spirit of Love and Truth. Send us out to be your loving, healing hands. May we become a blessing in your Name to all whom we meet. Dear Lord, make us instruments of your Peace; where there is hatred, let us sow Love; where there is injury, Pardon; where there is doubt, Faith; where there is despair, Hope; and where there is sadness, Joy. So it is.

Mother's Day

"As a mother comforts her child, so I will comfort you."

Isaiah 66:13

Do you believe that God is feminine as well as masculine? How would this affect your view of the Divine?

"If you want to find richer meaning and purpose in your life, just keep loving."

Alan Cohen

Divine Mother, you were with our Father from the beginning and together you gave birth to all of Creation. How often have we forgotten you and ignored your teachings of Compassion, gentle Power and the balance of all things? Today we need your Wisdom more than ever as our world spins out of control. Be the glue that holds us together. Be the healing balm for your despoiled Earth. Gather us under your wings and embrace us with your loving arms so that we may learn from you once again. Teach us to walk gently on your good Earth and honor all your creatures. Show your wayward children that Peace is possible only if we take our place in the human tapestry and weave it together in your Love. May the fountain of your Compassion overflow in our hearts and water our desert Earth. So it is.

Memorial Day

"This day is holy to our Lord; and do not be grieved, for the joy of the Lord is your strength."

Nehemiah 8:10

What does this day of remembrance mean to you? How do you remember those who have touched your life and have now passed on? What gifts have they entrusted to you?

"Every happening great and small is a parable whereby God speaks to us, and the art of life is to get the message."

Malcolm Muggeridge

God of Time and Space, we pause in our mad rush through life to remember with love and thankfulness those who have walked this path before us. They have gifted us with a wonderful legacy and we are grateful. We give thanks for lives well-lived, for lives cut short and snuffed out too soon, for sacrifices offered for country and family. In all things, O God, we affirm your Divine Order and Truth. In our sadness and grief, we cry out that we do not understand, but we know that there is a higher Truth and a greater Purpose. Comfort our hearts and lift us up on the wings of eagles. May we truly see as you see and give thanks for what has been, what is and what is to come. So it is.

Father's Day

"So he set off and went to his father. But while he was still far off, his father saw him and was filled with compassion; he ran and put his arms around him and kissed him."

Luke 15:20

What qualities make a good father? How has your experience in your personal life affected your feeling and definition of God?

"Love and compassion are necessities, not luxuries. Without them, humanity cannot survive."

The Dalai Lama

Loving and Forgiving Father, when we call on you we often bring the baggage of the past. Teach us how to leave that past behind and begin again in love, forgiveness and trust. Show us the way home from our many wanderings. Heal our broken hearts and our fractured minds. Bring us back to you in wholeness and completeness for in you we find our true Self and our true Home. As we are healed at depth we return to where we began as your beloved children, free at last to live in Peace, Joy and Love. We affirm that this is our reality. We commit ourselves to Peace in our time. We covenant with you, our Father, to be your ambassadors of Love and Joy here on Earth. So it is.

Independence Day

"As servants of God, live as free people."

1 Peter 2:16

How would you define freedom? Have you ever felt that you were not free? What were the circumstances that enslaved you and what was/is the solution?

"How would you live if you felt you could trust life fully? If you believed you were totally protected and secure, that forevermore your life would be filled with love and prosperity? Think of how your fears would dissolve, of how totally accepting of yourself and others you would be—it wouldn't matter if they met your expectations or not. Think of how you would venture forth knowing you would succeed. Think of how your heart would open, of how free you would feel. How free you would be to love. All of this is the treasure that life offers us. We just lack the consciousness to experience it."

Susan L. Taylor

O God of all Nations, on this day of celebration we stop our busy lives to say "Thank you" for the precious gift of our freedom. We remember those who have paid the ultimate price to preserve these freedoms. Today we pledge ourselves to walk humbly as servants and citizens of your world. We pray that the leaders of our nation will be guided and directed in paths of Peace and Justice. We pray for all your children everywhere, our dear brothers and sisters, who are not free and who face deprivation and struggle that we can barely imagine. May your Kingdom come, O Lord our God, on Earth as in heaven with Liberty and Justice for all. So it is.

Labor Day

"*We are workers with you for your joy, because you stand firm in the faith.*"

2 Corinthians 1:24

Is there a difference for you between your work and your job? How do you balance work and play in your life?

"The world is moved not only by the mighty shoves of the heroes, but also by the aggregate of the tiny pushes of each honest worker."

Helen Keller

Holy God, you have given us work to do in your world. We pray now for the courage and the strength to complete what you have placed in our hands. May we build well upon a sure foundation. May our vision be guided by our knowledge of your Purpose. May our feet walk on your chosen Path even if it be narrow and overgrown. May our words be your words of Truth and Wisdom even if they are bold and unsettling. We are your instruments, dear God. Use us for the greater Good. So it is

Veterans Day

"Let each of you look not to your own interests, but to the interests of others. Let the same mind be in you that was in Christ Jesus."

Philippians 2:4-5

If Jesus were walking among us today, how would he feel about our world, the conflicts and the turmoil between peoples? What does it mean to you to have the same mind as Christ Jesus in this regard?

"The love of one's country is a splendid thing. But why should love stop at the border?"

Pablo Casals

Almighty and Everlasting God, we praise you as the God of all humanity and the Source of all Goodness. On this day we remember those who have sacrificed their lives for what they believed was right and true. Freedom is so precious and so few of your children can experience it and fully live free. Remind us again and again how fortunate we are, no matter what the cost and what the minor inconveniences may be. Teach us to stand strong for your Truth and Justice in a world that knows so little about what is right and true. Teach us to bend but not break with the winds of change so that we may embrace those different from us with understanding and love. We know that war is not the answer and that the opposite of love is not hate but fear. Remove the fear in our hearts and minds, and fill us to overflowing with your Light, Love and Peace. Let there be Peace on Earth and let it begin with each one of us. So it is.

Thanksgiving Day

"*Those who observe the day, observe it in honor of the Lord. Also those who eat, eat in honor of the Lord, since they give thanks to God.*"

Romans 14:6

What part does God play in your Thanksgiving Day? Reflect on the blessings that you have received as a child of God and remember to say "Thank you, God!"

"Home is a shelter from storms—all sorts of storms."

William J. Bennett

Generous and Ever-Loving God, you spread your banquet table before us and invite us to eat our fill. We are humbled by the abundance that you lay before us and amazed at the blessings that you shower upon us. On this special day of thanksgiving, remind us that every day can be an opportunity to give thanks for the good in our lives. Teach us to truly count our blessings and see life as a glass half-full instead of half-empty. We know that you are there walking beside us even when the challenges come and life is far from easy or perfect. We trust in your Love and Care knowing that tomorrow is another day, a better day. For all we have received may we be truly thankful. We lift up our hearts to you and say "Thank you, thank you, thank you God." So it is.

About the Author

Rev. Mother Maryesah Karelon has been a student of mystical Christianity, spirituality and healing for more than 30 years. She received her Master of Divinity degree in 1976 from Colgate Rochester Divinity School in Rochester, New York, and was subsequently ordained as a Presbyterian minister in 1978. After serving in several parishes in Western New York, she returned to further graduate studies in counseling and since then has been led into deeper explorations of metaphysics. She was ordained as a priest in the teaching and healing Order of Melchizedek in 1987, which led to a life-changing trip to Egypt later that same year. Her interest in the sacred ancient mysteries continued with the Coptic Fellowship International and most recently has led her to give birth to the Order of St. Mary Magdalene, a non-denominational organization dedicated to spiritual wholeness through the balance of the masculine and feminine energies. To contact her or for further information about the Order of St. Mary Magdalene, please visit the website **www.magdalenerose.org**.

Scripture Index

Acts of the Apostles
- 2:1-4 - 383
- 2:28 - 84
- 7:33 - 277
- 13:39 - 148
- 20:35 - 367

1 Chronicles
- 22:16 - 145
- 28:20 - 215

Colossians
- 1:5-6 - 165
- 1:11-12 - 327
- 1:17 - 88
- 3:12-13 - 244
- 3:15 - 57
- 4:17- 353

1 Corinthians
- 1:10 - 199
- 2:9 - 291
- 2:12 - 144
- 2:13 - 239
- 3:7 - 296
- 3:10 - 53
- 3:16 - 24
- 3:17 - 362
- 4:5 - 298
- 6:19-20 - 240
- 12:31 - 120
- 13:4,7-8 - 54
- 13:12 - 60
- 14:33 - 118
- 15:10 - 205
- 15:44 - 337
- 16:14 - 314

2 Corinthians
- 1:24 - 393
- 3:17 - 276
- 3:18 - 209
- 4:15 - 374
- 4:18 - 26
- 5:5-7 - 147
- 5:17 - 180
- 6:2 - 182
- 9:6 - 142
- 9:8 - 259
- 9:15 - 375
- 13:11-12 - 265

Daniel
- 2:22 - 156

Deuteronomy
- 4:29 - 286
- 31:6 - 86
- 32:2 - 152

Ecclesiastes
- 3:15 - 321
- 5:20 - 73

Ephesians
- 1:5-6 - 266
- 2:10 - 331
- 3:16-17 - 135
- 3:18-19 - 313
- 3:20-21 - 279
- 4:1-3 - 168
- 4:4-6 - 154
- 4:24 - 76
- 4:32 - 22
- 5:1-2 - 299

- 5:8-9 - 234
- 6:7-8 - 92

Exodus
- 35:34-35 - 76
- 40:4 - 332

Ezekiel
- 17:5-6 - 18
- 34:12 - 308
- 36:26 - 221
- 37:14 - 113

Galatians
- 5:13 - 350
- 5:22-23 - 51
- 5:25 - 326

Genesis
- 1:3-4 - 15
- 9:14-15 - 62
- 17:7 - 283
- 28:15 - 82
- 33:11 - 345

Habakkuk
- 2:2-3 - 287

Hebrews
- 11:1 - 245
- 11:8,10 - 81
- 12:28 - 257
- 13:5-6 - 14

Hosea

14:7 - 115

Isaiah

6:8 - 130
12:2 - 32
18:4 - 140
26:4 - 161
27:2-3 - 258
30:15 - 204
32:18 - 248
40:31 - 55
41:10 - 347
42:9 - 56
42:16 - 181
43:1-3 - 278
43:19 - 13
44:3 - 289
52:7 - 82
54:10 - 256
55:11 - 306
55:12 - 262
56:7 - 198
57:14 - 34
58:8 - 268
58:11 - 87
60:1 - 369
61:1 - 243
65:17 - 76
66:13 - 389

James

1:2-4 - 234
1:5-6 - 28
1:17 - 134
1:18 - 232
3:17-18 - 33
4:8 - 89

Jeremiah

17:14 - 21
24:7 - 316
29:11 - 59
29:13-14 - 71
30:17 - 146
31:13 - 289
33:3 - 121
33:6 - 206

Job

5:8 - 71
6:11 - 354
11:17-18 - 372
11:18 - 340
22:21 - 209
32:8 - 78
33:4 - 260
42:1-2 - 167

Joel

3:1 - 158

John, Gospel of

1:3-5 - 365
1:5 - 323
1:16 - 151
3:6-7 - 149
3:8 - 219
4:13-14 - 246
4:14 - 366
4:24 - 116
7:24 - 220
7:37-38 - 74
8:12 - 96
8:32 - 241
10:10 - 242
10:14-15 - 318
14:12 - 208
14:20 - 309
14:23 - 386
14:26 - 155
14:27 - 119
15:1-4 - 272
15:5,7 - 280
15:9 - 95
15:11 - 107
15:12 - 106
15:16 - 61
16:13 - 63
16:24 - 218
16:33 - 101
16:33 - 380
18:37 - 131
20:22 - 294

1 John

1:1 - 170
1:5 - 123
1:7 - 108
3:2 - 16
3:18 - 273
4:7 - 333
4:11-12 - 45
4:18 - 65

3 John

1:2 - 359

Judges

18:6 - 37

1 Kings

9:3 - 48

2 Kings

20:5 - 177

Leviticus

23:3 - 256

Luke, Gospel of

1:46-47 - 351
1:78-79 -17
2:7 - 387
2:12 - 368
2:13-14 - 385
2:19-20 - 388
4:1 - 102
4:18-19 - 19
5:38 - 143
6:19 - 111
6:37 - 72
6:38 - 235
6:45 - 163
8:16 - 162
8:17 - 27
10:5 - 348
10:27 - 187
11:36 - 226
12:35-36 - 102
15:20 - 391
17:20-21 - 175
23:46 - 381

Malachi

3:10 - 129
4:2 - 357

Mark, Gospel of

4:26-27 - 244
4:28 - 299
4:31-32 - 43
6:31 - 58
10:27 - 267
11:22-23 - 231
11:24 - 47
11:25 - 85
12:29-31 - 23
13:11 - 307

Mary Magdalene, Gospel of

8:1-10 - 214
8:11-24 - 328
9:12-18 - 30

Matthew, Gospel of

1:23 - 384
4:1-11 - 378
4:4 - 153
5:9 - 164
5:16 - 79
5:44-45 - 264
6:10 - 183
6:14 - 200
6:21 - 317
6:25 - 363
6:26 - 31
6:28-29 - 174
6:33 - 36
7:7 - 202
9:16-17 - 43
9:21-22 - 21
11:29 - 247
12:50 - 122
14:23 - 360
17:20 - 179
18:3 - 104
18:12 - 109
18:19-20 - 50
19:26 - 47
21:9 - 379
22:37-39 - 301
23:26 - 303
25:40 - 173
28:20 - 229

Micah

6:8 - 157

Nehemiah

8:10 - 390

1 Peter

1:23 - 137
2:16 - 392
3:4 - 25
3:8 - 324
3:9 - 325
4:10 - 358

Philip, Gospel of

Verse 7-8 - 364
Verse 10 - 285
Verse 44 - 49

Philippians

1:3-4 - 139
1:9 - 169
2:1-2 - 305
2:4-5 - 394
3:13-14 - 189
4:6 - 260
4:9 - 248
4:19 - 94

Proverbs

2:6 - 293
3:1 - 112
3:8 - 302
3:13,17 - 117
3:26 - 341
4:18 - 349
4:20,22 - 91
4:23 - 123

Proverbs (cont.)

4:23-26 - 190
16:3 - 227
16:24 - 236
17:17 - 211
19:20 - 329
19:21 - 77
23:18 - 349
25:11 - 304
29:18 - 44

Psalms

1:3 - 52
4:6 - 26
5:7 - 225
8:4-5 - 222
16:7-8 - 195
16:11 - 178, 201
17:8 - 283
17:15 - 116
20:4 - 103
23:1-5 - 263
24:1 - 274
25:5 - 284
26:11-12 - 110
27:1 - 334
27:14 - 288
30:11 - 386
32:6 - 184
32:8 - 265
33:21-22 - 233
34:4 - 290
36:7 - 161
37:24 - 211
40:8 - 228
42:1-2 - 295
42:8 - 271
43:3 - 307
46:1-2 - 218
51:10 - 212
52:8 - 125
52:9 - 346
57:8 - 207
62:1-2 - 35
62:5 - 88
62:8 - 176
63:5 - 335
63:7-8 - 186
66:19 - 196
78:16 - 141
81:28 - 38
84:3 - 270
85:8 - 195
86:12-13 - 315
90:14 - 90
91:1-2 - 373
91:11-12 - 132
105:4-5 - 238
107:30 - 36
116:7 - 336
118:19-24 - 382
119:18 - 300
119:54 - 226
119:66 - 105
119:76 - 319
119:105 - 138
121:1-2 - 355
126:2 - 171
128:2 - 261
130:4-5 - 65
139:9-10 - 250
143:10 - 269
146:5 - 188

Revelation

4:11 - 239
7:17 - 54
21:5 - 213
21:1, 3-4 - 370

Romans

1:20 - 356
5:5 - 94
6:4 - 292
8:6 - 29
8:9 - 361
8:19 - 19
8:21 - 275
8:24-25 - 80
8:26 - 197
8:28 - 32
8:38-39 - 320
12:2 - 216
12:6-8 - 46
12:9-10 - 330
13:11-12 - 124
14:6 - 395
14:19 - 111
15:7 - 332

Song of Songs

2:11-13 - 136
8:6-7 - 106
8:13 - 217

1 Thessalonians

1:6-7 - 338

2 Thessalonians

1:11-12 - 237
3:16 - 322

Thomas, Gospel of

Saying 1 - 339
Saying 2 - 114
Saying 3 - 93
Saying 5 - 83
Saying 9 - 297
Saying 17 -15

Thomas, Gospel of (cont.)

Saying 22 - 133
Saying 24 - 121
Saying 26 - 352
Saying 38 - 150
Saying 50 - 66
Saying 57 - 274
Saying 70 - 203
Saying 75 - 175
Saying 77 - 185
Saying 97 - 255
Saying 106 - 249
Saying 113 - 230

1 Timothy

2:1-2 - 64

Zechariah

4:6 - 58

Subject Index

Abundance/Prosperity - 31, 52, 94, 137, 153, 174, 206, 242, 246, 259, 299, 317, 335, 336, 345, 363

Angels - 132, 186, 279, 385

Balance - 27, 51, 102, 117, 133, 147, 210, 214, 220, 222, 239, 249, 285, 321, 345, 350, 389, 393

Beauty - 83, 151

Blessings - 16, 47, 52, 57, 84, 129, 151, 158, 200, 202, 207, 218, 231, 242, 246, 257, 259, 261, 280, 289, 291, 300, 325, 327, 330, 336, 346, 366, 375, 387, 388, 395

Body Temple - 24, 89, 90, 226, 240, 275, 362

Calling - 14, 19, 44, 50, 61, 71, 77, 78, 81, 110, 130, 149, 154, 157, 168, 205, 227, 237, 259, 266, 273, 276, 295, 307, 318, 325, 328, 338, 388, 393

Challenges - 18, 31, 32, 44, 59, 73, 76, 79, 88, 118, 136, 145, 147, 153, 166, 167, 179, 183, 187, 197, 199, 212, 218, 228, 233, 234, 250, 259, 265, 267, 272, 274, 278, 287, 288, 290, 296, 301, 319, 320, 330, 334, 341, 347, 352, 353, 355, 363, 370, 375, 378, 381, 392

Change - 13, 19, 21, 24, 33, 43, 44, 56, 75, 84, 104, 121, 124, 143, 152, 173, 180, 188, 198, 209, 212, 213, 216, 221, 231, 243, 268, 292, 298, 326, 341, 351, 362, 366, 382, 384

Choices - 13, 21, 22, 27, 33, 73, 77, 81 105, 110, 112, 125, 142, 148, 153, 172, 177, 182, 255, 274, 276, 279, 285, 293, 299, 304, 305, 316, 329, 332, 335, 338, 340, 348, 353, 355, 361, 368, 378

Comfort - 14, 31, 32, 55, 119, 132, 161, 184, 186, 196, 211, 218, 229, 250, 256, 260, 263, 278, 289, 290, 319, 320, 322, 340, 341, 347, 355, 366, 372, 373, 389, 390, 395

Compassion - 20, 54, 63, 74, 95, 106, 109, 123, 173, 200, 236, 243, 249, 256, 308, 314, 318, 319, 368, 373, 389, 391

Courage - 56, 86, 101, 131, 179, 215, 263, 288, 353, 363, 380, 385

Divine Presence - 26, 35, 37, 48, 50, 58, 62, 66, 71, 74, 78, 82, 84, 88, 89, 113, 116, 135, 138, 140, 141, 162, 167, 176, 195, 201, 211, 218, 219, 221, 225, 229, 230, 239, 250, 258, 260, 261, 270, 271, 277, 283, 284, 286, 289, 290, 294, 308, 309, 319, 334, 347, 351, 356, 364, 373, 375, 381, 383, 384, 387

Dreams/Visions - 34, 44, 63, 142, 158, 196, 287

Earth/Creation - 19, 62, 115, 136, 141, 152, 239, 240, 274, 275, 336, 356, 364, 371

Faith - 21, 26, 28, 37, 47, 81, 94, 147, 161, 174, 179, 228, 231, 234, 237, 244, 245, 249, 260, 317, 333, 334, 347, 351, 380, 382

Family of God - 16, 66, 108, 122, 133, 211, 275, 333, 375, 383, 386, 389, 390, 391, 394, 395

Forgiveness - 22, 38, 65, 72, 85, 200, 264, 380, 391

Freedom - 148, 210, 241, 275, 276, 350, 392

Generosity - 37, 94, 134, 206, 235, 332, 345, 367

Gifts - 46, 51, 77, 92, 120, 122, 134, 144, 202, 244, 291, 345, 359, 367, 383

Goals - 34, 50, 75, 77, 103, 114, 157, 189, 202, 217, 232, 235, 290, 295, 306, 338, 353, 355, 357, 379

Grace - 53, 91, 151, 168, 205, 283, 289, 294, 308, 358, 366, 374, 375, 381

Gratitude - 52, 53, 57, 139, 207, 257, 279, 315, 327, 332, 346, 374, 375, 390, 395

Growth - 18, 33, 43, 44, 48, 83, 87, 104, 112, 115, 125, 143, 150, 156, 180, 203, 209, 212, 217, 232, 261, 263, 265, 266, 269, 271, 274, 277, 284, 292, 296, 297, 300, 326, 341, 346, 364, 383, 390

Guidance - 30, 54, 56, 59, 71, 78, 87, 91, 105, 155, 162, 178, 189, 195, 196, 226, 228, 239, 247, 248, 272, 284, 293, 294, 300, 307, 313, 326, 329, 352, 368, 391

Happiness - 171, 188, 189, 207, 261, 332, 335, 367

Healing - 21, 85, 91, 95, 111, 146, 164, 177, 203, 206, 265, 268, 290, 302, 303, 320, 357, 375, 385, 390, 391

Heart - 45, 72, 74, 95, 106, 129, 163, 164, 190, 221, 295, 299, 316, 378, 387, 388

Holiness/Wholeness - 30, 46, 85, 90, 114, 116, 140, 219, 244, 249, 256, 277, 303 309, 313, 337, 339, 346, 359, 363, 370, 382, 383, 385, 387

Hope - 15, 35, 43, 59, 80, 82, 89, 113, 165, 166, 188, 233, 245, 267, 283, 315, 339, 340, 341, 349, 355, 366, 372, 384

Humility - 296, 324, 352

Inner Awareness - 17, 24, 25, 29, 44, 49, 54, 55, 56 60, 64, 65, 66, 71, 76, 79, 81, 93, 107, 113, 115, 118, 121, 135, 138, 144, 149, 164, 170, 178, 196, 197, 203, 208, 209, 212, 214, 219, 221, 227, 237, 238, 241, 248, 255, 262, 266, 270, 280, 284, 286, 290, 295, 301, 302, 303, 306, 313, 320, 328, 335, 337, 339, 341, 359, 361, 363, 365, 375, 378, 383, 387, 388

Integrity - 28, 50, 53, 106, 110, 131, 137, 176, 211, 324, 335, 378

Joy - 73, 84, 107, 108, 137, 171, 201, 219, 262, 290, 305, 335, 379, 382, 386, 388

Light/Darkness - 15, 17, 26, 38, 66, 79, 96, 108, 122, 123, 162, 181, 185, 225, 226, 234, 268, 298, 307, 323, 334, 338, 349, 350, 365, 369, 390

Love - 23, 28, 37, 45, 54, 55, 65, 90, 94, 95, 106, 107, 161, 169, 175, 187, 211, 215, 236, 250, 257, 264, 273, 295, 299, 301, 314, 329, 330, 331, 333, 358, 368, 372, 374, 386, 387, 389, 391, 394

Manifestation - 17, 26, 46, 47, 51, 80, 87, 93, 103, 111, 116, 129, 141, 142, 144, 158, 163, 167, 168, 171, 216, 222, 226, 227, 236, 245, 261, 266, 280, 291, 303, 304, 306, 348, 350, 383, 386

New Beginnings - 13, 34, 56, 76, 89, 137, 180, 213, 292, 366, 368, 370, 382, 383

Opportunity - 16, 25, 34, 61, 102, 103, 121, 130, 191, 217, 246, 258, 266, 276, 291, 292, 304, 339, 346, 348, 351, 357, 368, 382, 383, 393

Patience - 65, 80, 103, 287, 288, 354, 379

Partnership - 14, 17, 92, 108, 130, 133, 215, 240, 244, 250, 275, 279, 284, 294, 300, 338, 359, 364, 371, 386, 389, 393

Peace/Harmony - 33, 37, 38, 64, 82, 111, 118, 119, 164, 165, 199, 209, 214, 248, 249, 264, 265, 305, 324, 335, 348, 349, 385, 394

Peace/Serenity - 29, 57, 65, 101, 140, 181, 195, 247, 248, 270, 278, 279, 317, 322, 328, 336, 340, 356, 360, 365, 380

Positive Focus - 27, 32, 48, 73, 83, 103, 111, 118, 119, 123, 129, 155, 158, 166, 171, 174, 181, 196, 199, 230, 232, 234, 257, 262, 267, 287, 302, 315, 323, 333, 338, 340, 350, 366, 375, 381

Prayer/Meditation - 22, 47, 59, 64, 78, 86, 117, 139, 165, 169, 177, 184, 185, 196, 197, 198, 237, 238, 260, 266, 278, 327, 360

Priorities - 36, 102, 112, 125, 172, 220, 255, 270, 279, 284, 299, 316, 317, 329, 331, 340, 350, 360, 361

Rest - 36, 58, 204, 247, 248, 256, 336, 340

Secrets - 27, 60, 83, 120, 121, 156, 298

Self-Esteem - 16, 23, 75, 116, 187, 222, 240, 267, 292, 297, 325, 337

Service - 19, 23, 45, 53, 62, 74, 76, 92, 95, 96, 109, 131, 146, 163, 165, 173, 175, 208, 213, 216, 227, 228 236, 243, 249, 273, 275, 299, 302, 309, 314, 318, 328, 331, 333, 358, 367, 373, 388, 393, 394

Silence/Solitude - 35, 36, 59, 88, 102, 136, 139, 143, 185, 247, 336, 360

Simplicity - 36, 101, 104, 172, 360, 373

Spiritual Path - 15, 20, 22, 25, 29, 47, 49, 61, 71, 82, 89, 105, 109, 113, 114, 116, 120, 122, 130, 137, 138, 145, 149, 150, 152, 155, 157, 170, 175, 178, 182, 184, 187, 189, 190, 201, 208, 219, 225, 227, 228, 230, 235, 238, 242, 245, 256, 258, 261, 269, 271, 276, 284, 286, 295, 297, 309, 310, 323, 331, 333, 339, 348, 357, 359, 361, 370, 373, 375, 382

Surrender - 30, 58, 60, 71, 88, 132, 169, 183, 204, 205, 241, 269, 285, 361, 380, 381

Time - 124, 145, 146, 182, 220, 229, 245, 321, 322, 349, 364, 367, 375

Tolerance - 96, 123, 154, 198, 264, 394

Trust - 28, 32, 33, 58, 125, 161, 174, 176, 183, 204, 233, 259, 307, 329, 339, 373, 380, 392

Truth - 63, 93, 112, 131, 148, 150, 154, 170, 235, 241, 284, 300, 307, 337

Vineyard - 18, 258, 272, 280

Wisdom - 15, 33, 48, 78, 86, 117, 156, 190, 236, 293, 321

www.ingramcontent.com/pod-product-compliance
Lightning Source LLC
Chambersburg PA
CBHW020346170426
43200CB00005B/64